Colloquial
Portuguese

Colloquial Portuguese: The Complete Course for Beginners has been carefully developed by an experienced teacher to provide a step-by-step course to Portuguese as it is written and spoken today.

Combining a clear, practical and accessible style with a methodical and thorough treatment of the language, it equips learners with the essential skills needed to communicate confidently and effectively in Portuguese in a broad range of situations. No prior knowledge of the language is required.

Colloquial Portuguese is exceptional; each unit presents a wealth of grammatical points that are reinforced with a wide range of exercises for regular practice. A full answer key, a grammar summary, bilingual glossaries and English translations of dialogues can be found at the back as well as useful vocabulary lists throughout.

Key features include:

- A clear, user-friendly format designed to help learners progressively build up their speaking, listening, reading and writing skills
- Jargon-free, succinct and clearly structured explanations of grammar
- An extensive range of focused and dynamic supportive exercises
- Realistic and entertaining dialogues covering a broad variety of narrative situations
- Helpful cultural points explaining the customs and features of life in Portugal
- An overview of the sounds of Portuguese

Balanced, comprehensive and rewarding, *Colloquial Portuguese* is an indispensable resource both for independent learners and students taking courses in Portuguese.

Audio material to accompany the course is available to download free in MP3 format from www.routledge.com/cw/colloquials. Recorded by native speakers, the audio material features the dialogues and texts from the book and will help develop your listening and pronunciation skills.

THE COLLOQUIAL SERIES
Series Adviser: Gary King

The following languages are available in the Colloquial series:

Afrikaans	German	Romanian
Albanian	Greek	Russian
Amharic	Gujarati	Scottish Gaelic
Arabic (Levantine)	Hebrew	Serbian
Arabic of Egypt	Hindi	Slovak
Arabic of the Gulf	Hungarian	Slovene
Basque	Icelandic	Somali
Bengali	Indonesian	Spanish
Breton	Irish	Spanish of Latin
Bulgarian	Italian	America
Burmese	Japanese	Swahili
Cambodian	Kazakh	Swedish
Cantonese	Korean	Tamil
Catalan	Latvian	Thai
Chinese (Mandarin)	Lithuanian	Tibetan
Croatian	Malay	Turkish
Czech	Mongolian	Ukrainian
Danish	Norwegian	Urdu
Dutch	Panjabi	Vietnamese
English	Persian	Welsh
Estonian	Polish	Yiddish
Finnish	Portuguese	Yoruba
French	Portuguese of Brazil	Zulu (forthcoming)

COLLOQUIAL 2s series: *The Next Step in Language Learning*

Chinese	German	Russian
Dutch	Italian	Spanish
French	Portuguese of Brazil	Spanish of Latin America

Colloquials are now supported by FREE AUDIO available online. All audio tracks referenced within the text are free to stream or download from www.routledge.com/cw/colloquials. If you experience any difficulties accessing the audio on the companion website, or still wish to purchase a CD, please contact our customer services team through www.routledge.com/info/contact.

Colloquial
Portuguese

A Complete Language Course

Second Edition

João Sampaio and Barbara McIntyre

Routledge
Taylor & Francis Group

LONDON AND NEW YORK

First published 1995
by Routledge
2 Park Square, Milton Park, Abingdon, Oxon, OX14 4RN

and by Routledge
711 Third Avenue, New York, NY 10017

Reprinted in 1998, 2000, 2001

Second edition first published 2002

Reprinted 2003

Routledge is an imprint of the Taylor & Francis Group, an informa business

© 1995, 2002 João Sampaio and Barbara McIntyre

The publisher has made every effort to trace copyright holders and would
be glad to hear from any who have not been traced.

British Library Cataloguing in Publication Data
A catalogue record for this book is available from the British Library

Library of Congress Cataloguing in Publication Data
A catalogue record for this book has been requested

ISBN: 978-1-138-96011-4 (pbk)

Illustrations by
Matthew Crabbe

Typeset in Times Ten by
Florence Production Ltd, Stoodleigh, Devon

Contents

Introduction

This book has been written to provide a beginners' course in Portuguese suitable for self-study, using a practical and modern method. It consists of thirteen lessons containing dialogues, reading comprehensions and exercises covering essential grammar points and vocabulary. Any differences of grammar and vocabulary found in Brazilian Portuguese are highlighted and the language used is kept simple but idiomatic. A simplified pronunciation guide is included with free audio to accompany the book available at www.routledge. com/cw/colloquials. The audio will allow you to listen to and practise speaking Portuguese.

The purpose of the course is to provide the student with a sound base of conversational Portuguese in a relatively short period of time, sufficient to cope in general holiday/business situations. The dialogues and reading texts present grammar and vocabulary in a systematic manner and each lesson is built around everyday situations such as visiting the bank or buying a drink in a café.

We recommend studying a little at a time but often – say about an hour a day – but, of course, individual preferences vary. First answer the exercises orally, then write them down before checking in the key at the end of the book. Certain exercises have no key as the answers are usually self-evident. As each lesson is completed, revise with the help of the concluding 'How much can you remember?' section. If you find that you can't remember a particular grammar point or structure, go back and revise the relevant part of the lesson before moving on to a new one. All the grammatical points raised are summarized in the compact reference grammar section at the back of the book.

Start a notebook for vocabulary, perhaps under different headings such as 'colours' or 'food', for ease of learning and reference. Two glossaries (Portuguese–English and English–Portuguese) are provided. Keep all your exercises in a second notebook. For help on pronunciation, consult the guide at the beginning of the book and listen carefully to the audio that accompanies the course. These are, of course, optional but are of great assistance in improving listening and speaking skills.

The authors would like to thank Carlos Alves, Eric Smith, Ester Soares, Jane Dennis, Louisa Semlyen, Alberto Simões, Barclay Duff (for providing a lap-top computer), the Portuguese Tourist Board and our respective wife (Patsy) and husband (Angus) for their encouragement. A special thank you to Maria Cristina Sousa.

A guide to pronunciation

1 Vowels

a If this is stressed, it is pronounced like the *a* in *father* but shorter: **fado** (pronounced *fahdoo*). If it is unstressed, it is pronounced like the *e* in *rather*: **mesa** (pronounced *meza*) ('table').

ã This is pronounced like the *e* in *rather* but nasalized: **maçã** ('apple').

e 1 If this is stressed, it sounds either like the *e* in *sell*: **preto** (pronounced *prehtoo*) ('black') or like the *ey* in *prey*: **saber** (pronounced *sabeyr*) ('to know'). If it is unstressed, it sounds like the *ey* in *prey*: **bebida** (pronounced *beybeeda*) ('drink').

2 At the end of a word, **e** is not pronounced in European Portuguese: **tarde** (pronounced *tard*) ('late/afternoon'). In Brazil, however, the final **e** is pronounced like *ee* in *peep*: **cidade** (pronounced seedahjee) ('city').

3 The word for 'and', **e**, is pronounced as *ee* in *sweep*.

i This is pronounced like the *e* in *evil*: **decidir** ('to decide'). When it is unstressed, it sounds like the *i* in *pin*: **idade** (pronounced *idahd*) ('age').

o If this is stressed or has an acute accent (´), it is pronounced like the *o* in *opera*: **fome** ('hunger'). When it is unstressed, it is pronounced like the *oo* in *book*: **fato** ('suit').

u This is usually pronounced like the *oo* in *roof*: **rua** ('street'). In the following four groups, however, it is not pronounced: **gue, gui, que** and **qui**.

2 Consonants

b This is pronounced as in *bank*: **obrigado** (pronounced *obree-gahdoo*) ('thank you').

c 1 This can be: soft, like the *s* in *slow* before an **e** or **i**: **cidade** (pronounced *seedad*) ('city'). If the **c** has a cedilla (**ç**), it is always soft;

2 hard, as in *card* before an **o** or **a**: **cá** (pronounced *cah*) ('here').

d This is pronounced as in *sad*: **tenda** (pronounced *tendah*) ('tent'). In Brazil, however, it is pronounced like the *ji* in *jinx*, especially at the end of a word: **dificuldade** (pronounced *deefeeculdahjee*) ('difficulty').

f This is pronounced as in *fair*: **fechado** (pronounced *feshadoo*) ('closed').

g 1 This is soft before an **e** or **i**, as in the English *s* in *pleasure*: **gente** (pronounced *zhent*) ('people');

2 hard before an **o**, **u** or **a**, as in *get*: **gato** (pronounced *gahtoo*) ('cat').

h This is never pronounced: **homem** (pronounced *omaing*) ('man').

1 When it follows a **c** it is pronounced like *sh* in *shore*: **chuva** (pronounced *shoova*) ('rain').

2 When it follows an **n**, it is pronounced like *ni* in *onion*: **banho** (pronounced *banyoo*) ('bath').

3 When it follows an **l**, it is pronounced like *lli* in *million*: **mulher** (pronounced *moolyair*) ('woman').

j This is pronounced like the *s* in *measure*: **jovem** (pronounced *zhovaing*) ('young').

l This is pronounced as in *look*: **fácil** (pronounced *faahseel*) ('easy'). In Brazil, the letter **l** at the end of a word sounds fainter.

m Except at the end of a word, this is pronounced as in *machine*: **maio** (pronounced *myyoo*) ('May'). At the end of a word it sounds like *ng* in *sung*: bem (pronounced *baing*) ('good').

n This is pronounced as in *no*: **nada** (pronounced *naahdah*) ('nothing').

p This is pronounced as in *put*: **pato** (pronounced *pahtoo*) ('duck').

q This is pronounced as in *quick* and is always followed by **u**: **quarenta** (pronounced *kwarentah*) ('forty').

r This is pronounced as in *rain*: **rir** (pronounced *reer*) ('to laugh'). Double **r** has a harder, more rolling sound: **carro** (pronounced *cahrroo*) ('car').

s 1 At the beginning of a word this is pronounced like the *s* in *sun*: **socorro!** (pronounced *sockoroo*) ('help!').

2 Between two vowels it is pronounced like the *s* in *present*: **casa** (pronounced *caahzah*) ('house').

3 At the end of a word it is pronounced like *sh* in *push*: **livros** (pronounced *leevroosh*) ('books').

t This is pronounced as in *teacher*: **tudo** (pronounced *toodooh*) ('everything').

v This is pronounced as in *video*: **videocassete** (pronounced *veedeeocasset*) ('video-cassette player').

x 1 At the beginning of a word this is pronounced like the *sh* in *shone*: **xale** (pronounced *shal*) ('shawl').

2 In the prefix **ex** when followed by a vowel, it is pronounced like the *z* in *zoo*: **executivo** (pronounced *ezekooteevoo*) ('executive').

3 Within a word and between two vowels, it can be pronounced either like the *sh* in *shone*: **roxo** (pronounced *rawshoo*) ('purple') or like the *cks* in *racks*: **tóxico** (pronounce *tokseekoo*) ('toxic').

4 When it is followed by **ce** or **ci**, it is not pronounced: **excêntrico** (pronounced *esentreecoo*) ('eccentric').

z 1 At the beginning and in the middle of a word, this is pronounced like the *z* in *zoo*: **zanga** (pronounced *zangah*) ('anger'); **dizer** (pronounced *deezair*) ('to say').

2 At the end of a word it is pronounced like the *s* in *measure*: **luz** (pronounced loozh) ('light').

Diphthongs

ãe This is pronounced like the *ie* in *pie* but nasalized: **mãe** ('mother')
ão This is pronounced like the *ow* in *crowd* but nasalized: **limão** ('lemon')
õe This is pronounced like the *oi* in *boil* but nasalized: **lições** ('lessons')
ou This is pronounced like the *ow* in *crow*: **comprou** ('you bought')
ei This is pronounced like the *ay* in *pray*: **dei** ('I gave')
eu This is pronounced *ayooh* (the first part rhymes with *hay*): **eu** ('I')
ai This is pronounced like the *ie* in *pie*: **pai** ('father')

Stress

This normally falls on the penultimate syllable – *me*sa ('table'), ja*ne*la ('window') – except when:

1 words end in **ade**: **ci***da***de** ('city')
2 words end in **l, r** or **z**: **panta***nal* ('swampland'), **liber***tar* ('to free'), **fe***liz* ('happy')

3 words end in **um** or **uns**: **ne*nhum*** ('no one'), **al*guns*** ('some')
4 there is an accent, indicating where the stress should fall: **fácil** ('easy'), **inglês** ('English').

Spoken Portuguese tends to run words together: **Lia o livro** ('He was reading the book') sounds like: *lee-er-oo-lee-vroo*.

Accents

The English names of accents are as follows:

acute (é) grave (à) tilde (ã) circumflex (ê).

1 Olá, tudo bem?

Hello, how are you?

In this lesson you will learn about:

- greetings, introductions, farewells
- ordering something to eat and drink
- using the present indicative tense of **ser** (to be)
- nationalities
- subject pronouns
- the definite and indefinite articles

Dialogue 1 (Audio 1: 1)
Boa noite, como está?

A crowd has gathered in the foyer of the Cinema Tropical in Lisbon to see the film **Os Três Mosqueteiros** (The Three Musketeers). *Some of the crowd greet each other*

ALICE: Boa noite, como está?
ANTÓNIO: Boa noite, estou bem obrigado, e você?
ALICE: Estou bem, obrigada[1]
LUISA: Faz favor, como se chama?
ISABEL: Chamo-me Isabel, e você?
LUISA: Chamo-me Luisa, muito prazer.
JORGE: Olá pá!
JOSÉ: Olá, estás bom?
JORGE: Óptimo![2]
CARLOS: *(from Brazil)* Oi[3], Alice, tudo bem?
ALICE: Ora viva Carlos, como vai?
CARLOS: Muito bem, obrigado.

---

1 You say **obrigado** if you are male and **obrigada** if you are female.

2 This is spelt **ótimo** in Brazil. Throughout this book we shall use the abbreviations (Br) for Brazilian spellings and equivalents and (Pt) for European Portuguese.
3 This is the Brazilian equivalent of **Olá!**

ALICE: *Good evening, how are you?*
ANTÓNIO: *Good evening, I'm fine thanks, and you?*
ALICE: *I'm well, thank you.*
LUISA: *Excuse me, what's your name?*
ISABEL: *My name is Isabel, what's yours?*
LUISA: *My name is Luisa, pleased to meet you.*
JORGE: *Hi there, mate!*
JOSÉ: *Hi, how's things?*
JORGE: *Great!*
CARLOS: *(from Brazil) Hi, Alice, everything OK?*
ALICE: *Hi there Carlos, how's it going?*
CARLOS: *Very well, thanks.*

Exercise 1

If you have the recordings, listen again to the dialogues. Each time you hear the words or phrases listed in the chart below, tick them off. (If you don't have the recordings, re-read the dialogues, then cover the English and try writing the English translations, and vice versa.)

boa noite	estás bom?	como se chama?	tudo bem?	como está?	chamo -me	estou bem obrigado /a

Exercise 2

Translate the following into English then back into Portuguese.
(Use the dialogues on pages 7–8 as a guide.)

A: Faz favor, como se chama?
B: Chamo-me Jorge, e você, como se chama?
A: Chamo-me Luisa. Muito prazer.
A: Boa noite, como está?
B: Estou muito bem obrigado, e você?
A: Estou muito bem, obrigada.

Greetings

Depending on what time of day it is, you say:

Bom dia   Good morning/Hello!
(during the morning until lunch time)
Boa tarde Good afternoon/Good evening/Hello!
(during the afternoon until dusk)
Boa noite Good evening/Good night/Hello!
(from nightfall until daylight)

These greetings can also be used as farewells:

Bom dia!   Good morning! i.e. Goodbye!
(when taking leave)

When used as farewells, **bom dia**, **boa tarde** and **boa noite** are more informal than **adeus** which means 'goodbye'.

In Portuguese, either **boa tarde** or **boa noite** can be used to express the English 'good evening'. Essentially, although it may be fairly late in the evening – say after 7.00 p.m. – if an element of daylight still lingers, **boa tarde** is used. So, if it is 6.45 p.m. and dusk is falling but some light still remains:

Boa tarde! Good evening!

If it is 10.15 p.m., dusk has already fallen and the streetlights are on:

Boa noite! Good evening!

Dialogue 2 (Audio 1: 2)
Estou bem, obrigado

What responses would you give to the following questions? If you have the recordings, use the pause button after each question to give yourself time to think of a reply. If you don't have the recordings, cover up the responses given by B and imagine how you might answer the questions

1

A: Boa noite, como está?
B: Estou bem, obrigado.

2

A: Olá Paula! Estás boa?[4]
B: Estou bem, obrigada.

3

A: Boa tarde, chamo-me Isabel, e você, como se chama?
B: Boa tarde, chamo-me ...

1

A: *Good evening, how are you?*
B: *I'm fine, thanks.*

2

A: *Hi there Paula! How are you?*
B: *Fine, thanks.*

3

A: *Good afternoon, my name is Isabel, what's yours?*
B: *Good afternoon, my name is ...*

---

4 **Está(s) boa?** (How are you?) is the form of question asked of a female person and **Está(s) bom?** is the form asked of a male person.

Pronunciation (Audio 1: 3

Portuguese is a language which abounds in nasal sounds. If you have the recordings, listen to the following words:

fim	end	**bem**	well, fine	**opinião**	opinion
com	with	**ontem**	yesterday	**mão**	hand
homem	man	**sim**	yes	**pão**	bread
assim	thus	**bom**	good	**televisão**	television

Rules for pronunciation

1 The letter **-m** at the end of a Portuguese word sounds like **-ng** in English. For example:

bem is pronounced *baing*
sim is pronounced *seeng*
bom is pronounced *bong*
falam is pronounced *fahlang*
In each case the final **-g** is not pronounced.

2 The letters **-ão** at the end of a Portuguese word (the accent is called a 'tilde') sound like 'Ow!' in English with the sound being produced simultaneously from the mouth and the nose. For example:

não is pronounced *now*
pão is pronounced *pow*

Subject pronouns

We need to use four abbreviations in the following list and elsewhere in this book. They are: (m), which means 'masculine'; (f), which means 'feminine'; (s), which means 'singular'; and (pl), which means 'plural'.

eu	I
tu	you (ms + fs)
você[5]	you (ms + fs)
o senhor	you (ms)
a senhora	you (fs)
ele	he, it

ela	she, it
nós	we
vocês	you (mpl + fpl)
os senhores	you (mpl)
as senhoras	you (fpl)
eles	they (mpl)
elas	they (fpl)

5 This form for 'you' is most widely used in Brazil.

Subject pronouns are often omitted in Portuguese, as the verb ending gives information about who is being referred to. For example:

Somos de Londres   We are from London

Vós ('you' (pl)) is another way of expressing **vocês** or **os senhores/as senhoras**. It is still used in some parts of northern Portugal but largely it is found in prayers, speeches and classical literature.

One of the most noticeable differences between English and Portuguese is the variety of ways of expressing 'you', which can be translated as **você** (formal + informal), **tu** (informal), or **o senhor/a senhora** (formal), as well as their plural forms. For the time being, use **você** for 'you'.

The verb ser

One of the most frequently used verbs in Portuguese (as in English) is the irregular verb **ser** ('to be'). The present indicative tense of **ser** is as follows:

eu	**sou**	I am
tu	**és**	you are (ms + fs)
você	**é**	you are (ms + fs)
o senhor	**é**	you are (ms)
a senhora	**é**	you are (fs)
ele	**é**	he is, it is
ela	**é**	she is, it is
nós	**somos**	we are
vocês	**são**	you are (mpl + fpl)
os senhores	**são**	you are (mpl)

as senhoras	**são**	you are (fpl)
eles	**são**	they are (mpl)
elas	**são**	they are (fpl)

Exercise 3

Now match the correct subject pronoun to its form of the verb **ser**. The first has been done for you.

	ele	nós	vocês	tu	eu	elas	você
é	3						3
são							
és							
sou							
somos							

Regular and irregular verbs

As in English, verbs can be either regular or irregular. An irregular verb is one which does not follow the normal pattern of stem + endings. The term 'present indicative' is the equivalent of the simple present in English and signifies a mood of certainty and fact. For example:

Ela é muito rica	She is very rich
O autocarro parte amanhã	The bus leaves tomorrow

Uses of the present indicative tense

1 To express facts:

Gosto de viajar
I like travelling

2 A normal occurrence:

O banco fecha às 3 horas
The bank closes at 3 p.m.

3 Something happening at some future date which has an aura of intent about it:

Vou às compras mais tarde
I'll go shopping later

4 Something which has been going on and still is:

Estuda português há anos
He has been studying Portuguese for years (and is still doing so)

Dialogue 3 (Audio 1: 4)
Sou angolano

Listen to the next four mini-dialogues where people of various nationalities are chatting about where they are from

1

Q: Bom dia. Sou de Angola. Sou angolano.[6] Donde é?
A: Olá! Sou de França. Sou francesa.[6]

2

Q: Bom dia. Chamo-me Fernanda. Sou brasileira. Como se chama?
A: Chamo-me Stig. Sou da Holanda. Muito prazer.

3

Q: Olá! Tudo bem? Sou do Brasil. Você também é do Brasil?
A: Bom dia. Como vai? Não, não sou do Brasil. Sou de Moçambique. Sou moçambicano.

4

Q: Olá! Chamo-me Cristina. Qual é a sua nacionalidade?
A: Muito prazer. Chamo-me Tracey. A minha nacionalidade é britânica.

6 Nationalities do not require a capital letter.

1

Q: *Good morning. I'm Angolan. I'm from Angola. Where are you from?*
A: *Hi! I'm from France. I'm French.*

2

Q: *Good morning. My name is Fernanda. I'm Brazilian. What's your name?*
A: *I'm Stig. I'm from Holland. I'm pleased to meet you.*

3

Q: *Hi! How's things? I'm from Brazil. Are you from Brazil too?*
A: *Good morning. How's it going? No, I'm not from Brazil. I'm from Mozambique. I'm Mozambican.*

4

Q: *Hi! My name's Cristina. What nationality are you?*
A: *Pleased to meet you. My name is Tracey. My nationality is British.*

Negatives

To make a sentence negative, put **não** ('no/not') before the verb:

Não sou inglês	I'm not English
Não, não sou do Brasil	No, I'm not from Brazil

Exercise 4

Now imagine you are in the group. How would you say: 'Hi! How are you? I'm fine, thanks. My name is ... What's your name? Are you from France? Oh, you're from England! I'm from Holland. Pleased to meet you!' You should find all the necessary expressions in the material covered so far.

Forming feminine adjectives

In the dialogues about nationalities, the endings used were not always the same. This is because they change according to whether a male or female person is speaking or is being addressed:

Sou inglês
I'm English (male person speaking)

Sou inglesa
I'm English (female person speaking)

Você é angolana?
Are you Angolan? (asked of a female person)

As you can see from the above examples, to form the feminine of a nationality ending in -**ês**, the circumflex accent (^) is dropped and an -**a** is added. In the case of an adjective ending in -**o**, the -**o** is dropped and replaced with an -**a**. (Some nationalities do not conform to this rule but they need not concern us at this stage.)

Exercise 5a

Now match up the correct Portuguese phrase with its English equivalent in the following examples.

Sou brasileira	Are you English? (f)
Sou português	I am Dutch (m)
Ele é angolano	She is Scottish
Você é inglesa?	I am Portuguese (m)
Ela é escocesa	I am Brazilian (f)
Sou holandês	He is Angolan

Introducing someone

Apresento-lhe a Joana
I'd like you to meet/This is Joana

Apresento-lhes ...
I'd like you to meet ... (when you are introducing someone to more than one person)

Exercise 5b

Now try introducing the following people using the information given below each figure. Say in Portuguese: 'I'd like you to meet (name). He/she is from (country). He/she is (nationality).'

Tom
England
English

Gabriella
Italy
Italian

Alberto
Angola
Angolan

Hans
Germany
German

Vocabulary

Itália	Italy	**italiano/a**	Italian
Angola	Angola	**angolano/a**	Angolan
Alemanha	Germany	**alemão/alemã**	German

Exercise 6

Can you give the following in Portuguese? Wherever 'you' occurs, for the moment use the **você** form. Answers are in the key at the end of the book.

1 Are you English? (f) _____
2 I am Scottish (m) _____
3 He is Portuguese _____
4 Is she Brazilian? _____
5 You are Angolan (f) _____

Now cover up the English and translate the Portuguese into English.

Sou de, sou do, etc.

You may have noticed in Dialogue 3 that you cannot always say simply **sou de** ('I'm from'). Certain countries need the Portuguese word for 'the', which will either be **o** (m) or **a** (f). This then joins with **de** to produce the following:

Sou da (de + a) Holanda	I'm from Holland
Você é do (de + o) Brasil?	Are you from Brazil?

Some countries are plural:

os Estados Unidos	the United States
Sou dos Estados Unidos	I'm from the United States
de + os → dos	

There is no real pattern as to why some countries require the definite article or why some are considered masculine while others are feminine. Just note them as they arise.

'Yes' and 'no'

Instead of replying with a bald 'yes' (**sim**) or 'no' (**não**), in Portuguese you repeat the verb:

Você é japonês?	Are you Japanese?
Sou, sim	Yes

The gender of nouns

All Portuguese nouns are either masculine or feminine, even if you are referring to an inanimate object, 'it'.

Como é o computador?	What's the computer like?
(Ele) é muito útil	It's very useful (*lit.*: 'he')

Nouns ending in **-o, -im, -om** and **-um** are generally masculine. Those ending in **-a, -ã, -gem, -dade, -ice, -ez, -ção** and **-são** are generally feminine, although there are exceptions.

The definite article

English does not have the problem of distinguishing between the gender of words. In Portuguese, the word for 'the' changes according to what is being referred to and every noun is either masculine or feminine.

For words in the singular you have a choice of either:

o (masculine words)	(pronounced *oo*)
a (feminine words)	(pronounced *er*)
o livro (m) the book	**a casa** (f) the house

and for words in the plural:

os (masculine words)	(pronounced *oosh*)
as (feminine words)	(pronounced *ersh*)
os livros (mpl) the books	**as casas** (fpl) the houses

The indefinite article

Again, this changes according to whether a noun is masculine or feminine:

um (masculine words)	(pronounced *oom*)
uma (feminine words)	(pronounced *oomah*)

Examples

um jornal (m) a newspaper   **uma revista** (f) a magazine

Unlike in English, these articles have a plural form translated as 'some' or not translated at all:

uns (masculine words)	(pronounced *oonsh*)
umas (feminine words)	(pronounced *oomash*)

Examples

uns óculos   (some) spectacles
umas canetas (some) pens

Exercise 7

Match up the following words with their correct article, definite or indefinite, in the box below.

1	_____ **telemóvel** (ms)	the mobile phone
2	_____ **mulher** (fs)	the woman
3	_____ **bolachas** (fpl)	(some) biscuits
4	_____ **relógios** (mpl)	the watches
5	_____ **gelados** (mpl)	(some) ice creams
6	_____ **colinas** (fpl)	the hills

os	a	uns	as	umas	o

Forming the plural

(a) Nouns ending in a vowel (but not **ão**) add **s**

singular		*plural*	
o gato	the cat	**os gatos**	the cats
a cidade	the city	**as cidades**	the cities

(b) Nouns ending in **r** or **z** add **es**

o sabor	the flavour	**os sabores**	the flavours
a voz	the voice	**as vozes**	the voices

(c) Nouns ending in **m** become **ns**

o homem	the man	**os homens**	the men

(d) Nouns already ending in **s** add **es** if the stress is on the last syllable:

o país	the country	**os países**	the countries
o lápis	the pencil	**os lápis**	the pencils

In the second example, the spelling of the noun is unchanged because the stress falls on the penultimate syllable.

Exercise 8

Can you give the plural forms of the following?

1 **uma nuvem**	a cloud	2 **o prato**	the dish
3 **um pente**	a comb	4 **a praia**	the beach

Exercise 9

Now give the singular forms of these words. The first has been done for you:

1	**os tapetes**	the carpets	→	**o tapete**
2	**as cadeiras**	the chairs		
3	**os lápis**	the pencils		
4	**umas revistas**	(some) magazines		
5	**uns carros**	(some) cars		

Pronunciation (Audio 1: 5)

If you have the recordings, listen to the different pronunciations of the letter **s** in Portuguese.

s at the beginning of a word is as in the English 'same':
sou (I am)

s at the end of a word is as in the English 'push':
inglês (English)

s between two vowels is as in the English 'zebra':
irlandesa (Irish)

Exercise 10

Bearing in mind who is being referred to in each case, do you think that the sentences below are all correct? Provide the correct version of each sentence where necessary.

1 **Kathleen é irlandês**
2 **Jorge é português**
3 **Isabel é portuguesa**
4 **Ela é holandês**
5 **Você** (Matthew) **é inglês e** [and] **eu** (Jane) **sou escocês**
6 **Andrew é escocês mas** [but] **Jules é francesa** (French)

Exercise 11

Read the following short passage and answer the questions which follow:

> **Chamo-me Jorge. Sou do Brasil. Sou brasileiro. Apresento-lhe o Paulo. Ele é de Portugal; é português. Qual é a nacionalidade da Isabel? Ela é italiana? Ah, ela é brasileira também.**

1 True or false? Jorge introduces himself by stating that he is from Italy.
2 What does he say about Paulo?
3 What information does he want to know about Isabel?
4 What is he surprised to find out?

Food and drink

Getting the waiter's attention:

Faz favor!	Excuse me!
Por favor!	Excuse me!

What you will be asked:

Que deseja?	What would you like? (to one person)
Que desejam?	What would you like? (to more than one person)

Asking for something to eat and drink:

um café	a black coffee
uma bica	an espresso
um chá	a tea
uma cerveja	a beer
uma imperial	a half pint of (draught) beer
uma água mineral	a mineral water
uma água mineral com gás	a fizzy mineral water
uma água mineral sem gás	a still mineral water
um galão	a large white coffee
uma média (Br)	a large white coffee
uma sande de fiambre (Pt)	a ham sandwich
uma sande de queijo (Pt)	a cheese sandwich
uma sanduíche (Br + Pt)	a sandwich
uma tosta mista	a toasted ham and cheese sandwich
um mixto quente (Br)	a toasted ham and cheese sandwich
um prego	a steak sandwich
um bolo	a cake

Saying 'please', 'thanks' and 'how much?'

(se) faz favor	please
por favor	please
(muito) obrigado/a	thank you (very much)
quanto é?	How much is it?

∩ Dialogue 4 (Audio 1: 6)
Faz favor!

See if you can discover what Jorge and Cristina are ordering

JORGE:	Faz favor!
EMPREGADO:	Boa tarde. Que desejam?
JORGE:	Boa tarde, um café e um bolo, por favor.
EMPREGADO:	E a senhora?
CRISTINA:	Um galão e uma sanduíche de fiambre, se faz favor.
EMPREGADO:	Mais alguma coisa? (*Anything else?*)
JORGE:	Mais nada, obrigadinho.
	(*Nothing else, thanks very much.*)

obrigadinho (obrigado + inho)   thanks very much
(**obrigadinha** if you are a female speaker)

Go through Dialogue 4 again. Now it's your turn to order for them:

(a) For Jorge, ask for a small black coffee and a cake.
(b) For Cristina, ask for a large white coffee and a ham sandwich, and reply, 'Nothing else, thanks very much' to the waiter's last question.

Exercise 12

Here is a bill (**uma conta**) from a cake shop (**uma pastelaria**) but it has a few things missing from the list below in English. Can you discover which things and add them to the list in Portuguese:

a steak sandwich	a cake, a white coffee
a ham sandwich	a tea, a beer
a cheese sandwich	a fizzy mineral water

Pastelaria Gomes

---

1 sanduíche de fiambre   ....
1 prego   ....
1 galão   ....
1 chá   ....

How much can you remember?

1 Fill in the missing words:

LIDIA: _____ se chama?
PABLO: _____ -me Pablo.
LIDIA: _____ espanhol? (Spanish)
PABLO: Sou. _____ de Madrid. E você?
LIDIA: Sou _____, sou de Portugal.

2 What greeting would you give in Portuguese?

It is 9 a.m. in the morning _____!
Now it is 6 p.m. in the evening _____!
And now it is 11 p.m. at night _____!

3 Ask someone you have just met:

If he is English. Find out where he is from. Ask his name. Say you are (name) and you are from Italy.

4 (a) Name three drinks you might order.
(b) Would you eat: **uma bica, um bolo, uma imperial**?
(c) Would you drink: **uma sanduíche, uma cerveja, um galão**?

5 Can you provide the questions which match the following replies?

1 Boa tarde, estou bem obrigado.
2 Chamo-me Isabel.
3 Sou de Paris.
4 Tudo bem, obrigado.
5 A minha nacionalidade é espanhola.

6 Now talk about yourself. Say what your name is, what nationality you are, and where you are from.

7 Read this short passage, answer the questions which follow and then translate it into English:

> **Carlos e Fernanda são brasileiros. Vivem no Rio de Janeiro no Brasil. Vêm a Portugal todos os anos para visitarem o irmão deles, José, que vive no Porto.**

1 What nationality are Fernanda and Carlos?
2 Where do they come from?

3 Why do they visit Portugal and how often do they make the trip?

Vocabulary

vivem	they live
vêm	they come
a	to
todos os anos	each year
o irmão deles	their brother
que vive no Porto	who lives in Oporto

Vocabulary

In order to build up your vocabulary, why not start a small notebook which contains various headings? For example:

p 1. *Greetings*	*p 2.* *Drinks*	*p 3.* *Various*
Está bem? (Pt) **Tudo bem?** (Br) How are you?	**um chá** a tea	**Sim** Yes **Bem** Well

Use your dictionary to add to your word lists. For example, you might want to know how to ask for other drinks not listed in this lesson, or to extend the list of nationalities. As you consult your dictionary, make a point of noting down at the same time the gender of a word (i.e. whether it is masculine or feminine). For example, for 'house' you will find **casa** (f). You already know from this lesson the word for the English 'a' which can be either **um, uma, uns** or **umas** depending on the noun involved, and the different forms for 'the' in Portuguese: **o, a, os, as**. In this case, **casa** is feminine singular:

uma casa   a house   **a casa**   the house

2 Gosto de viajar

I like to travel

In this lesson you will learn about:

- using the verbs **ser** and **estar**
- expressing likes and dislikes
- using the present indicative of regular verbs
- describing yourself and saying what you do
- telling the time
- the days of the week

The following Portuguese speakers were asked to give a brief description of their lives, likes, dislikes and personalities by the local radio station. **O locutor** *('the radio announcer') asks them to* **Fale-me de si** *('tell me a bit about yourself')*

 Dialogue 1 (Audio 1: 7)
Álvaro

O Locutor: Fale-me de si.

Álvaro: Canto o fado.[1] Trabalho num[2] clube em Albufeira no[3] Algarve. Sou casado mas separado. Moro num apartamento perto da praia. Gosto de tocar a guitarra; de arte. Não gosto de violência; de intolerância. Personalidade? Sou bastante tímido mas gosto muito de me divertir.

I sing fado. I work in a club in Albufeira in the Algarve. I'm married but separated. I live in a flat near the beach. I like playing the guitar; art. I don't like violence; intolerance. Personality? I'm quite shy but I like a good laugh.

1 **o fado**: a type of melancholy Portuguese folk music
2 **num clube: em + um → num** ('in a').
   Similarly, with the feminine indefinite article: **em + uma → numa**
   Moro numa casa I live in a house
3 **no Algarve: em + o → no** ('in the').
   Similarly, with the feminine definite article: **em + a → na**
   Trabalho na pastelaria I work in the cake shop
   em can also mean 'on': **na televisão** on the TV

 ## Dialogue 2 (Audio 1: 8)
Paulo

O LOCUTOR: Fale-me de si.
PAULO: Sou electricista.[4] Trabalho numa companhia no centro do Funchal, na Madeira. Sou casado. Moro numa casa moderna. Gosto de desportos; de jogar futebol.[5] Não gosto da comida chinesa; de palavras cruzadas. Personalidade? Sou extrovertido[6] e bastante preguiçoso.

I'm an electrician. I work in a company in the centre of Funchal in Madeira. I'm married. I live in a modern house. I like sports; playing football. I don't like Chinese food; crosswords. Personality? I'm an extrovert and quite lazy.

4 **Sou electricista** 'I'm *an* electrician'. There is no need for 'a/an' with professions.
5 **tocar** means 'to play (music)' while **jogar** means 'to play (sport)'.
6 **Sou extrovertido** 'I'm *an* extrovert'. There is no need to say 'a' or 'an' when one is describing oneself in Portuguese.

 ## Dialogue 3 (Audio 1: 9)
Graça

O LOCUTOR: Fale-me de si.
GRAÇA: Sou vendedora. Trabalho numa loja de brinquedos nos[7] arredores de Lisboa, em Portugal. Não sou casada.[8] Sou solteira. Moro num apartamento alugado. Gosto de viajar; de cinema. Não gosto de

tempo frio; de transporte público. Personalidade?
Sou faladora e descontraída.
*I'm a shop assistant. I work in a toy shop on the
outskirts of Lisbon in Portugal. I'm not married. I'm
single. I live in a rented flat. I like travelling; the
cinema. I don't like cold weather; public transport.
Personality? I'm talkative and laid-back.*

7 **Nos arredores: em + os** (mpl) → **nos** ('in the')
Similarly, with the feminine plural definite article:

Há nova tecnologia nas fábricas
There is new technology in the factories

em + as → **nas** ('in the')

8 **Não sou casada**: remember that, if the speaker is feminine, the adjective usually changes at the end from **o** to **a**.

The present indicative tense of regular verbs

Revise **regular and irregular** verbs and the uses of the present indicative tense in Lesson 1.

	trabalhar	*to work*
eu	**trabalho**	I work
tu	**trabalhas**	you work
você	**trabalha**	you work
o senhor	**trabalha**	you work
a senhora	**trabalha**	you work
ele	**trabalha**	he, it works
ela	**trabalha**	she, it works
nós	**trabalhamos**	we work
vocês	**trabalham**	you work
os senhores	**trabalham**	you work
as senhoras	**trabalham**	you work
eles	**trabalham**	they work
elas	**trabalham**	they work

Trabalhar is an example of a regular Portuguese **-ar** verb. The letters **-ar** are removed from the stem (**trabalh-**) and are replaced by: **-o**, **-as**, **-a**, **-amos** and **-am**. These five endings are all you need to learn for the present indicative tense of any regular verb ending in **-ar**.

Two more groups of verbs exist in Portuguese, which end in either **-er** or **-ir**. The present indicative of these two groups of verbs are formed in the same way as that of **-ar** verbs:

-er verbs:
vender ('to sell') → **vend-** plus the ending: **-o, -es, -e, -emos** and **-em**

-ir verbs:
partir ('to leave') → **part-**, plus the endings: **-o, -es, -e, -imos** and **-em**

These endings are added to the stem of the verb as in the case of the **-ar** verb **trabalhar**. Here are two more examples:

comer	*to eat*	**decidir**	*to decide*
como		**decid**o	I
comes		**decid**es	you
come		**decid**e	he, she, it, you (s)
comemos		**decid**imos	we
comem		**decid**em	they, you (pl)

Exercise 1

Write out in full, referring to the above chart, the following verbs: **viver** ('to live') and **dividir** ('to divide').

The verb gostar de ('to like')

Gostar de is another example of an **-ar** verb but this verb is one which is always followed by the preposition **de** ('of/from'):

Gosto de cantar	I like to sing (I like singing)
Gosto de viajar	I like to travel (I like travelling)

If **gostar de** is followed by the complete form of the verb – i.e. the infinitive form: 'to sing', 'to dance', etc. – the **de** will remain unaltered as in the examples above. If referring to a *specific* noun, however, the **de** contracts with the definite article, **-o, -a, -os** or **-as**, according to whether the noun is masculine, feminine or in the plural.

Examples:

gosto de + verb	. . . **trabalhar**
	. . . **nadar**
	. . . **beber café**
gosto de + noun	. . . **bolos** (in general)
	. . . **revistas**
	. . . **música**
	. . . **computadores**
gosto de + noun (specific)	**gosto** *da* **música jazz**
	gosto *da* **poesia do T S Eliot**

Vocabulary

nadar	to swim	**revistas** (fpl)	magazines
computadores (mpl)	computers		

Exercise 2

Can you fill in the correct form of **de**?

Gosto d ——— roupa (f)	I like clothes
Gostamos d ——— fruta (f)	We like fruit
Gostam d ——— viajar	They like travelling
Gosta d ——— cinema francês	He likes French cinema
Gostas d ——— rádio (m)	You like the radio
Gostam d ——— casas modernas (fpl)	They like modern houses

Exercise 3

Re-read Dialogues 2 and 3. Imagine that Paulo and Graça have exactly the same likes and dislikes, and then describe them: 'they like . . .'/'they don't like . . .' For example: **Gostam de desportos.**

Exercise 4

Can you give your likes/dislikes from the list below? Write out in full **gosto de/não gosto de** . . .

a música 'rock'	rock music
ver as telenovelas	to watch soaps on TV

a política	politics
ler poesia	to read poetry
os filmes de Woody Allen	Woody Allen films
a energia nuclear	nuclear energy
escrever cartas	to write letters
Posto de edição electrónica	desk-top publishing

(Re-read or listen again to the dialogues at the beginning of the lesson as a guide.)

Exercise 5

Re-read Dialogue 1. Now you have to describe Álvaro's life to someone else. 'He sings . . .';'he doesn't like . . .', etc. Try to translate the rest of the details Álvaro reveals about himself in Portuguese.

Exercise 6

Read the following passage, then answer the questions below:

A família Gonçalves vive em Algés, nos arredores de Lisboa. A mãe (Lucília) é telefonista num consultório médico. O pai (José) é mecânico numa garagem.

1 Where does the family live exactly?
2 What do the parents do for a living?

Exercise 7

Can you write these potted histories for two singers, one male, one female:

JORGE: Sou cantor . . .

    casado Lisboa casa tímido a ópera (sim gosto) o futebol (não gosto)

CLARA: Sou cantora . . .

    solteiro Luanda (Angola) casa preguiçoso o andar[9] (sim gosto) o desporto (não gosto)

9 **o andar** walking

The endings of adjectives and nouns

Remember that the adjectives describing Clara ('single', 'lazy') will change because she is a female speaker (refer to the section about nationalities in the first lesson). Nouns denoting professions also alter according to who is speaking or being referred to. There are a variety of ways in which adjectives can end, as the following demonstrate.

(1) The masculine singular form ends in **-o** (but not **-ão**):

masculine:			feminine:	
honesto	(s)	→	**honesta**	(-o → -a)
honestos	(pl)	→	**honestas**	(-os →-as)
o engenheiro	(s)	→	**a engenheira**	engineer
os engenheiros	(pl)	→	**as engenheiras**	engineers

(2) The masculine singular form ends in **-e**

inteligente	→	**inteligente** (no change takes place)	
inteligentes	→	**inteligentes**	
o gerente	→	**a gerente**	manager
os gerentes	→	**as gerentes**	managers

(3) The masculine singular form ends in **-r**

falador	→	**faladora**	(add **-a**)
faladores	→	**faladoras**	
o professor	→	**a professora**	teacher
os professores	→	**as professoras**	teachers

(4) The masculine singular form ends in **-a**

pessimista	→	**pessimista**	
		(no change takes place)	
pessimistas	→	**pessimistas**	
o jornalista	→	**a jornalista**	journalist
os jornalistas	→	**as jornalistas**	journalists

The position and agreement of adjectives

Adjectives usually follow the noun and agree in gender and number with the noun to which they refer:

a arquitectura moderna   **um atleta vigoroso**
modern architecture   a powerful athlete

as aulas de condução car*as*   os vinhos tint*os*
expensive driving lessons   red wines

When an adjective refers jointly to a masculine and a feminine noun, the adjective always takes the masculine plural form:

três canetas (fpl) e dois lápis (mpl) vermelh*os*

Exercise 8

Graça wants to change her job (o emprego) so she consults Álvaro who, before taking up fado singing, tried out quite a few different occupations. How would Graça write out a similar curriculum vitae? And which job does she finally choose?

Álvaro   Graça

Curriculum vitae
médico
jornalista
padeiro
gerente
pintor
carpinteiro

Curriculum vitae
uma médica . . . ?
Não.
uma . . . . . . ?
uma jornalista.
Sim!

Vocabulary

o médico	doctor	o gerente	manager
o pintor	painter	o jornalista	journalist
o carpinteiro	carpenter	o padeiro	baker

Cardinal Numbers

Memorize the following numbers from 1 to 50:

		pronounced:
um, uma[10]	1	oom, oomah
dois, duas[10]	2	doish, dooersh
três	3	tresh
quatro	4	kwahtroo
cinco	5	seenkoo
seis	6	saysh
sete	7	set
oito	8	oitoo
nove	9	nov
dez	10	desh
onze	11	onz
doze	12	doz
treze	13	trez
catorze	14	katorz
quinze	15	keenz
dezasseis	16	dizasaysh (Br dezesseis)
dezassete	17	dizaset (Br dezessete)
dezoito	18	dizoitoo
dezanove	19	dizanov (Br dezenove)
vinte	20	veent
vinte e um/uma	21	veent-ee-oom/oomer
vinte e dois/duas etc.	22	veent-ee-doish/dooersh
trinta	30	treenta
trinta e cinco	35	treenta-ee-seenkoo
quarenta	40	kwarenta
cinquenta	50	seenkwenta

10 'One' and 'two' (**um/a, dois/duas**) agree with what is being referred to: **um***a* **rua** (f) ('a street') / **um café** (m) ('a coffee')

Exercise 9

Here are three advertisements from a newspaper (**um jornal**) for various staff (**o pessoal**). Can you answer the following questions with the aid of the vocabulary below?

Vocabulary

precisam-se	wanted/required
exigem-se	wanted/required
admite pessoas	staff wanted/required
cabeleireiros/as	hairdressers
vendedores/as	sales assistants
com prática	with experience
alguma prática	some experience
boa apresentação	good appearance
ambição e dinamismo	ambition and dynamism
facilidade de comunicação	good communicator
boa remuneração	good remuneration
para vários cargos	for various posts
com conhecimentos de produtos de plantas/flores	with knowledge of plant and flower products
com carro de preferência	car owner preferred
marque entrevista	for interview (telephone ...)

1 Can you find the advertisement for hairdressers? Is the pay good?
2 What qualities are required by the multinational firm?
3 Which advertisement would prefer applicants to have their own transport?

Days of the week: Os dias da semana

Exercise 10

Look at this page from Paulo's diary (**a agenda**). He had already marked in his commitments for the week but suddenly remembers that he must arrange a meeting ...

segunda-feira	
terça-feira	*comprar um presente*
quarta-feira	*escrever uma carta*
quinta-feira	*ir à universidade*
sexta-feira	
sábado	*descansar*
domingo	*visitar amigos*

Vocabulary

comprar um presente	to buy a gift
ir à universidade	to go to the university
descansar	to rest
visitar amigos	to visit friends
escrever uma carta	to write a letter
quarta-feira	Wednesday (there is no need for the article)
na **segunda-feira**	*on* Monday (the article is needed when 'on' is used)
nos **domingos**	*on* Sundays
trabalho na quarta(-feira)	I work on Wednesday
hoje	today
quinze dias	fortnight
todos os dias	everyday
que dia é hoje?	what date is it today?
quantos são hoje?	what date is it today?

1 What days does he have free?
2 Is he available on Thursday?
3 He is extremely busy on Friday. True or false?
4 What does Paulo do at the weekend (o fim de semana)?

Contraction

When **a** means 'at/to' and precedes the definite article **o/a/os/as**, the words contract as follows:

vou à universidade (fs)	I'm going to the university (**a** + **a**)
joga ao ténis (ms)	he plays tennis (**a** + **o**)
vai às lojas (fpl)	he goes to the shops (**a** + **as**)
brincam aos 'cowboys' (mpl)	they play cowboys and indians (**a** + **os**)

Days of the week are feminine except for **sábado** and **domingo**. The '**-feira**' element can be dropped:

Vou na segunda   I'm going on Monday

Dialogue 4
Um encontro

*Paulo wants to arrange a meeting (**marcar um encontro** or **arranjar uma reunião**) with someone who works on the floor below him. First he has to describe himself over the telephone*

PAULO: Como é que nos vamos reconhecer? Eu sou muito alto, um pouco gordo, moreno e tenho uma barba.

JOANA: E eu sou bastante baixa, magra, uso óculos e tenho cabelo frisado. Então, junto do elevador na sexta à uma hora. Até logo!

PAULO: *How will we recognise each other? I'm very tall, well-built, dark and I have a beard.*

JOANA: *And I'm quite small, slim, wear glasses and I have curly hair. So, next to the lift on Friday at one. See you then!*

Vocabulary: **à uma hora**   at one o'clock

Muito and pouco

Used adjectivally **muito** and **pouco** agree with the noun referred to:

Tenho muitos vídeos	I have a lot of videos
Há muita gente na rua	There are many people in the street
Lêem poucas revistas	They read few magazines
A loja tem pouca variedade	The shop has little variety

If used adverbially, however, both **muito** and **pouco** are invariable:

Somos muito altos
We are very tall

Estas luvas são muito caras
These gloves are very expensive

Usamos pouco a varanda
We do not use the verandah much

Conhece pouco as obras de Shakespeare
He knows little about Shakespeare's works

Adjectives

Study the following descriptions of physical appearance (**a aparência física**):

(Eu) Sou de estatura média
I am of average build

(Ele/Ela/Você) é alto/alta
He/she is; You are tall

Tenho cabelo ('hair') preto/loiro/ruivo/castanho
I have black/blonde/red/brown hair

Tenho cabelo comprido/curto/liso/encaracolado
I have long/short/straight/curly hair

Tenho olhos ('eyes') azuis/verdes/castanhos
I have blue/green/brown eyes

Tem (he/she has; you have), etc.

Vocabulary

alto/a	tall	**médio/a**	average
baixo/a	short	**feio/a**	ugly
magro/a	slim/thin	**bonito/a**	handsome/pretty
gordo/a	fat		

Exercise 11

Here are some contrasting types of character. Using your dictionary, can you match the pairs? The first one has been done for you.

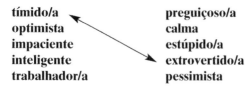

tímido/a	**preguiçoso/a**
optimista	**calma**
impaciente	**estúpido/a**
inteligente	**extrovertido/a**
trabalhador/a	**pessimista**

Telling the time

Study the following sentences:

Que horas são?	What time is it?
	(*lit.*: What hours are they?)
São três horas	It's three o'clock
São nove horas	It's nine o'clock
São cinco menos um quarto[11]	It's a quarter to five
É uma hora	It's one o'clock (**uma** because **hora** is feminine)
É meio-dia	It's midday
É meia-noite	It's midnight
A que horas?	At what time?
à uma e cinco	at five past one
às três e meia	at half past three

Expressing minutes past the hour:

São duas *e* vinte	It's twenty *past* two

Expressing minutes to the hour:

São cinco *menos* dez	It's ten *to* five

---

11 The expression '**falta um quarto para** (**as cinco**)' can also be used.

The word **horas** is optional (as in English) in these cases:

às três (horas) at three (o'clock)
às duas (horas) da tarde at two (o'clock) in the afternoon

The 24-hour clock can be used, as in the UK, when referring to departure and arrival times of trains and the like:

O comboio (Br: o trem) sai às quinze e cinquenta
The train leaves at 15.50

Exercise 12

Look at the following clocks. What are these times in Portuguese?

Other expressions concerning time

em ponto (precisely)

menos um quarto   **e um quarto**
quarter to   quarter past

e meia half past

You can also add on:

da manhã   in the morning
da tarde   in the afternoon
da noite   in the evening
às duas horas da tarde at two o'clock in the afternoon

You can refer to parts of the day with no mention of time by saying **de manhã, de tarde, de noite**:

De manhã vou ao escritório
In the morning I go to the office

Vocabulary

esta manhã/tarde/noite	this morning/afternoon/evening
Até amanhã!	See you tomorrow!
Até amanhã de manhã!	See you tomorrow morning!
Até logo!	See you later!
Até breve! já!	See you soon!
Até à próxima!	See you next time!
um minuto	a minute
É cedo	It's early
É tarde	It's late

A clock can be:	**certo**	**atrasado**	**adiantado**
	correct	slow	fast

Exercise 13

Look at the following list of programmes on **Canal TV2** (Channel TV2) for **sábado** (Saturday) and answer the following questions in Portuguese:

TV 2

09.02 - Universidade Aberta
12.15 - Cine Sábado:
 «Tarzan na Selva
 Misteriosa»
13.30 - Musical: Jason
 Donovan - ao vivo
14.35 - Eerie Indiana
14.55 - Agatha Christie:
 «Poirot»
15.40 - O Tempo
15.45 - TV2 Desporto. Inclui:
 Cerimónia de
 Abertura dos Jogos
 Olímpicos de Inverno
22.45 - Desenhos Animados /
 Boa Noite
22.55 - O Tempo

Vocabulary

os anúncios da televisão	TV adverts
os programas da televisão	TV programmes
as notícias	the news
o tempo	the weather
cine sábado	Saturday cinema
os Jogos Olímpicos de Inverno	the Winter Olympics
a cerimónia de abertura	the opening ceremony
os desenhos animados	cartoons
a universidade aberta	the open university
ao vivo	live

1 What time would you switch on if you were a sports fan?
2 You are keen to find out what the weather has in store. When should you tune in? (Two times are possible.)
3 When is the only live programme on?
4 You are going to be out between **meio-dia** and **duas e meia**. How many programmes will you miss?

The verb estar

Portuguese has *two* verbs for 'to be', one of which you already know, **ser**. The other is **estar**. The present indicative tense of **ser** and **estar** is as follows:

ser	*estar*	
sou	estou	I am
és	estás	you are, etc.
é	está	
somos	estamos	
são	estão	

How do you decide when to use which verb?

1 **O gato é preto**   The cat is black
2 **O gato está doente**   The cat is ill

1 Here the verb **ser** is used to denote an unchanging state regarding the colour of the cat – his fur is black, and he will remain black. This is a permanent characteristic.
2 Here the verb **estar** is used because although the cat is ill at present, he will most probably recover and no longer be ill. This is a temporary state.

Expressing location

1 **O banco é na esquina**   The bank is on the corner
2 **O cão está no sofá**   The dog is on the sofa

In the first example, **ser** is used because the bank is an unchanging feature on the corner. This is taken to be a permanent state. In the second example, **estar** is used instead of **ser** because the dog is, at the moment, on the sofa. He may, however, decide to jump off half an hour later in order to go for a walk. This state may change at anytime.

Exercise 14

Can you fill in the correct part of the verbs **ser** or **estar**?

A janela ——— aberta   The window is open
O carro ——— azul   The car is blue
A menina ——— inglesa   The girl is English
Ele ——— triste   He is sad
Elas ——— na cozinha   They are in the kitchen
Estremoz ——— uma   Estremoz is a city in Portugal
   cidade em Portugal

Exercise 15

Read the following passage, answer the questions on it then translate it into English:

Sou médico e moro num apartamento no Rio de Janeiro. Trabalho num hospital no centro da cidade. Sou bastante alto e moreno. Gosto de computadores. Não gosto de estar doente.

1 How does the speaker describe his looks?
2 What does he do for a living and where exactly does he work?
3 He does not like computers. True or false?

How much can you remember?

1 How would you say the following in Portuguese?

1 I like jazz music; I don't like politics.
2 I work in a company in Oporto on Wednesdays.
3 He is Swedish, quite shy, but an optimist.

2 What do you think the following mean?

1 precisa-se	2 inteligente	3 feio
4 o jornal	5 calma	6 o apartamento
7 uma revista	8 baixo	9 a praia

3 How do you form the plurals of these words?

1 a casa	2 pessimista
3 o cinema	4 o pintor

4 Can you give the the feminine of these?

1 o médico	2 o senhor	3 o cantor
4 o jornalista	5 solteiro	6 tímido

5 Can you give the following times in Portuguese?

12.30 p.m.   2.15 p.m.   15.45   9.00 a.m.

and translate:

duas e meia	meia-noite	nove e vinte
uma hora	sete e dez	três horas

3 Parabéns!

Congratulations!

In this lesson you will learn about:

* expressing age, date and place of birth
* family relationships
* using the preterite tense
* using possessive adjectives and pronouns
* asking for a table and ordering food in a restaurant

Dialogue 1 (Audio 1: 10)
Donde é a Maria?

A new colleague, Maria, has started work in the same office as Miguel. They start to chat

MIGUEL: Donde é a Maria?
MARIA: Sou do Porto.
MIGUEL: Ah sim! Também eu. Nasci na Foz do Douro, nos arredores. Tenho trinta e dois anos.
MARIA: Quando é o dia dos seus anos?
MIGUEL: A dez de Novembro. E você?
MARIA: Hoje é o dia dos meus anos!
MIGUEL: Então muitos parabéns! Quantos anos faz?
MARIA: Faço trinta anos.

MIGUEL: *Where are you from, Maria?*
MARIA: *I'm from Oporto.*
MIGUEL: *Ah! So am I. I was born in Foz do Douro, in the suburbs. I'm 32.*
MARIA: *When is your birthday?*

MIGUEL: *The 10th of November. And you?*
MARIA: *It's my birthday today!*
MIGUEL: *Well, congratulations! How old are you?*
MARIA: *I'm 30.*

Expressing age

Portuguese does not use the verb 'to be' (**ser**) but instead the verbs **ter** ('to have') or **fazer** ('to make/do') to express age and date of birth:

Q: **Quantos anos tem?**
A: **Tenho 30**
lit.: How many years do you have? I have 30

Q: **Quantos anos faz?**
A: **Faço 30**
lit.: How many years do you make? I make 30

Vocabulary

o dia de anos	birthday (*lit*: the day of years)
Parabéns!	Happy birthday/Congratulations!
Feliz aniversário! (Br)	Happy birthday!
o aniversário	anniversary

Revise the numbers 1–50 in Lesson 2.

Exercise 1

Listen again to the dialogue (or, if you don't have the recordings, re-read the dialogue) then try to match the English expression in the left-hand column with its Portuguese equivalent on the right.

1 Miguel is 32   É o dia dos meus anos
2 How old is Maria?   Quando é o dia dos seus anos?
3 When is your birthday?   O Miguel tem 32 anos
4 It's my birthday   Quantos anos faz a Maria?

🎧 Names of months (Audio 1: 11)

These are very similar to the names of English months:

Janeiro   Fevereiro   Março   Abril   Maio   Junho   Julho

Agosto   Setembro   Outubro   Novembro   Dezembro

Exercise 2

Here are the details of four people whose ages, birth dates and places of birth all differ. Imagine that you are each person in turn and say in Portuguese: 'I was born in (place)', 'my birthday is on (date)' and 'I am (age)'.

1 Ana. Age 13. Born on 6 May in Madeira.
2 Robert. Age 24. Born on 14 August in Ireland.
3 Pedro. Age 42. Born on 1 March in Spain.
4 Maria. Age 36. Born on 29 December in Brazil.

Exercise 3

Can you translate the following dialogue into English?

ANTÓNIO: Chamo-me António, e você, como se chama?
MANUELA: Chamo-me Manuela. Donde é você?
ANTÓNIO: Sou de Lisboa, e você?
MANUELA: Sou de Coimbra. Tenho dezanove anos. Que idade tem?
ANTÓNIO: Tenho vinte e cinco anos.

Irregular verbs

Here is the present indicative of three common irregular verbs:

ter to have	*fazer* to do/make	*ir* to go
tenho I have	**faço** I do (I make)	**vou** I go
tens you have	**fazes** you do	**vais** you go
tem you have	**faz** you do	**vai** you go
he, she, it has	he, she, it does	he, she, it goes
temos we have	**fazemos** we do	**vamos** we go
têm they, you have	**fazem** they, you do	**vão** they, you go

There is a second verb meaning 'to have' – **haver** – in Portuguese. Whereas **ter** expresses possession, however, **haver** is mainly used in the third person **(há)**, meaning (1) there is/are; (2) for; (3) ago:

Há muitas lojas em Londres
There are many shops in London

Há quanto tempo está em férias?
(for) How long have you been on holiday?

O comboio partiu há dez minutes
The train left 10 minutes *ago*.

Idiomatic uses of ter

As well as expressing age, **ter** is used in a number of idiomatic expressions instead of the verb 'to be':

ter fome[1]	to be hungry	**ter sede**	to be thirsty
ter cuidado	to be careful	**ter vontade de**	to be keen to
ter sono	to be sleepy	**ter pressa**	to be in a hurry
ter frio	to be cold	**ter calor**	to be warm
ter sorte	to be lucky	**ter medo**	to be afraid
ter razão	to be right	**não ter razão**	to be wrong
ter saudades de	to miss, to long for		

1 In Brazil you are more likely to hear **estar com: estou com fome** I am hungry (*lit*: I am with hunger). Sometimes, also used in Portugal

Dialogue 2 (Audio 1: 12)
A família

António is asking Cristina about her family

ANTÓNIO: Bom dia, Cristina. Diga-me por favor, quantas pessoas há na sua família?
CRISTINA: Há cinco. Os meus pais, a minha irmã, o meu irmão e eu.
ANTÓNIO: São todos do Brasil?
CRISTINA: Não, eu nasci no Brasil mas os meus irmãos[2] são de Portugal.

ANTÓNIO: Que idades têm vocês todos?
CRISTINA: Eu sou a mais velha³ e tenho vinte e três anos. O meu irmão Zé (José) tem vinte anos e a minha irmã mais nova⁴, a Cámi (Maria do Carmo), tem dezasseis.
ANTÓNIO: *Hello, Cristina. Tell me please, how many people are there in your family?*
CRISTINA: *There are five. My parents, my sister, my brother and myself.*
ANTÓNIO: *Are they all from Brazil?*
CRISTINA: *No, I was born in Brazil but my brother and sister are from Portugal.*
ANTÓNIO: *How old are they all?*
CRISTINA: *I'm the oldest, I'm 23. My brother Zé is 20 and my younger sister, Cámi, is 16.*

2 **os meus irmãos** my brothers *or* my brother(s) and sister(s)
3 **a mais velha** the eldest (f) (**o mais velho** (m))
4 **mais nova** younger (f) (**mais novo** (m))

Exercise 4

Listen again to the dialogue above. If you don't have the cassettes, re-read the dialogue and answer the questions in English.

1 How many people are there in Cristina's family?
2 What are the names of her brother and sister?
3 How old are her brother and sister?
4 Where were they all born?

Possessive adjectives and pronouns

These possessives reflect ownership of a particular item, e.g. 'your gloves', 'his drink', etc., and agree in gender and number with the noun referred to.

Singular	*ms*	*fs*	*mpl*	*fpl*
my/mine (+ noun)	o meu	a minha	os meus	as minhas
your(s)	o teu	a tua	os teus	as tuas
his/her(s)/your(s)	o seu	a sua	os seus	as suas

Plural

our(s)	o nosso	a nossa	os nossos	as nossas
your(s)	o vosso	a vossa	os vossos	as vossas
their(s) your(s)	o seu	a sua	os seus	as suas

Examples

their friend	a sua amiga
her car	o seu carro
his houses	as suas casas
your books	os seus livros

In the example **o seu carro**, confusion may arise as to whose car is being referred to because this can be translated as: 'his car', 'her car', 'their car' or 'your car'. To avoid ambiguity the following alternative for 'him/her/their' can be used:

de + ele/ela	(of him/of her)
de + eles/elas	(of them/(mpl and fpl))
o carro dele	his car
o carro dela	her car
o carro deles	their car
o carro delas	their car

Although the personal pronoun **vós** (you) has all but disappeared from everyday speech, you will see that its equivalent set of possessive adjectives and pronouns are very much in use: **o vosso, a vossa, os vossos, as vossas**. These pronouns are used to express the informal 'you' plural.

Omission of the article

If the possessive stands on its own, usually at the end of a sentence and is preceded by the verb **ser**, the definite article is dropped:

Este é meu	This is mine
	(i.e. **Este (livro) é meu**)
Esta é minha	This is mine
	(i.e. **Esta (carta) é minha**)

In cases where ownership requires emphasizing, however, then the article reappears:

Este é o meu   This is mine (i.e. not yours)

The possessive adjective is omitted when:

1 a relationship is obvious:

Ela vai a Lisboa com o filho (not **o seu filho**)
She's going to Lisbon with her son.

2 referring to parts of the body:

os braços   my arms (not **os meus braços**)

Exercise 5

Here are some items belonging to two individuals. Try to fill in the correct possessive adjectives:

CRISTINA: **Na minha mala de mão há:**
                In my handbag I have:

                ... **porta-moedas** (m)   my purse
                ... **maquilhagem** (f)   my make-up
                ... **óculos** (mpl)   my spectacles
                ... **vitaminas** (fpl)   my vitamin pills

ANTÓNIO: **Nos meus bolsos há:**   In my pockets I have:
                ... **carteira** (f)   my wallet
                ... **agenda** (f)   my diary
                ... **chaves** (fpl)   my keys
                ... **óculos de sol** (mpl) my sunglasses

The important thing to remember with these adjectives is that they agree with the *noun* referred to and *not the person* who is the owner of the keys, wallet, etc.

Exercise 6

With the help of the vocabulary below, translate the following into English.

JOSÉ: Olá, Teresa. Tem uma família grande ou pequena?
TERESA: Tenho uma família grande: três filhos e uma filha. O
            Vasco é o mais velho e a Clara é a mais nova ... as
            idades variam entre os trinta e os quinze anos.

JOSÉ: O marido da Teresa é reformado, não é? A Teresa ainda trabalha?

TERESA: Sou dona de casa. Tenho sempre que fazer!

Vocabulary

grande	big	pequena/o	small
o filho	son	a filha	daughter
o marido da Teresa		your husband	
		(*lit.*: (the husband of Maria)	
a esposa		wife	
as idades variam		the ages vary	
o mais velho		the oldest	
a mais nova		the youngest	
entre os trinta e os quinze anos		between 30 and 15 years of age	
ser reformado (Br: aposentado)		to be retired	
dona de casa		housewife	
tenho sempre que fazer		I always have lots to do	

More numbers

Memorise the following numbers from 60 to two billion:

		pronounced:
sessenta	60	sisenta
setenta	70	sitenta
oitenta	80	oytenta
noventa	90	noventa
cem	100	saing
cento e um/a	101	sentooeeoom/ah
cento e quinze, etc.	115	sentooeekeenz
cento e setenta	170	sentooeesitenta
duzentos/as	200	doozentoosh/ersh
trezentos/as	300	trezentoosh
quatrocentos/as	400	kwatrosentoosh
quinhentos/as	500	kinyentoosh
seiscentos/as	600	saysentoosh
setecentos/as	700	setsentoosh
oitocentos/as	800	oitoosentoosh
novecentos/as	900	novsentoosh

mil	1,000	meel
mil e um/a	1,001	meeleeoom/ah
dois mil	2,000	doyshmeel
cem mil	100,000	saingmeel
trezentos mil	300,000	trezentooshmeel
um milhão	1 million	oom meelyow
dois milhões	2 million	doysh meelyoysh
um bilião	1 billion	oom beelyow
dois biliões	2 billion	doish beelyoysh

Like 1 and 2, the numbers 200 to 900 alter according to whether the thing referred to is masculine or feminine, singular or plural:

um café (m)	a (one) coffee
duas bicas (fpl)	two black coffees
setecentos livros	700 books(mpl)
setecentas cadeiras	700 chairs (fpl)

 Dialogue 3 (Audio 1: 13)
Onde foram vocês ontem?

Listen to, or read, the following conversation where people talk about what they did yesterday

MARIA: Onde foram vocês ontem?
GRAÇA: Fomos dar um passeio de carro muito agradável pela Costa do Sol. E vocês?
JORGE: Nós passámos o dia na praia. Tomámos banhos de mar e banhos de sol. Foi óptimo!
PAULO: Nós também passámos um dia excelente. Gostámos muito da paisagem.

MARIA: *Where did you go yesterday?*
GRAÇA: *We went for a very pleasant trip in the car to the Costa do Sol (the Sun Coast). What did you do?*
JORGE: *We spent the day on the beach. We swam and sunbathed. It was great!*
PAULO: *We also had an excellent day. We loved the scenery.*

The preterite tense

The verbs in the above dialogue are in the preterite tense. You form this from any regular verb by removing the -ar, -er or -ir endings from the infinitive form and replacing them with the following endings:

regular verbs			irregular verbs
passar	comer	partir	ir + ser⁵
'to spend'	'to eat'	'to leave'	'to go' + 'to be'
pass*ei*	com*i*	part*i*	fui
pass*aste*	com*este*	part*iste*	foste
pass*ou*	com*eu*	part*iu*	foi
pass*ámos*	com*emos*	part*imos*	fomos
pass*aram*	com*eram*	part*iram*	foram

5 The verbs **ir** and **ser** are exactly the same in the preterite tense.

You will see that the irregular verbs on the right do not follow the normal pattern of stem + endings in the case of the three regular verbs. Many irregular verbs in the preterite tense bear little resemblance to the verb in its infinitive form: for example, **querer** ('to want') has these forms in the preterite:

quis   quiseste   quis   quisemos   quiseram

Commitment to memory is, unfortunately, the only way to remember such verbs!

The preterite tense is used to refer to actions or events that took place in the past and which have an air of finality and completeness about them:

Ontem foi ao banco   Yesterday he went to the bank
(See personal pronouns, p. 224)

Exercise 7

Follow the model given below and change the plural part of the verb in each case into the 1st person singular (**eu**) part of the verb:

Gostámos muito do jantar → **Gostei muito do jantar**
We really liked the meal → I really liked the meal

1 **o restaurante onde fomos ontem**
the restaurant where we went yesterday

2 **Onde foram vocês?**
   Where did you go?
3 **Nós passámos o dia na praia**
   We spent the day on the beach
4 **Tomámos banhos de sol**
   We sunbathed

Exercise 8a

Give the preterite tense of the following: **encontrar** ('to find')
esconder ('to hide') **decidir** ('to decide')

Exercise 8b

Look at the following drawing: the people on the left have lost
something whilst those on the right have found something. Now
try to answer the questions below, replying in the following way:

   Foi ... (name) It was ...

Vocabulary

quem   who   **achar**   to find

| perder | to lose | o casal Sousa | the Sousas (the Sousa couple) |
| o dinheiro | money | o gelado | ice cream |

1 **Quem perdeu o dinheiro?** (Who lost the money?)
2 **Quem achou o jornal?** (Who found the newspaper?)
3 **Quem perdeu os óculos?**
4 **Quem achou a scooter?**
5 **Quem perdeu o gelado?**
6 **Quem achou o dinheiro?**
7 **Quem perdeu a scooter?**
8 **Quem perdeu o jornal?**
9 **Quem achou os óculos?**
10 **Quem achou o gelado?**

Meals (Audio 1: 14)

The names of meals (**as refeições**) in Portuguese are as follows:

o pequeno-almoço	breakfast
o almoço	lunch
o jantar	dinner
o lanche	afternoon snack
a ceia	supper

Dialogue 4 (Audio 1: 15)
Que desejam?

JORGE: Faz favor!
O EMPREGADO[6]: Que desejam?
JORGE: Queríamos[7] uma mesa para três.
O EMPREGADO: Muito bem. Esta mesa serve?
MARIA: Está óptima. Tem a lista?
O EMPREGADO: Aqui tem a lista. Já querem encomendar o jantar?
GRAÇA: Sim. Para mim, um caldo verde[8] e um bacalhau-à-Gomes de Sá[9].
MARIA: Eu não quero sopa. Queria só as sardinhas assadas. Não tenho muita fome.
JORGE: Uma sopa de feijão, um frango piri-piri com batatas fritas e uma cerveja imperial muito fresca. Estou cheio de fome e cheio de sede!

Later on, the dinner finished, Jorge calls the waiter:

JORGE:	Queria a conta se faz favor.
O EMPREGADO:	Ora bem ... o total são vinte e cinco mil escudos[10] (25.000$00).
JORGE:	Aqui tem trinta contos[11]. Dê-me dois mil e quinhentos escudos (2.500$00) e pode guardar o troco[12].

JORGE:	*Excuse me!*
WAITER:	*Can I help you?*
JORGE:	*We'd like a table for three.*
WAITER:	*That's fine. Will this table do?*
MARIA:	*This is great. Do you have the menu?*
WAITER:	*Here it is. Are you ready to order?*
GRAÇA:	*Yes. I'll have cabbage soup and* bacalhau-à-Gomes de Sá.
MARIA:	*I don't want soup, I just want grilled sardines. I'm not very hungry.*
JORGE:	*Bean soup, spicy chicken, chips and a glass of really cold beer. I'm starving and really thirsty!*

Later ...

JORGE:	*I'd like the bill please.*
WAITER:	*Let's see now ... the total is 25,000 escudos (25.000$00).*
JORGE:	*Here's 30,000. Give me 2,500 escudos and you can keep the change.*

6 **o empregado** 'waiter'
7 **queríamos ...** 'we would like ...'
8 **caldo verde** 'cabbage soup'
9 **bacalhau à ...** 'dried salt cod [the Portuguese national dish] in the style of ...'
10 **o escudo ($)** the Portuguese unit of currency (100 centavos = um escudo); the equivalent Brazilian unit is **o real**, also comprising 100 centavos
11 **um conto** = 1.000$00 (one thousand escudos)
12 **o troco** change

Note: where a comma is used in English in four-figure numbers and above (e.g. 1,450, 10,450), a full stop is used in Portuguese (e.g. 1.450, 10.450).

Exercise 9

Below is a menu (**a lista** or **a ementa**) similar to the one that the three friends above chose from. In Portuguese, call the waiter over, ask for a table for one and then order the items listed and later ask for the bill. You should be able to find all the expressions you

---

O Restaurante Sol

Entradas
caldo verde
sopa de feijão

✳

Peixe
bacalhau-à-Gomes de Sá
sardinhas assadas

✳

Carne
costeletas de porco
frango piri-piri

✳

Sobremesa
arroz doce
mousse de chocolate
fruta

---

need in the preceding dialogue.

YOU:	(Excuse me!)
O EMPREGADO:	**Bom dia. Que deseja?**
YOU:	(A table for one.)
O EMPREGADO:	**Esta mesa serve?**
YOU:	(This is great. Can I see the menu please?)
O EMPREGADO:	**Aqui tem a lista. Deseja encomendar?**
YOU:	(Yes please. I'd like the bean soup, grilled sardines with chips[13] and a bottle of white wine.)
YOU:	(Can I have the bill please?)

---

13 more commonly with **batatas cozidas** 'boiled potatoes'

Vocabulary

entradas (or aperitivos)	starters
peixe	fish
carne	meat
sobremesa	dessert
uma garrafa de	a bottle of
sopa de feijão	bean soup
vinho branco	white wine
costeletas de porco	pork chops
vinho tinto	red wine
arroz doce	rice pudding
fruta	fruit
mousse de chocolate	chocolate mousse

Asking questions

Q: **Como é o Museu Gulbenkian?**
What's the Gulbenkian Museum like?

A: **O Museu Gulbenkian é excelente.**
The Gulbenkian Museum is excellent.

In the above question the normal order of subject and verb changes because a question word (**como, onde**) is at the start of the sentence. This also happens in English.

Where there is no question word, there is no need to invert the order of subject and verb; it is enough to assume a questioning tone of voice. The word order remains the same for both the statement and the question:

Q: **Está muito doente?**
Is he very ill? (question)

A: **Está muito doente**
He is very ill

The most common interrogatives and relatives are as follows:

interrogatives (question words)		*relatives* (joining words)	
que?	what, which?	**quem**	who
(o) que?	what?	**que**	that, which, who(m)
quem?	who?	**o que**	what, that, which
de quem?	whose?	**quando**	when

quando?	when?	onde	where
onde?	where?	donde	from where
aonde?	to where?	porque	because, why
porque?[14]	why?	como	as, since
como?	how?	cujo/a/os/as	of which, whose
quanto/a/os/as	how much?	quanto/a/os/as	how much

Examples

Quem vai ao Brasil?
Who is going to Brazil?

Porque não comes?
Why aren't you eating?

Qual é a loja?
Which shop is it?

Que acha da peça?
What do you think of the play?

Ela sabe quem é
She knows who it is

Trabalha lá porque pagam bem
He works there because they pay well

Temos um tio cujo país favorito é a Espanha
We have an uncle whose favourite country is Spain

O café de que gostamos vai fechar
The cafe we like is going to close down

Exercise 10

Read the following passage and answer the questions which follow:

Uma óptima refeição

Primeiro, uma sopa de canja; depois um prato de peixe cozido com batatas e, em seguida, outro de carne assada com arroz e uma salada de alface com tomate. Para a sobremesa, há fruta: laranjas, maçãs, uvas.

14 **porquê, quê, o quê**: when alone or ending a sentence

62

Vocabulary

a sopa de canja	chicken soup	**um prato de**	a plate of
peixe cozido	boiled fish	**carne assada**	roast beef
com arroz	with rice	**para sobremesa**	for dessert
salada de alface e tomate		lettuce and tomato salad	
laranjas, maçãs, uvas		oranges, apples, grapes	

1 What does the first course consist of?
2 There is meat and fish on the menu. Which comes with potatoes and which is served with rice?
3 What does the salad consist of?
4 For dessert there are pears and chocolate mousse. True or false?

How much can you remember?

1 Translate into Portuguese:

1 How old are you? (There are two ways of asking this)
2 When is your birthday?
3 I'm in a hurry
4 I was born in London
5 My brother is 16. Their sister is 10
6 His keys and wallet
7 I'd like a table for two and the menu please

2 Can you fill in the blanks?

1 **Estou ... de fome**	I'm starving
2 **A ... irmã ...-se Clara**	My sister's name is Clara
3 **Não ... razão**	He is wrong
4 **Onde ... ?**	Where were you born?

3 Translate into Portuguese:

1 my brothers	4 my purse
2 his car	5 their books
3 your sunglasses	6 your pen

4 Name four months of the year in Portuguese

5 How do you say the following numbers in Portuguese:

66, 73, 101, 23, 7, 87, 2000, 207, 8, 90, 45, 679, 10, 1, 36

6 True or false?

o jantar	= breakfast	**a ceia**	= lunch
o pequeno-almoço	= supper	**o almoço**	= dinner

7 Translate the following:

Nasci em Londres. Tenho vinte e dois anos. O dia dos meus anos é a quinze de Maio. Quantos anos faz o Paulo? Ele faz quarenta anos. O dia dos seus anos é no dia um de Dezembro.

8 Read the following dialogue and answer the questions which follow:

JOSÉ:	Olá, Paulo! Estás bom?
PAULO:	Bem, obrigado. E tu?
JOSÉ:	Estou óptimo! Apresento-te o meu vizinho e amigo, o Sr Mendes.
PAULO:	Como está? Sente-se, se faz favor. Quer vinho ou cerveja?
SR MENDES:	Uma cerveja, se faz favor. Há um telefone aqui perto? Queria falar com a minha mulher[15].

está(s) bom?	how are you?	**sente-se**	sit down
o meu vizinho	my neighbour	**quer . . .?**	do you want . . .?
apresento-te	may I introduce . . .	**amigo**	friend
aqui perto	near here (in the vicinity)		

1 Who does José introduce?
2 What does Paulo invite Sr Mendes to do?
3 What does he then suggest?
4 What drink does Sr Mendes choose?
5 What does Sr Mendes want to do?

---

15 also, **a esposa** wife

4 Desculpe!

Excuse me!

In this lesson you will learn about:

- finding your way about
- getting a room in an hotel
- choosing the correct way of saying 'you'
- expressing future plans
- using the imperative

Dialogue 1 (Audio 1: 16)
Podia-me dizer . . .?

Álvaro is in São Paulo, Brazil, to give a performance of fado singing at the municipal theatre. But first, he has to find his way there

ÁLVARO:	Faz favor, podia-me dizer onde é o teatro municipal?
MARGARIDA:	Não sei, não conheço muito bem esta zona . . . ah! é ali em frente, à direita.
ÁLVARO:	Como? Pode falar mais devagar se faz favor?
MARGARIDA:	Você siga[1] sempre em frente e depois vire[2] à direita. É em frente de um[3] parque, junto de uma[3] pequena praça.
ÁLVARO:	Obrigado.
MARGARIDA:	De nada.[4]
ÁLVARO:	*Excuse me, could you tell me where the municipal theatre is?*
MARGARIDA:	*I don't know, I don't know this area very well . . . ah! it's there, opposite, on the right.*

ÁLVARO:	*Sorry? (Pardon?) Can you speak more slowly please?*
MARGARIDA:	*Continue straight ahead and then turn to the right. It's opposite a park, beside a small square.*
ÁLVARO:	*Thanks.*
MARGARIDA:	*No problem (It's a pleasure/not at all).*

1 **siga** ('follow') is the imperative form of **seguir**
2 **vire** ('turn') is the imperative form of **virar**
3 **de um, de uma:** in Brazil you are less likely to hear **de** contracting with an article than in Portugal.
4 You may also say **Não faz mal** ('That's OK')

Dialogue 2 (Audio 1: 17)
Desculpe

António is in Lisbon and wants to find a room for the night in **uma pensão** *(a guest house)*

ANTÓNIO:	Desculpe. Há uma pensão aqui perto?
ANA:	Não, não há. Mas há um hotel ali na Avenida da Liberdade.
ANTÓNIO:	Obrigado. Onde é?
ANA:	Olhe[5], é já ali, à esquerda, na esquina, antes do quiosque dos jornais. Mas primeiro, o senhor tem de[6] atravessar a rua.
ANTÓNIO:	Muito obrigado. Boa tarde.
ANA:	Não tem de quê.[7]
ANTÓNIO:	*Excuse me. Is there a guest house near here?*
ANA:	*No there isn't. But there is a hotel over there in the Avenida da Liberdade. (Avenue of Liberty).*
ANTÓNIO:	*Thanks, where is it?*
ANA:	*Look, it's right there, on the left, on the corner before the newspaper stand. But first you'll have to cross the road.*
ANTÓNIO:	*Thanks very much. Good afternoon.*
ANA:	*That's OK.*

5 **Olhe** ('Look!') is the imperative form of **olhar**
6 **tem de** (or **tem que**) is a combination of **ter** + **de/que** and is followed by the infinitive; it means 'to have to, must'
7 **Não há de quê** in Brazil

Exercise 1

Answer the following in relation to the two dialogues:
1 What two ways are there of getting attention?
2 If you can't understand or follow what someone says, what word do you use to convey this?
3 How do you say: 'I don't know'?
4 Find the words for 'here' and 'there'. Look in your dictionary for other ways to say these words.
5 How do you say 'no problem'.

Compound prepositions

Q: **Onde está o gato?**   Where is the cat?
A: **Está (ao lado) da caixa**   He is (beside) the box.

(**de + a = da**)

longe de	far from
atrás de	behind
em cima de	on top of
junto de/junto a	next to
em	in/on
dentro de	inside
ao lado de	beside
fora de	outside of
em frente de	in front of/opposite
perto de	near
debaixo de	underneath/below
à esquerda de	on the left of
à direita de	on the right of

As normal, the prepositions **de** and **a** contract with the definite article. For example:

em frente da janela (f)	in front of the window
perto dos edifícios (mpl)	near the buildings
junto à loja (f)	next to the shop

Exercise 2

Can you say in Portuguese which position **o gato** is in?

O gato está (debaixo da caixa), etc.

Exercise 3

Give the opposites of:

longe de, em cima de, atrás de, dentro de

Getting someone's attention

The following terms are used in different situations:

Faz favor!	Please/Excuse me!
	(When you just want to attract someone's attention)
Desculpe!	Excuse me!
	(If you have either to interrupt to get someone's attention or to make your request even more polite)

Com licença! Excuse me!
(When you have to ask someone to move out of the way)

The imperative

In the case of regular verbs the imperative is formed as follows:

-*ar* verbs	-*er* verbs	-*ir* verbs	
1 **fala!**	**bebe!**	**parte!**	**tu**
2 **fale!**	**beba!**	**parta!**	**você/o senhor/a senhora**
3 **falem!**	**bebam!**	**partam!**	**vocês/os senhores/as senhoras/**

(to more than one person addressed as **tu**)

4 **falemos! bebamos! partamos!** 'Let us speak/drink/leave!'

The verbs conhecer and saber

The present indicative of these two verbs is as follows:

Saber ('to know' facts)

sei   sabes   sabe   sabemos   sabem

Você sabe quantas pessoas estão aqui?
Do you know how many people are here?

Conhecer ('to know' places, people, about a subject)

conheço   conheces   conhece   conhecemos   conhecem

Ele conhece a Joana
He knows Joana

Forms of address for 'you'

Unlike English, which simply has one way of expressing 'you' – regardless of who is addressed, be it child, friend, adult or pet dog – Portuguese has the following forms which you use according to the type of person you are addressing:

		Use for
You	**tu** (pl **vocês**)	very close relationships
You	**você(s)**	informal 'you' between friends and people of the same age. In Brazil, used widely
You	**o Jorge; a Cristina**	

Friendly but formal 'you' found in Portugal but not in Brazil. It is formed using the definite article 'o' or 'a' + the given name

examples: **A Fernanda é do Brasil?**
Are you (*Fernanda*) from Brazil?

O Paulo gosta da informática?
Do you (*Paul*) like computing?

You	**o senhor** **os senhores** **a senhora** **as senhoras**	polite, formal 'you'. Also used along with titles, **doutor**, etc.: **o senhor doutor quer café?** and any professional person

Other forms of address:

English style	*Portuguese style*
Mrs, Ms, Miss (mature age)	**(a) (Senhora) Dona** + either given name or surname **Dona** + given name (Br)
Mr	**Senhor** + either given name or surname **Seu** + given name (Br)
Miss	**Menina** (or simply use given name) **Senhorita** (Br)

Exercise 4

Read the following then answer the questions which follow.

ANA: Boa tarde. Faz favor, pode-me dizer onde é o Chiado?[8]
JORGE: Ora bem. A senhora siga sempre em frente. Fique[9] neste[10] lado[11] da rua. No fim[12] desta[13] praça[14] vire[15] à direita e imediatamente à sua esquerda encontra[16] uma rua subindo[17] directamente para o Chiado.

8 **o Chiado** is an elegant district in the centre of Lisbon
9 **fique** is the imperative of **ficar** ('to stay/remain'); it is used along with **ser** to signify position
10 **neste** derives from **em + este** ('on + this')
11 **o lado** 'side'
12 **no fim de** 'at the end of'
13 **desta** derives from **de + esta** ('of + this')
14 **praça** 'square'
15 **vire** is the imperative of **virar** ('to turn')
16 **encontra** is from **encontrar** ('to find')
17 **subindo** 'going up'

1 What does Ana ask first?
2 Ana interprets Jorge's directions as: 'Cross the road. At the end of the square turn to the left and immediately on your right you will find a road going directly up into the Chiado district.' Is she completely right?

Contractions

The demonstrative **este,** etc., contracts with **em** with the following results:

em + este → **neste**	in/on this
em + esta → **nesta**	
em + estes → **nestes**	in/on these
em + estas → **nestas**	

Este, etc., also contracts with **de** with these results:

de + este → **deste**	of/from this
de + esta → **desta**	
de + estes → **destes**	of/from these
de + estas → **destas**	

Exercise 5

A Look at the city plan on page 71. Can you give directions to someone who wants to go:

1 from the railway station to the shoe shop
2 from the school to Largo do Rato
3 from the cinema to the hospital
4 from the car park to the supermarket
5 from the bus station to the Post Office

Vocabulary

a sapataria	shoeshop
o cinema	cinema
a estação de caminho de ferro	railway station
a estação ferroviária(Br)	railway station

a escola	school
o parque de estacionamento	car park
a estação das camionetas	coach station
a estação dos autocarros	bus station
os correios, o correio	post office
o supermercado	supermarket
a biblioteca	library
o banco	bank
o Jardim da Estrela	Estrela (star) park
a mercearia	grocer's (shop)
a padaria	baker's (shop)
a loja de modas	dress shop

B Can you say where places are located? For example:

Onde é o supermercado?   Where is the supermarket?

É em frente da biblioteca   It's opposite the library

1 **Onde é o cinema?**
(It's next to the theatre)

2 **Onde é o parque de estacionamento?**
(It's behind the police station)

3 **Onde é a pastelaria?**
(It's opposite the bank)

C Use **perto de** to answer the following:

1 **Onde é a biblioteca?**   (**É perto do/da ...**)
2 **Onde é a catedral?**
3 **Onde é o Jardim da Estrela?**

D Use **ao lado de** to answer these questions:

1 **Onde é o teatro?**
2 **Onde é a escola?**
3 **Onde é a padaria?**

The future tense using ir + infinitive

The use of **ir** + infinitive expresses intention to do something in the future. The 'true' future tense (e.g. 'I shall write', 'he will visit') will be dealt with later.

Vou fazer o jantar
I am going to cook dinner

Vai trabalhar esta noite
He is going to work tonight

Vou ao cinema ver um filme
I am going to the cinema to see a film

The present indicative also expresses the immediate future:

Telefono esta noite
I'll telephone tonight

Dialogue 3
Vou visitar Luanda em negócios

*Sr Silva goes to a travel agency **(uma agência de viagens)** regarding his business trip **(uma viagem de negócios)** to Luanda.*

SR SILVA: Boa tarde. Vou visitar Luanda em negócios. Preciso dum quarto simples com casa de banho. Vou viajar de avião, claro.

O AGENTE: Deseja um hotel de primeira ou de segunda classe?

SR SILVA: De segunda classe e só com pequeno-almoço[18].

O AGENTE: E quanto tempo vai ficar em Luanda?

SR SILVA: Vou ficar uma semana.

O AGENTE: Bom. Vou fazer as reservas. Dê-me[19] o seu nome e número de telefone, se faz favor.

SR SILVA: *Hello. I'm going to visit Luanda on business. I need a single room with bathroom. I'll be travelling by plane naturally.*

AGENT: *Would you like a three star or five star hotel?*

SR SILVA: *Three star, and with breakfast only.*

AGENT: *And how long are you going to stay in Luanda?*

SR SILVA: *I'll be staying for a week.*

AGENT: *Fine. I'll make the reservations. Give me your name and telephone number please.*

18 **o pequeno-almoço** 'breakfast' (Br **o café da manhã**)
19 **Dê-me** 'give me'

Exercise 6

Now it's your turn to say in Portuguese:

We are going to London and need a room with a bathroom. We are going to stay for two days. We would like (**queríamos**) a five star hotel.

Exercise 7

Can you put these words in order to make a correct sentence:

viajar	de	vou	semana	e	uma	ficar	vou	avião

Dialogue 4 (Audio 1: 18)
Posso ajudá-lo?

Sr Silva manages to arrive in Luanda but minus a few items. He
goes to the police station **(a esquadra)**[20] *to report to the Lost Property*
department **(os perdidos e achados)**

O POLÍCIA: Posso ajudá-lo? (*Can I help you?*)
SR SILVA: Ah, meu Deus! Perdi o meu passaporte. Ah! Nossa
Senhora! Não consigo encontrar os meus cheques de
viagem nem os meus cartões de crédito. O que vou
fazer? Procurei por toda a parte . . . Felizmente, ainda
tenho a minha carteira com algum dinheiro e a minha
pasta. Mas, onde está a minha pasta? Não acredito!
Perdi a minha pasta também!

20 **a delegacia** (Br) 'Police Station'

Exercise 8

Here is the English translation of Sr Silva's dialogue. Some words
have been substituted by a drawing. Can you guess what the missing
words are? Write them down in English and Portuguese.

My God! I've lost my _____. Heavens! I can't find my _____ nor my _____. What am I going to do? I've looked everywhere ... Fortunately, I still have my _____ with some money and my _____. But, where is my _____? I don't believe it! I've lost my _____ as well!

Exercise 9

Listen again to the dialogue if you have the recordings. If not, cover over the English and answer the following in Portuguese.

1 What items has Sr Silva lost?
  (Answer in full: 'He has lost ...')
2 What items does he think he still has?
3 What else has he lost?

Dialogue 5 (Audio 1: 19)
Tem quartos vagos?

*Sr Silva proceeds to his hotel but on arrival discovers that his room has not in fact been booked (**reservado**) and he has to reserve a room (**reservar um quarto**) himself*

SR SILVA:	Tem quartos vagos? Queria um quarto simples se faz favor.
O EMPREGADO:	Para quanto tempo? Uma semana? E o senhor quer que género de quarto? Com chuveiro[21]?
SR SILVA:	Prefiro com banho. Qual é o preço?
O EMPREGADO:	Um quarto simples com casa de banho e pequeno-almoço são onze mil escudos. Faz favor de assinar aqui. E o seu passaporte?
SR SILVA:	Perdi o meu passaporte. Tenho que ir amanhã de manhã à embaixada ...
O EMPREGADO:	Que pena! Aqui tem a chave, é o número dezanove. Boa noite, até amanhã.
SR SILVA:	*Do you have any vacancies? I'd like a single room please.*
EMPLOYEE:	*How long for? A week? And what kind of room would you like? With a shower?*
SR SILVA:	*I'd prefer a bath. How much is it?*

EMPLOYEE:	*A single room with bathroom and breakfast comes to 11 thousand escudos. Please sign here. And your passport?*
SR SILVA:	*I lost my passport. I have to go to the embassy tomorrow morning ...*
EMPLOYEE:	*What a shame! Here's the key, it's number 19. Good night, see you tomorrow.*

21 **a ducha** (Br) 'shower'

Exercise 10

Now it is your turn to ask for different types of rooms for varying periods of time. Begin your sentences with

Queria ... ('I'd like ...').

1 I'd like a double room with shower, TV and telephone for one week.
2 I'd like a single room with bath, shower and telephone for a fortnight.
3 I'd like a twin-bedded room with radio and TV for two nights. Do you have a lift?

Vocabulary

um quarto simples	
um quarto para pessoa só ⎫	a single room
um quarto individual ⎭	
um quarto de casal /	a double room
um quarto duplo	
um quarto de casal com	
duas camas	a twin-bedded room
com/sem ...	with/without ...
banho	bath
chuveiro	shower
casa de banho privativa	private bathroom
a pensão completa	full board
a meia pensão	half board
o ar condicionado	air conditioning
a televisão[22]	TV
o rádio	radio

vista para o mar	sea view
por quanto tempo?	for how long?
a partir de ... até ...	from ... until ...
para uma noite	for a night
para uma semana	for a week
para um mês	for a month
para quinze dias	for a fortnight
o fim de semana	the weekend
Há/Tem ...?	Do you have ...?
um parque de estacionamento	car park
um elevador	lift

22 **o televisor** 'television set'

Exercise 11

Some people at a hotel find their rooms have certain items missing. Can you ask for them in Portuguese?

Desculpe, mas não há ...
Excuse me, but there is/there are no ...

1 Excuse me, but there are no towels.
2 Excuse me, but there is no telephone/toilet paper.
3 Excuse me, but there is no television set.

toalhas (fpl) **luz** (fs) **papel higiénico** (ms)

Exercise 12

Some people at a hotel discover that certain things are not working properly. With the help of the following expressions, can you explain in Portuguese to the hotel manager what the problem is:

Desculpe, no meu quarto (the ...) **não funciona**
Excuse me, in my room (the ...) isn't working/is out of order

or use:

Desculpe, no meu quarto (the ...) **está avariado/a**
Excuse me, in my room (the ...) is out of order/is broken (down)

1 The blind isn't working/the TV is broken.
2 The telephone is broken/the radio is broken/the shower isn't working.
3 The toilet isn't working/the light isn't working.

| a retrete | toilet | o telefone | phone | a persiana | blind |
| o televisor | TV | o rádio | radio | | |

How much can you remember?

1 How do you say:

1 I'd like to reserve a double room with full board for six nights.
2 Give me your phone number. No problem.
3 I've lost my wallet, keys, passport and credit cards.
4 They reserved a twin-bedded room with shower.

2 True or false?

sem banho	=	with shower
um quarto de casal	=	a single room
vire à direita	=	continue straight on
no fim desta rua	=	behind this park

3 Match up the correct English verb to its Portuguese partner then give the first person singular preterite tense of each.

to reserve	confirmar (eu confirmei)
to cross	virar
to follow	subir
to turn	atravessar
to go up	seguir
to confirm	reservar

4 Can you remember how to say (using ir + infinitive):

1 They are going to cross the road
2 I am going to reserve a room
3 She is going to turn to the left

5 How would you translate:

Can you tell me how to get to the bank/post office/railway station/library/bus station?

6 What three ways are there in Portuguese to get someone's attention?

7 Can you remember how to say in Portuguese:

underneath, behind, on top of, next to, far from, beside, near to, to the right of, at the side of

8 Do you know what the following questions mean?

1 **Há um hotel aqui perto?**
2 **Pode-me dizer onde fica o teatro?**
3 **Onde é o mini-mercado?**
4 **Onde ficam os correios?**

9 True or false?

felizmente	= unfortunately
encontrar	= to lose
avião	= car
reservar	= to find
Que pena!	= That's fine!
quinze dias	= two months

10 Name five things you might find in a hotel room

11 Read the following dialogue and answer the questions in English

MANUEL: Faz favor! Podia-me dizer onde é o Hotel Continental?

O POLÍCIA: Com certeza. O senhor atravesse esta avenida, siga por aquela rua ali em frente, no fim da rua vire à sua esquerda e encontra o hotel muito perto à sua direita. Mas, o Hotel Marisol é ainda mais perto, deste lado da avenida.

MANUEL: Muito obrigado. O Hotel Marisol será mais caro?

O POLÍCIA: Não. Não é. O preço é o mesmo, mais ou menos.

Vocabulary

com certeza	of course
aquela rua ali em frente	that road there in front
encontra	you will find
muito perto	very close by
ainda mais perto	even closer
será mais caro?	will it be more expensive?

o preço é o mesmo	the price is the same
mais ou menos	more or less
o polícia (Br **o policial**)	policeman

1 What is Manuel looking for?
2 What directions is he given and by whom?
3 What alternative is suggested?
4 What is Manuel concerned about in his last question?

5 Posso ver ...?

Can I see ...?

In this lesson you will learn about:

- comparing things
- how to select, request and pay for things
- demonstratives
- sizes, quantities, weights and colours

Listen to or read the following dialogues where Helena is in a shoeshop (**uma sapataria**) in Campo Grande in Brazil looking for just the right pair of shoes (**os sapatos**) and Clara visits Amoreiras Shopping Center in Lisbon in search of a dress (**um vestido**).

 Dialogue 1 (Audio 1: 20)
Queria comprar ...

HELENA: Boa tarde. Queria comprar um par de sapatos castanhos. Vi uns na montra[1] ...
A EMPREGADA: Aqueles ali?
HELENA: Não, esses aí entre as sandálias vermelhas e as botas pretas.
A EMPREGADA: Que número calça?
HELENA: A minha medida é trinta e seis.
A EMPREGADA: Quer experimentar? Ah, ficam-lhe bem!
HELENA: Estes são bonitos mas estão um pouco grandes. Preciso dum tamanho abaixo ... ah, estes servem bem. Fico com eles. Posso pagar com cartão de crédito?

82

HELENA:	*I'd like to buy a pair of brown shoes. I saw some in the window.*
SALESLADY:	*Those ones there?*
HELENA:	*No, those ones there between the red sandals and the black boots.*
SALESLADY:	*What size do you take?*
HELENA:	*I take a 36.*
SALESLADY:	*Do you want to try them on? Ah, they really suit you.*
HELENA:	*These are nice but they are a bit big. I need a smaller size ... ah, these will do nicely. I'll take them. Can I pay by credit card?*

1 **a vitrina** (Br) 'window'

Vocabulary

Quanto custa/m?	How much is it/are they?
Que número calça?	What (shoe-) size do you take?
usar/levar	to wear (clothes)
usar/calçar	to wear (shoes)
a medida/o tamanho	size
um tamanho abaixo	a smaller size
um tamanho acima	a larger size
pagar com cartão de crédito	to pay by credit card

The verbs ver and poder

Ver *('to see')*

Present indicative tense
vejo vês vê vemos vêem   I see, you see, etc.

Preterite tense
vi viste viu vimos viram   I saw, you saw, etc.

Poder ('to be able/can')

present indicative tense
posso podes pode podemos podem I can, you can, etc.
preterite tense
pude pudeste pôde pudemos puderam I could, you could, etc.

Exercise 1

Here are some signs you might see in various shops. Can you decipher what they mean with the help of the list in English below?

| *saldo!* | preços baixos | *caixa* | aberto |
| saída | *entrada livre* | FECHADO | IVA[2] Incluído |

exit	low prices	VAT included
sale!	come in and browse	closed
cash desk	open	

2 **ICM** (Br) 'VAT'

Dialogue 2 (Audio 1: 21)
Posso ver alguns vestidos?

CLARA: Posso ver alguns vestidos se faz favor? Ah não, não gosto nada destes vestidos!

A EMPREGADA: Aqui tem outros mais modernos e noutras cores, verde, amarelo, azul ...

CLARA: Ai, não sei ... Ah sim, gosto mais destes vestidos. Prefiro o amarelo. Posso prová-lo?

A EMPREGADA: Com certeza. Qual é a medida da senhora? O número 38? Ora bem, aqui é o gabinete de provas.

CLARA: Penso que é muito giro e o preço é só dois mil escudos? É mesmo uma pechincha! Pago com cheque, está bem? Onde fica a caixa se faz favor?

CLARA: *Can I see some dresses please? Oh no, I don't like these at all.*

SALESLADY:	*We have other more modern ones here and in other colours, green, yellow, blue ...*
CLARA:	*I don't know! Oh yes, I like these dresses much more. I prefer the yellow one. Can I try it on?*
SALESLADY:	*Yes of course. What size are you? 38? Here is the fitting room.*
CLARA:	*I think it's really nice and the price is only 2,000 escudos? It's a real bargain! I'm paying by cheque, is that OK? Where's the cash desk please?*

Vocabulary

Ai, não sei ...	Oh, I don't know
uma pechincha	a bargain/a snip
pagar com cheque	to pay by cheque
Fica-me bem	It really suits me
Ficam-me bem	They really suit me
Não me fica bem	It doesn't really suit me
Não me ficam bem	They don't really suit me
É giro!	It's nice/cute!
Estou só a ver	I'm just looking

Expressing strong dislike

detesto ...   I hate ...

Note that in Portuguese a double negative is possible:

Não gosto *nada* de ...   I don't like ... *at all/in any way*

Expressing 'extremely' and 'really'

This is achieved by adding the suffix **-íssimo** (which agrees in number and gender with the root of an adjective):

Este colar é lind*íssimo*
This necklace is really beautiful

Esses carros são car*íssimos*
These cars are extremely expensive

Exercise 2

You want to buy a pair of black espadrilles (**as alpercatas**). Fill in your part of the dialogue using the previous dialogues as a guide.

YOU:	(a pair of (**um par de**) black espadrilles please)
A EMPREGADA:	**Que número calça?**
YOU:	(37)
A EMPREGADA:	**Quer experimentar?**
YOU:	(Yes please. They are a bit big. Do you have ... (**Tem** ...?) a smaller size?)
A EMPREGADA:	**Estas são um tamanho abaixo.**
YOU:	(Thanks. I like these ... I'll take them. How much are they? Can I pay by cheque?)

Making comparisons

Study the following examples:

1 **Esta camisa é *mais* garrida**
This shirt is more colourful

2 **Este vestido é *menos* alegre**
This dress is less colourful

3 **Esta blusa é *mais* cara *do que* aquela**
This blouse is *more* colourful *than* that one

4 **Este gira-discos[3] é *menos* sofisticado *do que* aquele**
This record-player is *less* sophisticated *than* that one

5 **Esta roupa é *a mais* prática**
(of all the clothes) These clothes are the most practical

6 **Este café é *tão* forte *como* este**
This coffee is *as* strong *as* this one.

7 **Ele tem *tantas* camisolas[4] *como* o seu irmão.**
He has *as many* sweaters *as* his brother.

---

3   **o toca-discos** (Br) record-player
4   **o suéter** (Br) sweater

Exercise 3

Can you create sentences like the ones above? The first one is done for you:

1 This pullover is cheaper than this one.
   Esta camisola é mais barata do que esta.
2 This train is quicker than this one.
3 This book is more interesting than this one.
4 These shoes are more modern than these ones.

barata	rápido	interessante	modernos
cheap	quick	interesting	modern

Demonstratives

This (one here)	*That (one there)*	*That (one over there)*
These (ones here)	*Those (ones there)*	*Those (ones over there)*

este (ms)	esse	aquele	envelope
esta (fs)	essa	aquela	cadeira
estes (mpl)	esses	aqueles	discos
estas (fpl)	essas	aquelas	luvas
isto	isso	aquilo	neuter forms (invariable)

The above demonstratives can be used on their own:
(**Quais** is the plural of **qual**)

Which (records) are you playing?
Quais (discos) toca?

I'm playing these (ones)
Toco estes

'Here', 'there', 'over there'

If you want to indicate where someone or something is, you use these words:

aqui here   **aí** there   **ali** over there
cá here   **lá** over there

Contractions

All the demonstrative forms above contract with both **em** and **de**. For example:

em + este esta estes estas → *n*este *n*esta *n*estes *n*estas
in this/in these, on this/on these

de + aquilo → *d*aquilo of/from that

See also the section on 'contractions' in Lesson 4.

Exercise 4

Can you fill in the missing words in the sentences below? Choose from:

como	tão	mais ... do ... que	mais ... do

1 **Estes sapatos são _____ caros _____ _____ estes**
2 **Ela é tão alta _____ o seu pai**
3 **O comboio é _____ rápido _____ que o autocarro**
4 **Ele é _____ inteligente como o seu irmão**

o comboio (Br trem) train   **o autocarro** bus

Irregular comparatives and superlatives

		comparative		*superlative*
muito	→	**mais**	→	**o mais**
very		more		the most
pouco	→	**menos**	→	**o menos**
little		less		the least

grande	→	maior	→	o maior
big		bigger		the biggest
pequeno	→	menor⁵	→	o menor
small		smaller		the smallest
mau/mal	→	pior	→	o pior
bad		worse		the worst
bom/bem	→	melhor	→	o melhor
good		better		the best

5 mais pequeno ('smaller') can replace menor

Certain of these adjectives have very different forms in the feminine:

mau → má	plurals: maus (mpl), más (fpl)
bom → boa	plurals: bons (mpl), boas (fpl)

Exercise 5

Can you give the opposites of these words?

pouco   mais   grande   maior   óptimo

Exercise 6

Some friends have been shopping for new clothes. Can you guess what they have bought? (Vocabulary is given at the end of the lesson.)

um blusão

uma T-shirt⁶

uns jeans⁷

umas meias

uns ténis

um fato[8]

uma camisa

uma gravata

umas luvas

uns sapatos

uma blusa

uma saia

um chapéu

umas botas

uma camisola[9]

umas calças

um cachecol

uns mocassins

---

6 **uma camiseta** (Br) 'T-Shirt'
7 **um jeans** (Br) 'jeans'
8 **um terno** (Br) 'suit'
9 **um suéter** (Br) 'sweater'

Exercise 7

Can you decipher what these colours are in Portuguese? (See if you are right at the end of the lesson.)

Grass is **verde**	The sun is **amarelo**
The sea is **azul**	Liquorice is **preto**
Clouds are **branco**	The danger sign is **vermelho**
The mole is **castanho**	The squirrel is **cinzento**

Shades

castanho claro	light brown
castanho escuro	dark brown

As normal, colours agree in gender and number with the thing referred to:

as calças pretas	black trousers (fpl)
o guarda-chuva vermelho	the red umbrella (ms)

What is it made from? (É feito/a de . . .?)

o algodão	cotton	**a seda**	silk
a lã	wool	**o couro**	leather
o linho	linen		

Examples

uma sweat-shirt de algodão	a cotton sweat-shirt
(é feita de algodão	it is made of cotton)

Exercise 8

Now it is your turn to ask for the following items. Use:

Pode-me mostrar?	Can you show me?
Posso ver?	Can I see?
Desejo/queria . . .	I'd like . . .

1 a green sweater
2 a cotton T-shirt
3 a pair of black shoes
4 a light-green blouse
5 a grey silk tie

Places to shop

o centro comercial	shopping centre
o supermercado	supermarket
o minimercado	minimarket
a padaria	baker's (shop)
a mercearia	grocer's (shop)
a peixaria	fish shop
o talho (Br o açougue)	butcher's (shop)
a frutaria (Br o fruteiro)	fruit shop
a tabacaria (Br a charutaria)	tobacconist's (shop)
a loja de ferragens	hardware shop
o quiosque de jornais	newspaper stand
a feira da ladra	flea market

Exercise 9

Consult your dictionary for the following. You should already know some of the words:

chemist's (shop), cake shop, bookshop, stationer, hairdresser, laundrette, post office

Exercise 10

Read the following passage, answer the questions which follow, then translate it into English.

Queria comprar uma camisa se faz favor. Tem outras cores? Prefiro a vermelha. A minha medida é quarenta. Onde é o gabinete de provas? O preço é muito bom. Posso pagar com cheque?

1 What item of clothing does the person want to buy?
2 Which particular colour does s/he prefer?
3 What information does s/he give to the shop assistant?
4 What two questions does s/he ask the shop assistant and what comment does s/he make about the price?

Exercise 11

Try to match up the correct pairs of shops in the box below.

baker's (shop)	a peixaria
tobacconist's (shop)	o minimercado
minimarket	a mercearia
butcher's (shop)	a padaria
fish shop	a tabacaria
grocer's (shop)	o talho

Exercise 12

Can you match up the types of things you might buy in the right-hand column with the list of shops on the left?

a tabacaria	a fruta
a farmácia	o pão
a frutaria	coisas em[10] segunda mão
a livraria	os cigarros
o correio	os remédios
a padaria	os livros
a feira da ladra	os selos

10 coisas *de* segunda mão (Br)

Dialogue 3 (Audio 1: 22)
Na frutaria

O EMPREGADO:	Que deseja, minha senhora?
ANA:	Dê-me três quilos de batatas e seis bananas. Tem alhos? Quatro, se faz favor, e dois quilos e meio de cebolas e um molho de salsa também.
O EMPREGADO:	*What would you like, madam?*
ANA:	*Give me three kilos of potatoes and six bananas. Do you have garlic? Four, please, and 2½ kilos of onions and a bunch of parsley too.*

Dialogue 4 (Audio 1: 23)
Na mercearia

ANA:	Queria uma dúzia de papo-secos se faz favor e um pão grande. Também duzentos gramas de presunto e um bocadinho de queijo. Chega! E um pacote de manteiga.
O EMPREGADO:	Pode ser um pacote de meio quilo?
ANA:	Pode ser. E uma caixa de fósforos, uma lata de sardinhas, um pacote de café. Tem descafeinado? ... Um pacote de açúcar e uma garrafa de vinho branco. Quanto é tudo?
ANA:	*I'd like a dozen rolls please and a large loaf. Also 200 grammes of **presunto** and a little bit of cheese. That'll do! And a packet of butter.*
SHOPKEEPER:	*Is a half-kilo packet ok?*
ANA:	*That's fine and a box of matches, a tin of sardines, a packet of coffee. Do you have decaffeinated? ... A packet of sugar and a bottle of white wine. How much is that in total?*

Quantities

um quilo de	a kilo of
meio quilo de	½ kilo of
dois quilos de	2 kilos of
três quilos e meio de	3½ kilos of

um litro de	a litre of
meio litro de	½ litre of
quatro litros de	4 litres of
um quarto de litro de	¼ litre of
uma fatia de	a slice of
250 gramas de	approx. ½ pound of
uma dúzia de	a dozen
uma porção de	a portion of
um bocadinho de	a little bit of
um pouco de	a little bit of
uma garrafa de	a bottle of
um pacote de	a packet of
uma lata de	a tin of
uma caixa de	a box of
um tubo de	a tube of
um boião (Br pote) de	a jar of

Exercise 13

Can you remember how to ask for the following items in Portuguese? The first has been done for you. Use **Dê-me, pode-me dar** or **queria** where appropriate:

1 I'd like 2 kilos of bananas.
Queria dois quilos de bananas.
2 A packet of butter and a packet of coffee.
3 Half a litre of wine.
4 Can I have 200 grammes of cheese.
5 3½ kilos of potatoes.
6 I'd like 2 kilos of onions.
7 A tube of toothpaste/I'd like some soap.
8 Give me 4 kilos of sugar.

a pasta de dentes toothpaste   **o sabão** soap

Tudo *and* todo

Tudo, which means 'everything', is invariable:

Quanto é tudo?   How much is it? (i.e. everything)

Todo, which means 'all/every', agrees with the noun in gender and number:

toda a gente	everyone
todo (o) mundo (Br)	everyone
todos os dias	every day

Translating 'some', 'any' and 'none'

1 In general:

algum (ms)	algum dinheiro	some/any money
alguma(fs)	alguma dificuldade	some difficulty
alguns (mpl)	alguns copos	some glasses
algumas (fpl)	algumas situações	some situations

Você tem alguma dúvida?   Do you have any doubt?

2 If a sentence is in the negative, you use:

nenhum (ms)	nenhuns (mpl)	none/not any
nenhuma (fs)	nenhumas (fpl)	

Ela não tem nenhuma dúvida
She doesn't have any doubt at all

3 The plural forms of the indefinite article – **uns**, **umas** – also express 'some' but their use in this respect is more specifically related to quantity:

umas ideias (Br **idéias**) **maravilhosas**
some (i.e. a few/a certain number of) great ideas

uns dicionários medíocres
some mediocre dictionaries

Uns or **umas** before a number = 'approximately':

uns quinze anos   approximately fifteen years old

Note that in Portuguese 'some' and 'any' are often omitted where they would be used in English:

Quer frango?	Do you want some chicken?
Tenho sal	I have some salt

O hotel não tem quartos vagos
The hotel does not have any vacancies

Someone/no one

alguém   someone
ninguém   no one

These are both invariable:

Ninguém chegou   No one arrived

How much can you remember?

1 Can you translate these:

1 Can I pay by credit card?
2 What size do you take?
3 They suit you; it suits me
4 I need a bigger size
5 I'll take them
6 Can I try it on? It's a real bargain

2 Fill in the blanks with the appropriate demonstrative form (this/that/these/those):

1 **Posso experimentar ... fato?**
   Can I try on this suit?
2 **... flores são lindas**
   Those flowers (over there) are lovely
3 **Ele conhece ... homem**
   He knows this man
4 **... meninas têm muita bagagem**
   These girls have a lot of luggage
5 **O que é ...?**
   What is this?

3 Fill in the missing comparative (**mais/menos/tão**, etc.)

1 **Ele é ... alto como o seu pai**
   He is as tall as his father
2 **O comboio é ... rápido do que o autocarro**
   The train is quicker than the bus
3 **Esta cidade tem ... trânsito do que aquela**
   This city has less traffic than that one
4 **Este filme é bom mas esse é ......**
   This film is good but that one is the best

4 Read the following passage and see if you can answer the questions which follow:

A Manuela quer comprar um vestido. Ela prova o vestido que lhe estava muito grande. Depois, decide comprar um par de sapatos de salto alto e uma malinha de mão. Compra ambos e vai-se embora.

1 What is Manuela looking for?
2 What is wrong with the one she tries on?
3 What does she decide to do instead?

Vocabulary

que lhe estava muito grande	which was much too big for her
(estava-lhe muito grande	it was much too big for her)
decide comprar	she decides to buy
um par de sapatos de salto alto	a pair of high heeled shoes
uma malinha de mão	a handbag
ambos	both
vai-se embora	she goes away/she leaves

A roupa *clothing*

o blusão	jacket	**as sandálias**	sandals
a T-shirt	T-shirt	**os mocassins**	moccasins
o casaco	coat	**as botas**	boots
uns jeans	jeans	**os sapatos**	shoes
as meias	socks	**o chapéu**	hat
o fato	suit	**o cachecol**	scarf
a camisa	shirt	**as luvas**	gloves
a blusa	blouse	**a gravata**	tie
a saia	skirt	**o cinto**	belt
a camisola	jumper	**a sweat-shirt**	sweat-shirt
as calças	trousers	**os ténis**	trainers

As cores *colours*

verde	green	**cinzento**	grey
azul	blue	**roxo**	purple
branco	white	**cor-de-rosa**	pink
amarelo	yellow	**cor-de-ouro/dourado**	gold/golden
preto	black	**cor-de-prata/prateado**	silver
vermelho/encarnado	red	**castanho** (Br **marrom**)	brown

6 Uma ida para Lisboa

A single to Lisbon

In this lesson you will learn about:
- different types of transport
- asking for a ticket on a train
- the future indicative tense
- hiring a car, buying petrol and dealing with basic car problems

Situation 1
No aeroporto

*Sr Costa is travelling to New York (**Nova Iorque**). As his memory is not too good he has made a list of what he must do once he reaches the airport terminal (**o terminal**) in order to catch his flight (**o vôo**).*

Preciso de ...

**verificar o horário de partidas
ir ao check-in
entregar a bagagem
mostrar o passaporte e o bilhete
pedir um lugar de não-fumadores
receber um cartão de embarque
ir ao controlo dos passaportes
visitar o duty-free
esperar na sala de espera
e, finalmente,
ir à porta de embarque número ...**

Exercise 1

Can you follow Sr Costa's plan of action? here are the verbs used:

verificar	to check	**pedir**	to ask for
ir	to go	**receber**	to get
entregar	to hand over	**visitar**	to visit
mostrar	to show	**esperar**	to wait

and some vocabulary:

partidas (fpl), **chegadas** (fpl)	departures/arrivals
bilhete (m)	ticket
lugar de não-fumadores (m)	a no-smoking seat
cartão de embarque (m)	boarding card
sala de espera (f)	departure lounge
porta de embarque (número ...) (f)	gate (number ...)

Now write down in English what Sr Costa plans to do.

Exercise 2

Can you remember what the following are in Portuguese?

duty-free, boarding card, departure board, non-smoking, passport control, departure lounge, departure gate

The future indicative tense

There are various ways of expressing futurity in Portuguese:

1 By using part of the verb **ir** + infinitive (you have already seen this in Lesson 4), which implies a degree of intention or certainty:

Vamos visitar a costa   We are going to visit the coast

2 By using the present indicative tense

Compro o presente hoje   I'll buy the present today

3 By using the verb **haver de** + infinitive. Although this is less widely used than the above methods, it implies a greater degree of intention or future obligation:

| **Hei-de ir a Portugal** | I will go to Portugal |
| **Eles hão-de assinar o cheque** | They shall sign the cheque |

4 By using the future indicative tense

Forming the future indicative

With the exceptions given below, the following endings are added to the infinitive of any verb:

-ei -ás -á -emos -ão

Thus: **falar*ei*** *I shall* talk,   **decidir*á*** *he will* decide

The exceptions to this rule are the following three verbs, of which the stem changes slightly:

fazer	(to do) →	***fa*rei**	I shall do/make
dizer	(to say/tell) →	***di*rei**	I shall say/tell
trazer	(to bring) →	***tra*rei**	I shall bring

It is more common to use methods 1 and 2 above to express futurity, especially in everyday speech. Note that the future tense of **ser** in the third person singular is used to express 'I wonder if ...?'

Será que ...?   (*lit.*:) Will it be that ...?

Exercise 3

Go back to Sr Costa's list of things to do. How would you describe his actions in the future, using the future indicative?

1 **Ele verificará o horário de partidas ...**, etc.
2 He will go to the check-in desk.
3 He will go to passport control.
4 He will visit the duty-free shop.

Dialogue 1 (Audio 1: 24)
Não compreendi bem

*Paulo is meeting a friend at the airport but has difficulty understanding the announcement over the public-address system (**o alto-falante**). He asks when the plane (**o avião**) is going to land (**aterrar**)*

PAULO:	Faz favor. Não compreendi bem o que disse o alto-falante. Que vôo anunciam? A que horas chegará o vôo de Heathrow, Londres?
O EMPREGADO:	A hora de chegada será às duas e meia. Está com meia hora de atraso.
PAULO	Que chatice! Há sempre um atraso.

Vocabulary

anunciam	they announce	**(anunciar)**	to announce
chegar	to arrive	**a hora de chegada**	arrival time
a chatice	nuisance	**sempre**	always
Está com (meia hora) de atraso		There's a delay of ...	

Exercise 4a

Part of the translation of Dialogue 1 is given below. Some of the words, however, are missing. Can you fill them in?

PAULO: ... me, I didn't catch what came over the ... What ... are they announcing? What ... will the ... from Heathrow ...?

Exercise 4b

Here are three things you might expect an air hostess, **a hospedeira,**[1] to say during a flight:

Façam favor de apertar os cintos de segurança!
Querem refrescos e bebidas alcoólicas?
Querem comprar cigarros, perfumes, loção para depois de barbear?

Now try to fill in the missing words in Portuguese and discover what she is saying:

Façam favor de (to fasten) **os** (safety belts)!
Querem (refreshments) **e** (alcoholic beverages)?
Querem (to buy) (cigarettes), **perfumes,** (after-shave lotion)?

---

1 **a aeromoça** (Br) 'air-hostess', **a moça** 'girl, young woman'

🎧 Dialogue 2 (Audio 1: 25)
No Controlo dos Passaportes

O FUNCIONÁRIO:	Mostre-me o seu passaporte. Qual é a sua nacionalidade?
RICARDO:	Aqui o tem. Sou italiano.
O FUNCIONÁRIO:	Quanto tempo vai ficar em Angola?
RICARDO:	Tenciono ficar três semanas.
O FUNCIONÁRIO:	Faça favor de passar à Alfândega.

Vocabulary

mostre-me	show me
aqui o tem	here it is
Qual é a sua nacionalidade?	What nationality are you?
Quanto tempo vai ficar?	How long are you going to stay?
tenciono ficar	I intend to stay
Faça favor de passar à Alfândega	Please go through to Customs

Exercise 5

Which questions fit these responses?

Q: _____
A: **Sou inglês.**

Q: _____
A: **Aqui o tem.**

Q: _____
A: **Vou ficar dois meses.**

🎧 Dialogue 3 (Audio 1: 26)
Na Alfândega

The passengers (os passageiros) collect their luggage from baggage reclaim (a reclamação de bagagem) and go through customs

O OFICIAL:	Bom dia. Tem alguma coisa a declarar?
ANA:	Não, não tenho nada a declarar.
O OFICIAL:	Que bagagem tem?
ANA:	Só tenho duas malas e este saco.
O OFICIAL:	A senhora pode seguir. Bom dia.

Vocabulary

alguma coisa a declarar	something to declare
só tenho ...	I've only got ...
malas (fpl)	suitcases
pode seguir	you can go on

Exercise 6

Read this short passage, try to answer in English the questions which follow, then translate the passage into English:

Vou viajar ao Canadá para visitar os meus pais. O vôo partirá de Londres às nove e meia e durará mais de cinco horas. Antes de embarcar tenho de ir ao check-in e ao controlo dos passaportes. Confesso que não gosto nada de voar, mas, neste caso, é preciso!

Vocabulary

vou viajar	I'm going to travel	**partirá**	will leave
neste caso	in this case	**é preciso**	it's necessary
os meus pais	my parents	**durará**	will last
antes de embarcar	before boarding	**confesso**	I have to admit

1 What does the writer intend to do? (first sentence)
2 When does the flight leave? How long is the journey?
3 What does the writer have to do before boarding?
4 The writer loves flying. True or false?

Past participles

We have already seen some of these in action in the previous lesson, representing signs seen in shops etc. For example:

fechado closed **saída** exit **entrada** entrance

To form these, take off the -**ar**, -**er** or -**ir** ending of an infinitive:

-ar verbs	*-er verbs*	*-ir verbs*
mandar 'to send'	**ter** 'to have'	**partir** 'to leave'
mand/ + ado	**t/ + ido**	**part/ + ido**

past participle	*past participle*	*past participle*
mandado	**t**ido	**part**ido

There are exceptions:

aberto	open (from **abrir** – to open)
dito	said (from **dizer** – to say)
feito	made/done (from **fazer** – to do/make)
posto	put (from **pôr** – to put)
visto	seen (from **ver** – to see)
vindo	came (from **vir** – to come)
escrito	written (from **escrever** – to write)
gasto	spent (from **gastar** – to spend)
ganho	earned (from **ganhar** – to earn)
morto	killed (from **matar** – to kill)

The future perfect tense

This is formed by the future tense of **ter** + past participle:

She will have eaten the food = **Terá comido a comida**
We shall have seen the film = **Teremos visto o filme**

Exercise 7

A mulher[2] (the wife) of Sr Costa imagines the progress of her husband on his return journey (**a volta** or **o regresso**) from New York. Can you help her by following the example below?

He will have (landed – **aterrar**) **Terá aterrado**
He will have (gone – **ir**) to passport control
He will have (reclaimed – **reclamar**) his luggage
He will have (gone through – **passar**) customs
He will have (said – **dizer**) that he has nothing to declare
He will have (caught – **apanhar**) a taxi

Signs Not all signs use the past participle; some use the infinitive:

puxar pull   **não fumar** no smoking

2 also, **a esposa** 'wife'

Exercise 8

Can you match the following signs with their equivalent in English?

proibido estacionar   ocupado   empurrar   cancelado

push   CANCELLED   engaged   NO WAITING

Dialogue 4 (Audio 1: 27)
Na estação de Caminho de Ferro³

TERESA:	Faz favor. Quando é o próximo comboio⁴ para Lisboa?
EMPREGADO:	Amanhã de manhã às 7.30; é um rápido.
TERESA:	Queria uma ida e volta, se faz favor. De que linha⁵ parte o comboio?
EMPREGADO:	Da linha quatro. Aqui tem o bilhete⁶ e o troco ... Quer um horário?

3 **a estação ferroviária** (Br) 'railway station'
4 **o trem** (Br) 'train'
5 **a plataforma** (Br) 'platform'
6 **a passagem** (Br) 'fare/ticket'

Vocabulary

o próximo comboio para	the next train for
amanhã de manhã	tomorrow morning
é um rápido	it's an express
uma ida e volta	a return (**uma ida** single)
de que linha parte o comboio?	which platform does the train leave from?
o bilhete e o troco	the ticket and the change
um horário	timetable

Expressing 'to miss'

To miss a train/bus etc. = **perder** ('to lose'):

    Perdi o meu comboio   I missed my train

To miss a person/place etc. = **sentir falta de** or **ter saudades de**:

    Tenho saudades do Brasil   I miss Brazil
    Sinto falta dele   I miss him

Exercise 9

Can you say in Portuguese:

When is the next train for Coimbra? How much is a return? I'd like a timetable please. We would like three singles to Lisbon. What platform does the train leave from?

Exercise 10

Look at the railway timetable below. Try to answer the following questions:

SIMBOLOGIA

⊞ — Estação Fronteiriça.
Ⓧ — Serviço de mini-bar.
Ⓨ — Serviço de bar.
IC — Comboio Intercidades.
IR — Comboio Inter-Regional.
Reg. — Comboio Regional.
Ⓡ — Reserva de lugar obrigatória.
⊠ — Não se efectua aos sábados, domingos e feriados oficials.
✕ — Não se efectua aos domingos e feriados oficials.
{ — Comboio nãao diário.

SIMBOLOGIA

[1] — Efectua-se diariamente nos meses de Julho e Agosto.
[2] — Efectua-se diariamente nos meses de Juiho e Agosto. Durante os restantes meses só se efectua aos domingos excepto se segunda-feira for feriado oficial, efectuando-se neste caso neste dia.

1 How would you translate **serviço de mini-bar?**
2 If **lugar** means 'seat' and **obrigatória** means 'obligatory', what do you think the R symbol stands for?

3 What four types of train are mentioned?

Vocabulary

intercidades	intercities	**não diário**	not daily
feriados oficiais	national holidays		
efectua-se	... runs ...	**não se efectua**	does not run ...
estação fronteiriça	border station	**(a fronteira**	border)

Other types of transport

Exercise 11

Below are some drawings of different means of transport labelled in Portuguese. Can you put the correct English translation with each drawing?

de carro

de metro[7]

de autocarro[8]

a pé

de táxi   de eléctrico[9]

Ando de ... I go by ... (from **andar** 'to walk')

---

7 **de metrô** (Br) 'by underground'

by underground	by taxi	by bus	by car
	on foot	by tram	

8 **de ônibus** (Br) 'by bus'
9 **de bonde** (Br) 'by tram'
a praça de táxis 'taxi rank' (**o ponto de táxis** Br)

To ask to go somewhere, use **para** (to/for) + place:

Para Coimbra se faz favor/a Pensão Suiça, etc.

Using por and para

Both **por** and **para** mean 'for' but there are subtle differences:
Para = purpose:

I'd like a car for the weekend
(i.e. *for the purpose of* driving it)
Queria um carro para o fim de semana

Por = because of:

Do I have to pay for the mileage?
(i.e. *because of* the mileage)
Tenho de pagar pela quilometragem?

If followed by the definite article, **por** contracts:

por + o = pelo   **por + a = pela**
por + os = pelos   **por + as = pelas**

Example

Obrigado pela boleia   Thanks for the lift

Por also expresses 'by/through/for' (projected time):

Anda pela cidade
He walks through the city

O livro foi escrito por Pessoa
The book was written by Pessoa

Vamos por quinze dias
We are going for a fortnight

Expressing 'to'

Para is used to imply long distance and a long stay:

Vou *para* Portugal
I'm going *to* Portugal

A implies a short distance and short duration:

Vou *às* compras
I'm going *to the* shops

Exercise 12

On the following page is a leaflet advertising car-hire rates. Read it and see if you can answer these questions:

1 Can you hire a two-door car? How much is it for seven days?
2 What does the daily rate include?
3 Is there a minimum age for drivers?
4 What is the minimum deposit?
5 Does the price include breakdown assistance?

LA Locauto rent a car portimão Tarifa válida só para o Algarve		telf. e fax 417148 417149	
Tipo de Carro	3 dias	7 dias	dia extra (+ de 7)
opel corsa twingo	13.500$00	27.000$00	3.700$00
renault clio 2 PORTAS	15.100$00	30.200$00	4.250$00
renault clio 4 PORTAS	17.100$00	34.200$00	4.750$00
ford fiesta 4 PORTAS	21.250$00	42.500$00	5.800$00
v w jetta 4 PORTAS	26.000$00	52.000$00	7.250$00

Os preços incluem diária, seguro contra todos os riscos e quilómetros ilimitados e IVA.
O(s) condutor(es) deverá(ão) ter mais de 25 anos e carta válida em Portugal emitida há mais de 3 anos. Depósito mínimo 40.000$00. Seguro de acidentes pessoais (PAI), 350$00 por dia. Assistência em viagem, 120$00 por dia.

Vocabulary

a tarifa/os preços	rate/prices
incluem	include
tipo de carro	make of car
portas	doors
quilómetros ilimitados	unlimited mileage
IVA	VAT
condutor deverá ter mais de 25 anos	driver must be 25 and over
depósito mínimo	minimum deposit
assistência em viagem	breakdown assistance
seguro de acidentes pessoais	personal accident insurance
carta válida em Portugal emitida há mais de 3 anos	
driving licence valid in Portugal issued more than 3 years ago	

a carta de condução	(Pt) driving licence
a carteira de motorista	(Br) driving licence
seguro contra todos os riscos	comprehensive insurance

Speed Limits in Portugal:
60 km/hour in towns
90 km/hour on ordinary roads
120 km/hour on motorways

Exercise 13

What do you think these road signs mean?

semáforos dê prioridade **obras** sentido único

desvio **AUTO-ESTRADA** **peões** limite de velocidade

To help you, here are the English equivalents:

diversion	traffic lights	pedestrians
roadworks	motorway	one-way street
give way	speed limit	

Situation 2 (Audio 1: 28)
A estação de serviço

Listen to what these people are saying
1 Dois mil escudos de super, se faz favor!
2 Queria dez litros de gasolina sem chumbo.
3 Faz favor de verificar o óleo.
4 Pode-me verificar a pressão dos pneus?
5 Preciso de mais água no radiador.
6 Pode encher se faz favor!

Vocabulary

estação de serviço (f)	petrol station
gasolina (f)	petrol (in general)
super (m)	unleaded petrol
(also: sem chumbo (m)	unleaded)
gasolina aditivada (f)	lead replacement/four-star petrol

gasóleo (m)	diesel
óleo (m)	oil
Tenho um furo (num pneu)	I've got a puncture
a pressão dos pneus	the tyre pressure
radiador (m)	radiator
tanque (m)	petrol tank
Pode encher se faz favor!	Can you fill it up please!

Exercise 14

Using the vocabulary above as a guide, can you discover what the people in Situation 2 are asking for?

Exercise 15

Now it is your turn to speak. Say:

you would like your oil checked and also the tyre pressure checked. You need more water in the radiator as well as three thousand escudos of unleaded petrol. You also think you have a puncture in a tyre.

Vocabulary

uma pane/uma avaria	a breakdown
Tive uma pane/avaria	My car is broken down
O meu carro está avariado	My car is broken down
O/A ... não funciona	The ... isn't working
consertar	to repair
um conserto	a repair
o indicador	indicator
o volante	steering wheel
o limpa-pára-brisas	windscreen wiper
o acelerador	accelerator
a embraiagem	clutch
o travão de pé	brake (foot)
o travão de mão	handbrake
a alavanca de velocidades	gearstick

How much can you remember?

1 Can you translate:

1 Three thousand escudos of unleaded petrol please
2 Where is passport control?
3 What flight are they announcing?
4 When is the next train for ...?
5 I have nothing to declare

2 Give the past participles of:

comer, dar, ser, visitar, esperar, verificar

Give the irregular past participles of:

fazer, escrever, ver, pôr, dizer

3 What do these mean in Portuguese?

ocupado, obras, empurrar, proibido estacionar, peões, desvio, dê prioridade

4 What responses would you give to these questions?

1 **Quer ida e volta?** (Say you want a single)
2 **Qual é a sua nacionalidade?** (Say you are Spanish)
3 **Quantos litros de gasolina deseja?** (10 litres)

5 Are these true or false?

1 **a hora de chegada**	=	safety belt
2 **um atraso**	=	the air hostess
3 **a sala de espera**	=	a no-smoking seat
4 **a hospedeira**	=	the departure lounge
5 **o cinto de segurança**	=	arrival time
6 **um lugar de não-fumadores**	=	a delay

7 Não me sinto bem

I don't feel well

In this lesson you will learn about:
- describing your daily routine
- using reflexive verbs
- using the imperfect tense
- explaining minor ailments
- using ordinal numbers

Dialogue 1 (Audio 2: 1)
A que horas se levanta?

One of the Portuguese football team O Sporting *describes part of his daily routine for a very inquisitive magazine (**uma revista**)*

1 A REVISTA: A que horas se levanta?
  JORGE: Levanto-me às sete horas.
2 A REVISTA: Onde se lava?
  JORGE: Lavo-me na casa de banho.
3 A REVISTA: Onde se veste?
  JORGE: Visto-me no meu quarto.
4 A REVISTA: Onde se senta para comer o pequeno–almoço?
  JORGE: Sento-me na cozinha, claro!
5 A REVISTA: A que horas sai de casa?
  JORGE: Saio de casa às oito horas.
6 A REVISTA: E depois?
  JORGE: Faço jogging por meia hora.

1

2

Exercise 1

With the aid of the drawings in Dialogue 1, can you answer the

5

6

Vocabulary

levantar-se	to get up	**lavar-se**	to wash
vestir-se	to get dressed	**sentar-se**	to sit
sair de casa	to leave home	**fazer jogging**	to jog

Exercise 2

Describe your day. Can you say:
What time you get up. What time you wash and where. Where you dress. What time you have breakfast and what you do after leaving home. (**Vou ao meu trabalho** I go to work/**Vou à universidade** I go to university/**Vou às compras** I go shopping/**Fico em casa** I stay at home.)

Formation of adverbs

These are generally formed by the addition of **-mente** to any feminine adjective:

masc. adjective	fem. adjective	adverb
choroso	**chorosa**	**chorosamente**
tearful	tearful	tearfully
duvidoso	**duvidosa**	**duvidosamente**
doubtful	doubtful	doubtfully

Where there is no change in the feminine adjective, for example in adjectives ending in **-z** or **-e**, simply add **-mente**:

feliz	**feliz**	**felizmente**
happy	happy	happily

Exercise 3

Can you form adverbs from the following:

invejoso	jealous	**sereno**	serene/placid
evidente	obvious	**triunfante**	triumphant

Reflexive verbs are so called because they join with a reflexive pronoun (myself, yourself, etc.) which refers back to the subject of the verb. For example:

(ele) lava-se   he washes (himself)

| (ela) chama-se | she calls herself (her name is . . .) |

The present indicative tense of **sentar-se** ('to sit down – *lit.*: to sit oneself down') is as follows:

(eu)	sento-me	I sit down
(tu)	sentas-te	you sit down
(ele/ela)	senta-se	he, she sits down
(você/o sr/a sra)	senta-se	you sit down
(nós)	sentamo-nos[1]	we sit down
(eles/elas)	sentam-se	they sit down
vocês/os srs/as sras)	sentam-se	you sit down

1 **-s** at the end of the 1st person plural is omitted before the reflexive pronoun

The impersonal use of reflexive verbs, using **se**, is frequently seen in signs and notices:

Fala-se francês	French spoken
	(*lit.*: French speaks itself)
Vende-se	For sale
	(*lit.*: it sells itself)

Reflexive pronouns

me	myself	**nos**	ourselves
te	yourself	**se**	themselves
se	him/herself	**se**	yourselves
se	yourself		

Exercise 4

Can you put Dialogue 1 into the preterite tense; for example:

Levantei-me às sete horas . . .

Expressing 'each other'

Reflexive pronouns can also be used in reciprocal actions to mean 'each other':

Encontraram-se na praça

They met (each other) in the square

To express 'to each other', to avoid ambiguity, **um ao outro** is added to the end of the sentence:

Deram um presente um ao outro
They gave each other a present

Um ao outro agrees with the people doing the giving:

um ao outro	=	two ms subjects or one m + one f subject
uma à outra	=	two fs subjects
uns aos outros	=	more than two mpl or a mixture of the sexes
umas às outras	=	more than two fpl subjects.

Position of reflexive pronouns

If you go back to Dialogue 1, you will see that sometimes the reflexive pronoun comes after the verb and sometimes before it. Reflexive pronouns are placed *before the verb* in the following contexts:

1 When a question is being asked:

Onde se lava?　　　　Where do you have a wash?

2 When the statement is in the negative:

Não se lembrou de ir às compras
He didn't remember to go for the shopping

3 When certain adverbs – such as **já** (yet/already), **também** (also/too), **nunca** (never) or **sempre** (always) – precede the verb:

Ela nunca se engana
She never makes a mistake

4 When a preposition precedes the verb:

Depois de me queixar o barulho parou
After I complained, the noise stopped

5 Following statements such as 'He said *that* . . .' or 'They believed *that* . . .':

Disseram que se esqueceram do número do telefone
They said they had forgotten the telephone number

Reflexive pronouns are placed after the verb in all other cases except one. Consider the following sentences:

Ele enganou-se   He was mistaken (Pt)
Ele se enganou   He was mistaken (Br)

The Portuguese version follows the rules here; because there is no question/negative/adverb/preposition involved, the reflexive pronoun *follows* the verb. Brazilian Portuguese, however, places the pronoun *before* the verb. For this to happen, the sentence has to begin with **ele** as it is not possible to begin a sentence with a reflexive pronoun.

Exercise 5

Fill in the missing parts of the verb **queixar-se** ('to complain')

present indicative	*preterite tense*
(nós) ... -nos	queixámo-nos
(eles/elas/vocês) ... -se	queixaram- ...
(tu) queixas- ...	... -te
(ele/ela/você) ... -se	... -se
(eu) ... -me	queixei- ...

Some common reflexive verbs

chamar-se	to be called
sentir-se	to feel (sorry, happy, etc.)
divertir-se	to enjoy oneself
zangar-se	to be annoyed/to get angry
sentar-se	to sit down
esquecer-se de	to forget
lembrar-se de	to remember
cansar-se de	to tire of
enganar-se	to be mistaken
queixar-se de	to complain
deitar-se	to lie down/go to bed
levantar-se	to get up

Exercise 6

Can you fill in the correct part of the verb and pronoun? Remember that sometimes the reflexive pronoun will come before the verb, sometimes after.

1 (Você) não (levantar-se) tarde
You didn't get up late
2 (Nós) (sentar-se) na primeira fila
We sat down in the first row
3 (Ela) disse que eles (deitar-se) às 11 horas
She said that they went to bed at 11 o'clock
4 (Ela) também (esquecer-se) do encontro
She also forgot about the meeting

Exercise 7a

Below are some actions that Joana performs in the course of a
rather strenuous day. What do you think the actions are?

Exercise 7b

Read the following passage, answer the questions which follow,
then translate it into English:

O football, ou futebol, é um desporto de bola no qual jogam
duas equipas sobre um terreno rectangular. O objectivo do jogo
é introduzir a bola na baliza adversária o maior número de vezes
possível (marcar golos).

1 What is the object of the game?
2 How many teams does it involve and where is it played?

andar   correr   levantar

4   5

empurrar   **puxar**

Vocabulary

um desporto de bola	a ball sport
no qual	in which
duas equipas	two teams
sobre	on
introduzir	to introduce
a baliza	net
o maior número de	the largest number of
vezes	times
(uma vez	once/one time)
possível	possible
marcar golos	to score goals

The imperfect indicative tense

To form this tense, remove the **-ar, -er or -ir** from the end of most
infinitives and add these endings:

for **-ar** verbs	*for* **-er + -ir** verbs
-ava	**-ia**
-avas	**-ias**
-ava	**-ia**
-ávamos	**-íamos**
-avam	**-iam**

Four verbs do not follow this pattern:

Ser (to be)	**era eras era éramos eram**
Ter (to have)	**tinha tinhas tinha tínhamos tinham**
Vir (to come)	**vinha vinhas vinha vínhamos vinham**
Pôr (to put)	**punha punhas punha púnhamos punham**

Using the imperfect tense

1 The imperfect is a past tense and expresses, for example: 'He was eating' or 'They were shopping'. Unlike the other past tense we have seen already (the preterite), the imperfect is used for actions in the past which are incomplete and which have no precise time limits:

Andava no parque   I was walking in the park

In this sentence the time when the walking began is unknown and the time when it ended is also unknown. Compare this to the preterite tense:

Andei a pé toda a manhã   I walked all morning

Here, the walking has been confined to a particular period of time – all morning.

2 The imperfect also translates 'used to':

Comia naquele restaurante todos os sábados
I ate (used to eat) in that restaurant every Saturday

The verb **costumar** (to usually do) can also be used:

Costumava comer naquele restaurante
I used to eat in that restaurant

Exercise 8

Give the imperfect tense of the verbs in brackets and say what the sentences mean in English.

1 **Nós (ler** – to read)
2 **Ela (ir** – to go) **ao teatro**
3 **Você (conduzir** – to drive) **lentamente** (slowly)
4 **Eu (estudar** – to study)
5 **Elas (ter** – to have) **muitos problemas**

3 The imperfect tense is used to describe the background to events, i.e. to describe what *was going on* when an event of some kind occurred (which is expressed by the preterite tense):

Chovia **quando** *chegámos* **à praia**
It *was raining* (description/background) when *we arrived* (event/ action) at the beach

Dormia **quando** *começou* **o terramoto**[2]
He *was sleeping* (description/background) when the earthquake *started* (event/action)

2 **o terramoto** (Br) 'earthquake'

Exercise 9

Can you say what the following three people were doing when the earthquake began?
1 ... **quando o terramoto começou (pintar)**
2 ... **quando o terramoto começou (beber)**
3 ... **quando o terramoto começou (fazer a barba** – to shave)

4 The imperfect tense also frequently replaces the conditional tense (see the next section) in everyday speech:

He would like three tickets
Queria três bilhetes (not: **Quereria três bilhetes**)

The conditional tense

This tense expresses: 'I should', 'I would', etc. It is formed by adding to the infinitive (whether **-ar**, **-er** or **-ir**) the endings:

-ia -ias -ia -íamos -iam

As with the future tense, the three exceptions to this rule are:

fazer → far-ia	I would/should do/make
dizer → dir-ia	I would/should say
trazer → trar-ia	I would/should bring

The conditional perfect tense

This is formed with the conditional of the verb **ter** + past participle to express: 'He would have liked', etc.:

Teríamos ficado muito cansados
We would have been very tired

Exercise 10

Give the 1st person plural (**nós**) of the conditional tense of the following verbs:

ir → iríamos   We would/should go

dar, ser, estar, ver, vir, ter, fazer

Ordinal numbers

primeiro/a	1st	**décimo/a primeiro/a**	11th
segundo/a	2nd	**vigésimo/a**	20th
terceiro/a	3rd	**trigésimo/a**	30th
quarto/a	4th	**quadragésimo/a**	40th
quinto/a	5th	**quinquagésimo/a**	50th
sexto/a	6th	**sexagésimo/a**	60th
sétimo/a	7th	**septuagésimo/a**	70th
oitavo/a	8th	**octagésimo/a**	80th
nono/a	9th	**nonagésimo/a**	90th
décimo/a	10th	**centésimo/a**	100th

The numbers agree with what is spoken about:

a terceira casa à esquerda the third house on the left
o quinto andar the fifth floor
os primeiros dois carros the first two cars

⋒ Situation 1 (Audio 2: 2)
Na farmácia

ANA: Faz favor. Tem alguma coisa para a febre do feno? Dói-me a garganta e não paro de espirrar ...
Excuse me. Do you have something for hay fever? My throat hurts and I can't stop sneezing ...

ISABEL: Tem algum remédio para queimadura de sol, se faz favor? E também cortei-me no dedo. Tem esparadrapo* e creme anti-séptico?
Do you have something for sunburn please? And I've also cut my finger. Do you have sticking plaster and antiseptic ointment?

JOSÉ: Atchim! Estou constipado e dói-me a cabeça. Pode ser a gripe?
Achoo! I have a cold and my head hurts. Could it be flu?

*Esparadrapo** (Br) used in Portugal, but correct word is **pensos rápidos** (Pt).

⋒ Situation 2 (Audio 2: 3)
No hospital

PAULO: Penso que parti o braço e sinto-me tonto.
MÉDICO: Parece uma fractura. Vamos tirar um raio x.
PAULO: *I think I have broken my arm and I feel dizzy.*
DOCTOR: *It looks like a fracture. We'll take an x-ray.*

⋒ Situation 3 (Audio 2: 4)
No consultório

JORGE: Estou com dores no ouvido e não me sinto bem.
MÉDICO: Ah, tem uma infecção. Precisa de antibiótico. É alérgico

a algum medicamento? Ora bem, esta receita é para
penicilina.

JORGE: *I have a pain in my ear and I don't feel well.*
DOCTOR: *Ah, you have an infection. You need an antibiotic. Are
you allergic to any medicines? Fine, this prescription is
for penicillin.*

Situation 4 (Audio 2: 5)
No dentista

MANUELA: Estou com dor de dentes.
DENTIST: É preciso arrancar o dente, mas antes de tudo, uma
injecção ...

MANUELA: *I've got toothache.*
DENTIST: *The tooth will have to be extracted but, first of all, an
injection ...*

Exercise 11

Re-read Situations 1 to 4. Can you describe in Portuguese this
person's ailments? The first one has been done for you:

1 I've got a headache   **dói-me a cabeça**
2 I've got toothache
3 My throat is sore
4 My arm is sore
5 I've got a pain in my stomach
6 My back hurts
7 My knee is broken

Vocabulary

estar de ressaca	to have a hangover
uma constipação	a cold
uma picada (de mosquito/de vespa)	a sting (mosquito/wasp)
Onde é que dói?	Where does it hurt?
magoar-se	to hurt (oneself)
Não me sinto bem	I don't feel well
Melhoras!	Get well soon!
(or **Estimo as suas melhoras!**)	

A CABEÇA
OS OLHOS
O NARIZ
OS DENTES
A BOCA
A MÃO
O JOELHO

AS ORELHAS
A GARGANTA
O DEDO
O BRAÇO
AS COSTAS
O ESTÔMAGO
A PERNA
O PÉ

In case of emergency . . .

For all emergencies in Portugal, dial 112. You can then ask for:

Os Bombeiros Fire brigade
A Ambulância Ambulance
A Polícia Police

Personal object pronouns

We have already met subject pronouns (**eu**, **tu**, **ele**, etc.) and reflexive pronouns (**me**, **te**, **se**, etc.). The chart below contains these sets of pronouns as well as the following new sets:
1 Direct object pronouns
2 Indirect object pronouns
3 Pronouns after a preposition
4 Pronouns after the preposition **com**

Sub -ject	Reflexive	Direct	Indirect	After a pre- position	After *com*
eu	me	me	me	mim	comigo
I	myself	me	to me	me	with me
tu	te	te	te	ti	contigo
you	yourself	you	to you	you	with you
ele	se	o	lhe	ele	com ele
he	himself	him/it	to him	him	with him
ela	se	a	lhe	ela	com ela
she	herself	her/it	to her	her	with her
você	se	o/a	lhe	si/você	consigo/com você
you	yourself	you	to you	you	with you
o sr/	se	o	lhe	o sr	com o sr
a sra	se	a	lhe	a sra	com a sra
you	yourself	you	to you	you	with you
nós	nos	nos	nos	nós	connosco[3]
we	ourselves	us	to us	us	with us
(vós)	(vos)	(vos)	(vos)	(vós)	convosco
you	yourselves	you	to you	you	with you
eles	se	os	lhes	eles	com eles
they	themselves	them	to them	them	with them
elas	se	as	lhes	elas	com elas
they	themselves	them	to them	them	with them
vocês	se	os/as	lhes	si/vocês	com vocês
you	yourselves	you	to you	you	with you

3 **conosco** (Br) with us

1 Direct object pronouns: o, os, a, as

Viu o filme?
Has he seen the film?

Viu-*o* ontem
He saw *it* yesterday

Conhece a Ana?
Do you know Ana?

Conheço-*a*
I do (know her)

Frequently the 'it' is omitted in Portuguese:

Gostou do clube?
Did you like the club?

Gostei, sim.
Yes I liked it.

2 Indirect object pronouns: lhe, lhes

Falou ao professor?
Did you speak to the teacher?

Sim, falei-*lhe* (or, **falei com ele**)
Yes I spoke *to him*

Deu os livros às crianças?
Did you give the books to the children?

Dei-*lhes* os livros mais cedo
I gave the books *to them* earlier

3 Pronouns after a preposition

Falaram de nós	They spoke about us
Tenho boas notícias para ele	I have good news for him
Pensavam em mim	They were thinking about me

4 Pronouns after the preposition com (with)

This preposition contracts with the pronouns **mim, ti, si, nós** and **vós**:

Quer falar comigo?
Do you want to speak to me?

Pensa que vai contigo ao café
He thinks that he is going with you to the cafe

Posso estudar consigo?
Can I study with you?

Cantou connosco
He sang with us

Vamos convosco?[4]
Are we going with you?

---

4 Vamos com vocês is more commonly heard.

Position of direct and indirect pronouns

The same rules apply for these pronouns as for the reflexive pronouns, i.e. they are placed:

1 *Before the verb if the sentence contains*: a question, negative, short adverb, preposition, relative clause ('He said that ...')
2 *After and joined to the verb with a hyphen*: in all other cases.

As with the reflexive pronoun, in Brazil (even when the conditions in 1 above do not apply) these direct and indirect object pronouns tend to be placed in front of the verb:

(Ele) comprou-os	He bought them (Pt)
Ele os comprou	He bought them (Br)

Remember that it is not possible to start a sentence with an object pronoun – the subject pronoun (here, **ele**) must begin the sentence.

Exercise 12

Replace the following words in brackets with the correct direct object pronoun:

1 **Ela lava a louça**	She washes the dishes
Ela lava-*a*	She washes them
2 **Eu arranjei um encontro**	I arranged a meeting
Arranjei- ...	I arranged it
3 **Tu vendeste a casa?**	Did you sell the house?
Vendi- ...	I sold it
4 **Você tinha as chaves**	You had the keys
Você tinha- ...	You had them

Remember that in Brazil the pronouns would tend to be placed before the verb: **Você as tinha** ('You had them').

Exercise 13

Fill in the correct indirect object pronoun:

1 I gave a watch to him – **Dei-** ... **um relógio**
2 I didn't tell you the news – **Não** ... **disse as notícias**
3 He bought the cakes for her – **Comprou-** ... **os bolos**
4 She explained the problem to us – **Explicou-** ... **o problema**

How much can you remember?

1 How do you say?

to get up, to dress, to wash, to sit down

2 Can you answer these questions in Portuguese?

1 What time did you get up this morning?
2 What time did you go to bed?
3 Where do you wash?

3 Can you translate this into English:

Normalmente, levanto-me às oito horas, lavo-me e visto-me. Como o pequeno-almoço na cozinha. Saio de casa às nove menos um quarto. Vou ao meu emprego no centro da cidade.

4 Can you ask these questions in Portuguese?

1 What time did you leave home?
2 Where did you sit down to have breakfast?
3 Where did you get dressed?

5 What do you think these verbs mean?

zangar-se, lembrar-se de, enganar-se, queixar-se, cortar-se, sentar-se, lavar-se

6 Fill in the correct verb endings in the imperfect tense:

respir _____	We were breathing (**respirar**)
com _____	You (**você**) were eating (**comer**)
part _____	I was leaving (**partir**)
anda _____	They were walking (**andar**)

7 Write out the imperfect of the verb **ter**.

Then write out the conditional of **ter** and **fazer**.

8 How would you say:

I have a cold;   my head hurts;   I feel dizzy;
I have a pain in my ear

9 Translate (the first one has been done for you):

falo-lhe	I speak to her/to him/to you
falei-te	
falaram-me	
falou-nos	
fala-lhes	

10 Read the following dialogue and answer the questions which follow:

LUCINDA: A que horas te levantas?
LUIS: Levanto-me às sete e meia.
LUCINDA: Porque te levantas tão cedo?
LUIS: Porque tenho de ir trabalhar e o meu escritório é muito longe. Sou contabilista.

Vocabulary

tão cedo	so early
tenho de ir trabalhar	I have to go and work
o meu escritório é muito longe	my office is very far away
sou contabilista	I'm an accountant

1 At what time does Luis get up?
2 What does Lucinda then ask Luis?
3 What reason does Luis give?

8 Não desligue . . .

Hold on . . .

In this lesson you will learn about:
- using the post office and 'phoning
- the perfect tense
- the pluperfect tense
- using the bank: changing money and opening a bank account

🎧 Dialogue 1 (Audio 2: 6)
Nos correios

CLIENTE:	Queria selos para mandar estas cartas para os Estados Unidos, se faz favor.
EMPREGADO:	Quantos selos deseja? Quatro?
CLIENTE:	Sim. Quanto é tudo?
EMPREGADO:	390$00 escudos.

🎧 Dialogue 2 (Audio 2: 7)
Na cabine telefónica três

EMPREGADO:	O senhor queria fazer uma chamada?
ÁLVARO:	Queria, sim, para Roma, Itália. Qual é o indicativo do país para Itália? Posso ver a lista telefónica?
EMPREGADO:	O indicativo do país é 0039, e depois tem de marcar o indicativo da zona para Roma, 6. Pode usar a cabine telefónica número três . . .

Dialogue 3 (Audio 2: 8)
Na Posta-Restante

CLIENTE: Faz favor. Tem algumas cartas dirigidas a David Sinclair?

EMPREGADO: Só um minuto, vou verificar ... ah sim, aqui estão duas cartas dirigidas ao senhor David Sinclair.

Vocabulary

selos (mpl)	stamps
cartas (fpl)	letters
para mandar para	to send to
os Estados Unidos	USA
fazer uma chamada/um telefonema	to make a phone call
aqui estão	here are
vou verificar	I'll go and check
Quanto é tudo?	How much does it come to?
	(*lit*: How much is everything?)
o indicativo do país	international code
o indicativo da zona	area code
marcar	to dial
a lista telefónica (Br o catálogo)	telephone directory
dirigidas a	addressed to
um telegrama	a telegram
o carteiro	the postman
só um minuto	just a second
um pacote/uma encomenda	parcel/packet
uma carta registada	a registered letter
(Br **uma carta registrada**)	
a caixa de correio	postbox
o código postal	post code

Exercise 1

Now it is your turn to ask for certain things in a post office:

1 You would like to call London. You need a telephone directory. You need to find out what the international code is for England as well as the code for London itself.

2 You would like 10 stamps to send letters to America.

3 You enquire whether there are any letters waiting for you in the poste restante.

The perfect tense

This tense is used for repeated events or states in the past which are still having repercussions almost up until the present. It most closely translates the English 'we have been', 'she has been', etc.

1 **Não me tenho sentido bem**
   I haven't been feeling well
   (i.e. I haven't been feeling well (lately))
2 **Têm viajado muito**
   They have been travelling a lot
   (i.e. They have been travelling a lot (recently))

Forming the perfect tense

Use the present tense of **ter** (**tenho, tens, tem, temos, têm**) + the past participle (**estado** (been), **visitado** (visited), **sido** (been), etc.). These past participles are invariable, i.e. they do not agree with who is speaking or what is being spoken about. (Remember, however, that past participles used adjectivally agree with the subject of the sentence: **a porta está fechada** (the door is closed).)

Examples

Têm comido pouco
They have been eating very little (recently)

Temos estudado
We have been studying (lately)

Tens telefonado muito
You have been telephoning a lot (recently)

Exercise 2

Fill in the correct past participle from the list below to complete these sentences:

1 **Tem**   (been travelling)   **muito**
2 **Temos** (been sending)   **cartas**
3 **Tens**   (been buying)   **tantas coisas**

4	**Tenho**	(been seeing)	**muitos documentários**
5	**Têm**	(been)	**bastante doentes**
6	**Tem**	(been training)	**ultimamente**

estado	treinado	viajado	comprado	visto	mandado

Using the perfect tense

The perfect tense is fairly restricted in its use. The preterite tense, on the other hand, translates both 'I wrote' and 'I have written' – actions which are complete and confined to a distinct period of time:

Ele escreveu as suas memórias
He has written (he wrote) his memoirs
(action over and finished – preterite)

Tem mandado muitas cartas
He has sent a lot of letters
(i.e. He *has been* sending a lot of letters (lately))

Making a call from a phone box

Here are the instructions you would find in **uma cabine telefónica** (a telephone box)

> **Introduza a moeda**[1]
> **Levante o auscultador**
> **Espere o sinal de marcar**[2]
> **Marque o número**

---

1 You may have a telephone card – **um cartão telefónico**. In this case you will be asked **Introduza o cartão**.
2 **o sinal de discar** (Br)

138

Exercise 3

The English translation of the above instructions has been mixed up. Can you sort it out?

Introduza a moeda	Wait for dialling tone
Levante o auscultador	Insert coin
Marque o número	Lift receiver
Espere o sinal de marcar	Dial number

Problems that may arise . . .

ser cortado (or **ser desligado**)	to be cut off
o sinal de impedido	engaged tone
o sinal de ocupado (Br)	engaged tone

Once through to the correct number say: **Está?** (Hello?/Are you there?) (**Alô?** (Br) Hello). If you answer a call say: Estou (Hello) (*lit.*: 'I am') (**Alô** (Br) Hello).

The pluperfect tense

This tense in Portuguese is called the **mais que perfeito**, i.e. 'more than perfect'. It is used for actions which have taken place *before* another past action and translates the English 'They had left', 'I had eaten', etc.

Forming the pluperfect

Use the imperfect tense of the verb **ter (tinha tinhas tinha tínhamos tinham)** + past participle:

Tinham organizado a festa quando ele chegou
They had organized the party when he arrived

Ainda não tinha terminado o trabalho quando o gerente telefonou
He still had not finished the work when the manager phoned

Exercise 4

Provide the missing words:

1 **Ele** _____ **comprado uma pizza para levar**
He had bought a take-away pizza

2 **Você** _____ **aberto uma conta bancária**
You had opened a bank account

3 **Ela** _____ **chumbado³ no exame de motorista**
She had failed the driving test

---

3 **chumbado** from **chumbar em** ('to fail') very colloquial
more common is: **reprovado** from **ser reprovado em** ('to fail')

Palavras Cruzadas

Can you work out these clues? The answers are in the Key.

horizontais
1 **Região de Portugal**
5 **Uma boa praia**
6 **Sessenta minutos**
8 **O que se respira**
9 **Almoçar ou jantar**

verticais
2 **Capital de Portugal**
3 **Doze meses**
4 **Orgulho**
7 **Gosto muito**

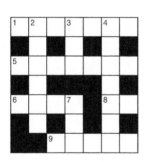

Provérbios

Can you work out what the following proverbs mean by filling in the blanks in the English translations:

Não deixes para amanhã o que podes fazer hoje
Don't _____ _____ till _____ what _____ _____
_____ _____

Mais vale tarde que nunca

_____ late _____ _____

Mais vale um pássaro na mão, que dois a voar

_____ _____ _____ _____ hand _____ worth_____

_____ _____ _____.

More on pronouns

Before moving on to some irregularities found when dealing with pronouns it might be a good idea to revise the section in Lesson 7 on direct and indirect object pronouns. The irregularities are as follows:

1 Where a direct object pronoun (**o, a, os, as**) follows a verb ending in either **-r, -s** or **-z**, those letters are dropped and an **l** is added to the beginning of the pronoun, joined to the verb with a hyphen.

Vou comprar o → **Vou comprá-lo**
I'm going to buy it (car – **o carro**)

Comes as → **Come-las**
You eat them (oranges – **as laranjas**)

Traz a → **Trá-la**
He brings it (shopping list – **a lista de compras**)

An accent is added to the infinitives of **-ar** (**á**) and **-er** (**ê**) verbs following contraction with a pronoun and also to parts of the verb **traz** (as above), **fez** ('he, she, you did') and **faz** ('he, she, you do').

'**Ela fê-lo!**' **gritou a criança.**
'She did it!' shouted the child.

Note, however, that the **-r** rule above does not apply to the present indicative of **ele/ela/você quer** ('he/she wants, you want'). Instead, an extra **-e** is added to the end of the verb: **você quere-o** ('you want it').

2 A direct object pronoun following a verb ending in a nasal sound, such as those ending in **-m, -õe** or **-ão**, has the letter **-n** added to the beginning of it and is joined to the verb with a hyphen.

Venderam os → **Venderam-nos**
They sold them (books – **os livros**)

Você põe os lá → **Põe-nos lá**
You put them there (cakes – **os bolos**)

Eles dão as   → **Eles dão-nas**
They give them (magazines – **as revistas**)

Order and treatment of object pronouns

When there is more than one object pronoun in the same sentence, the rule is that the indirect precedes the direct. Study the following sentences:

Comprou-lhe o C.D. (Pt)
Comprou-lhe o disco-laser (Br)
She bought the compact disc for him

Comprou-lho (lhe – for/to him **o** – it)
She bought it (the compact disc) for him

Você deu-me a informação
You gave me the information

Você deu-ma (me – to me **a** – it)
You gave it (the information) to me

The indirect pronoun joins with the direct pronoun and produces:

indirect direct
me +   o/a/os/as   → mo ma mos mas it/them to me
te +   o/a/os/as   → to ta tos tas it/them to you
lhe +   o/a/os/as   → lho lha lhos lhas it/them to him, her, you
nos +   o/a/os/as   → no-lo no-la no-los no-las it/them to us
(vos) + o/a/os/as   → (vo-lo vo-la vo-los vo-las)
lhes +   o/a/os/as   → lho lha lhos lhas it/them to them

Position of pronouns in future and conditional tenses

These are placed between the infinitive and the endings:

Limpá-lo-ei mais tarde   I shall wash it (car) later
Vendê-la-iam rápidamente   They would sell it (house) quickly

These constructions are not favoured in spoken, less formal, Portuguese. To avoid them the following may be used:
1) **ir** + infinitive (to replace the future)
    Vou limpá-lo mais tarde I shall wash it (car) later
2) the Imperfect (to replace the Conditional)
    Vendiam-na rápidamente They would sell it (house) quickly

Position of pronouns in compound tenses

Pronouns follow the verb **ter** and are attached to it with a hyphen (if none of the rules applies for placing the pronoun before the verb – see Lesson 7):

Tinha-o comprado	He had bought it *but*
não o tinha comprado	He had not bought it

 Dialogue 4 (Audio 2: 9)
No banco

CLIENTE:	Posso trocar um cheque de viagem?
EMPREGADO:	Tem o seu passaporte? Qual é a sua morada aqui, se faz favor?
CLIENTE:	Estou no Hotel Eva, na Avenida da Liberdade. Qual é a cotação?
EMPREGADO:	Quer trocar libras? O câmbio de compra é a 248$00 e o de venda é a 258$00. Faz favor de assinar aqui.

Vocabulary

Posso trocar⁴ um cheque de viagem?	
Can I cash a traveller's cheque?	
Qual é a sua morada aqui?	What's your address here?
Qual é a cotação?	What is the rate?
Qual é o câmbio?	What's the exchange rate?
Quer trocar libras?	Do you want to exchange pounds?
O câmbio de compra é a ...	The buying rate is ...
O câmbio de venda é a ...	The selling rate is ...
Faz favor de assinar aqui	Please sign here

---

4 **cambiar** 'to change/exchange'

Exercise 5

How would you say:

Hello, Can I change these traveller's cheques, please (**estes cheques de viagem**)? I am staying at the **Pensão Bonita**, in **Rua Gil Vicente**. What's the exchange rate?

Once you have made your transaction you will be told:

'O senhor/a tem de entregar a chapa na caixa para receber o dinheiro'.

You must take your token (**chapa**) and hand it over at the cashier's desk (**a caixa**) to receive your money.

Exercise 6

Read the following passage on Brazil then answer the questions which follow:

O Brasil, vibrante e dinâmico, é um país repleto de grandes matas e recursos naturais. O povo brasileiro consiste de uma mistura de raças. Isto gera uma cultura e folclore bastante variados e exuberantes.

Vocabulary

repleto de	full of
matas	forests
o povo	the people
recursos naturais	natural resources
gera	produces
consiste de	consists of
raças	races
bastante	quite

1 What qualities does the writer claim about Brazil?
2 What does s/he say about the terrain?
3 What, in the writer's opinion, produces Brazil's particular brand of culture? How is this described?

𝒬 Dialogue 5 (Audio 2: 10)
Abrindo uma conta

CLIENTE: Gostaria de abrir uma conta (bancária). Que é
             necessário fazer?
EMPREGADO: Tem uma referência a seu respeito e uma assinatura
             modelo formulário?
CLIENTE: Sim, tenho.

EMPREGADO: Está bem. Quer fazer um depósito à ordem ou um depósito a prazo?

CLIENTE: Um depósito à ordem com um livro de cheques e um cartão bancário. Queria também um cartão para o terminal caixa e um extracto de conta mensal.

Vocabulary

Gostaria de abrir uma conta bancária	I'd like to open a bank account
Que é necessário fazer?	What is required?
uma referência a seu respeito	a character reference
uma assinatura modelo formulário	specimen signature
um depósito à ordem	current account
um depósito a prazo	deposit account
um livro de cheques	a cheque book
um talão de cheques (Br)	a cheque book
um cartão bancário	a cheque card
o saldo	balance
um cartão para o terminal caixa	cash-point card
um extracto de conta (mensal)	a (monthly) statement

Exercise 7a

You want to open a current account with a cheque book and card. You also want a cash-point card and a monthly statement. What would you ask for?

Exercise 7b

What are you being asked here?

1 **Tem uma referência a seu respeito?**
2 **Quer um depósito a prazo?**
3 **Quer um cartão para o terminal caixa?**
4 **Tem uma assinatura modelo formulário?**

The present continuous tense

This tense consists of the present indicative of the verb **estar** + **a** + infinitive:

Estamos a cantar	We are singing
Estou a dar	I am giving
Está a ir	He is going

This tense conveys the idea of a continuous action. Don't, however, confuse it with the present indicative, which can translate the English 'he is (buying)/ he (buys)' which is simply: **compra**. In Brazil and in the Azores islands you are more likely to hear **estar** + gerund (see below) in place of **estar** + infinitive: **estou comprando** ('I am buying'); **está indo** ('he is going').

The gerund

This is equivalent to the English present participle (ending in '-ing'). It is formed by removing the final **-r** of any verb and adding **-ndo**:

estar → esta → esta*ndo*	being
partir → parti → part*indo*	leaving
beber → bebe → bebe*ndo*	drinking

The gerund is used to express a continuous action:

eating **comendo** buying **comprando** selling **vendendo**

The continuous action can also be expressed in other tenses besides the present:

Examples

estava a ir	he was going (imperfect)
estará a ir	he shall be going (future)

Exercise 8

Here are instructions for using a cash-point card (called **o cartão Multibanco**) issued by one particular Portuguese bank. Can you decipher these instructions? Some vocabulary is provided below.

146

Como utilizar o cartão Multibanco

Após introduzir o cartão e marcar o código pessoal

Levantamentos
(Conta à Ordem)

.Seleccione o montante desejado
pressionando as teclas que o assinalam.
.Caso não esteja indicado o montante
que deseja utilize a tecla
"Outros Levantamentos",
e usando o teclado com algarismos,
escreva a quantia pretendida.

Vocabulary

depositar	to deposit
levantar	to withdraw
levantamentos	withdrawals
após	after
seleccionar	to select
o montante desejado	the desired amount
Caso não esteja indicado	If the amount you wish is not
o montante que deseja utilize	shown, use the 'Other With-
a tecla 'Outros Levantamentos'	drawals' key
e usando o teclado com algarismos,	and using the numeric keyboard,
escreva a quantia pretendida	type in the desired amount

Exercise 9

What advice do you think is being given in Point 1 (see p. 147) under **Informações úteis**? (Useful information)

Vocabulary

pessoal	personal
intransmissível	untransferable

qualquer outro local ou documento	any other place or document
que possa ser perdido ou roubado	that may be lost or stolen
simultâneo com o cartão	along with the card
nem o comunique a ninguém	don't tell anyone
	(your pin number)

More plurals of nouns and adjectives

A Nouns or adjectives which end in **-ão** take one of three endings in the plural:

1 **-ão** → **-ões**	(the most likely possibility)
a atenção → as atenções	attention/s
a colecção → as colecções	collection/s
a organização → as organizações	organization/s
comilão → comilões	greedy
2 **-ão** → **-ães**	
o cão → os cães	dog/s
o pão → os pães	bread
3 **-ão** → **-ãos**	
o irmão → os irmãos	brother/s
a mão → as mãos	hand/s

B Nouns or adjectives which end in **-l** drop the **-l** and add **-is** in the plural:

o móvel	→ os móveis	(furniture)
comercial	→ comerciais	(commercial)
o guarda-sol	→ os guarda-sóis	(sunshade/s)
azul	→ azuis	(blue)
pastoril	→ pastoris	(pastoral)[5]
difícil	→ difíceis	(difficult)[5]

5 Note that words ending in **-il** have two possible endings – **-is** or **-eis**. This changes according to whether the **-il** is stressed. If it is stressed, you add **-is**. If unstressed, you add **-eis**. In the case of **difícil** the accent over the i informs you that the stress falls there and not on the **-il** at the end of the word.

Exercise 10

Give the plurals of the following:
1 **a televisão**
2 **o avião**
3 **a ligação**
4 **amável** (kind)
5 **portunhol** (a mixture of Spanish and Portuguese)
6 **radical** (radical)

Plurals of compound nouns

1 If a compound noun is a combination of verb + noun, only the noun takes the plural:

o guarda-roupa → **os guarda-roupas**
the wardrobe   the wardrobes

2 If the term is a combination of adjective + noun, both words become plural:

o cachorro-quente → **os cachorros-quentes**
the hot-dog   the hot-dogs

How much can you remember?

1 How would you say:

1 I want six stamps for Ireland
2 I'd like to make a phone call. Do you have the telephone directory?
3 What is the code for Scotland? What is the code for Edinburgh? Which booth?
4 I haven't been studying much (lately)
5 The receiver (phone); the number; dialling tone; to be cut off; to be engaged

2 Can you translate these into English:

1 **Ele tinha partido quando o carteiro chegou**
2 **Tínhamos posto (put) as chávenas na cozinha** (the cups in the kitchen)

3 Eu tinha comprado uma sanduíche para levar
4 Posso cambiar um cheque de viagem?
5 Qual é a cotação?
6 Um cartão bancário; o terminal caixa

3 Can you give the plurals of:

a ligação (link), o irmão, o pão, azul, o hotel

4 Can you give the singulars of:

as organizações, as mãos, os cães, difíceis

5 Read the following passage and see if you can translate it into English:

Esta manhã fui aos correios para fazer uma chamada. O empregado lá disse-me que eu tinha de esperar um pouco porque havia uma bicha.[6] Enquanto esperava, procurei o indicativo do país para Moçambique e também o indicativo da zona de Maputo. Marquei o número de telefone. Estava impedido. Marquei o número outra vez ... Ah! Esta vez tocava ... Eu disse 'Está?' Mas ninguém respondeu! Cortaram a ligação!

ser cortado	to be cut off
ser desligado	to be cut off
cortaram a ligação	I was cut off
enquanto esperava	while I was waiting
procurei	I looked for
tocava	it was ringing
uma bicha	a queue

6 **a fila** (Br) 'queue'

9 O fim de semana

The weekend

In this lesson you will learn about:

- buying tickets at the cinema, theatre, etc.
- discussing leisure activities and holiday plans
- using the passive
- talking about the weather and the seasons
- using the subjunctive

 Dialogue 1 (Audio 2: 11)
No cinema

JOSÉ:	A sessão está esgotada!
DUARTE:	Não. Não te preocupes. Vamos à próxima sessão que começa às nove e meia.
EMPREGADA:	Quantos bilhetes desejam? Querem balcão ou plateia?
JOSÉ:	Três plateias, se faz favor. No meio da sala, ao centro.

Vocabulary

estar esgotado/a	to be sold out
a sessão	the show
Não te preocupes	Don't worry
a próxima sessão começa	the next show begins
o balcão	circle
a plateia	stalls
no meio da sala	in the middle of the hall
ao centro	in the centre

Dialogue 2 (Audio 2: 12)
No teatro

EMPREGADA:	Que bilhetes desejam e para quando?
JOÃO:	Dê-nos um camarote, por favor, para a próxima quinta-feira, na matinée das três e meia.

Vocabulary

Dê-nos um camarote	Give us a box
a próxima quinta-feira	next Thursday
a peça	the play

 Dialogue 3 (Audio 2: 13)
Na tourada

ANA:	Queríamos quatro bilhetes de bancada, se faz favor.
EMPREGADO:	Sol ou sombra?
ANA:	Na sombra que é mais fresquinha. Esta vai ser uma grande tourada!
EMPREGADO:	Se os senhores quiserem, podem também comprar um cartaz desta corrida. Temos um toureiro novo. Chama-se Pedrito de Portugal.

Vocabulary

quatro bilhetes de bancada	four seats (stadium, etc.)
sol ou sombra	in the sun or in the shade
mais fresquinha/o	nice and cool
Esta vai ser uma grande tourada!	This is going to be a great bullfight!
Se os srs quiserem	If you want
podem também comprar	you can also buy
um cartaz desta corrida	a poster of this bullfight
um toureiro novo	a new bullfighter

Exercise 1

Can you remember how to say in Portuguese:

1 Four seats in the stalls, in the middle.
2 I would like a box at the theatre for next Saturday's show. It's sold out!?
3 Six seats in the sun to see the bullfight today. Do you have a poster?

Dimunitives and augmentatives

Pedrito and **fresquinho** are both examples of the diminutive, which is widely used in Portuguese. The following are added to the end of a word to alter the meaning to 'little':

-inho -zinho -ito -zito

These endings will agree with the subject in number and gender. For example:

o gato	the cat	**o gatinho**	the kitten
a caixa	the box	**a caixinha**	the little box
as mesas	the tables	**as mesinhas**	the little tables

Adding a diminutive ending to a word can also produce a tone of affection:

uma bica	a coffee	**uma bicazinha**	a nice little coffee
um café	a coffee	**um cafézinho**	a nice little coffee

Conversely, to express an augmentative add **-ão** to the end of a word:

a caixa	the box	**o caixão**	the large box/coffin

 Dialogue 4 (Audio 2: 14)
No intervalo

Three people discuss a film ...

JOSÉ: Este filme é uma porcaria!
DUARTE: Não acho! Tem uns bons actores muito célebres.
JORGE: Mas a história não presta para nada! Estou de acordo com o José.
DUARTE: Ora essa! Estou farto disto, vou-me embora!

Vocabulary

uns bons actores muito célebres	some good, very famous actors
a história	the story/plot
não acho!	I don't think so!
vou-me embora!	I'm going!
(ir-se embora – to go away)	

Expressing yourself . . .

Negatively: **Não estou de acordo com/Não concordo com** . . . I don't agree with . . .

Estou farto (disto)!	I'm fed up (with this)!
É uma porcaria!	It's rubbish!
É uma bagunça!(Br)	It's rubbish!
(Isto) não presta para nada!	It's awful!/no good!
É terrível/horrível!	It's awful!
É tão chato!	It's so boring!
Não acho!	I don't think so!
Ora essa!	Come off it!
Cala-te!	Shut up!
detesto	I hate

Positively: **Estou (completamente) de acordo com/ Concordo (completamente) com** . . . I agree (completely) with . . .

É óptimo!	It's great!
É (muito) giro!	It's (really) nice/terrific/cute!
Que giro!	Terrific!
É bestial!	It's great!
Está bem	It's OK
Também acho que . . .	I also think that . . .
adoro	I love
É bacana (Br)	It's great
Acho que sim	I think so

Exercise 2a

Using the previous dialogues can you translate the following into Portuguese:

PAULO: *I think the film is boring. The plot is awful and the acting (a actuação) is rubbish.*

ISABEL: *I don't agree. The plot is not awful, it's great! I also think that the acting is OK. In fact* **(na verdade)** *the film is really great!*

PAULO: *Come off it, it's so boring I'm going home!*

Exercise 2b

Look at the publicity for the following events then answer the questions:

TEATRO ABERTO

DE QUARTA A SÁBADO ÀS 22 H.
DOMINGOS – MATINÉE 16 H.

BILHETEIRA DAS 14 H. ÀS 22 H | TELS: 797 09 69 / 797 88 98

novo
grupo

apresenta

o Tempo
e oQuarto

de BOTHO STRAUSS

Versão: João Lourenço/Vera San Payo de Lemos
Dramaturgia: Vera San Payo de Lemos
Figurinos: António Filipe; **Cenário:** António Casimiro
Encenação: João Lourenço

Elenco· Alexandra Lencastre ● António Filipe ● Canto e Castro ● Diogo Infante
● Élio Correia ● João Lagarto ● José Gomes ● Melim Teixeira ● Paulo Neto
● Sofia de Portugal ● Teresa Roby ● Virgílio Castelo ● Zita Esteves

«O melhor espectáculo em cena nos palcos de Lisboa.
A não perder.» (E.V. *Expresso*)

1 Which poster would you choose if you wanted to participate in a carnival atmosphere? How many days does the event run? What is the last event and what prize is involved?

2 What time is the play on and what is the theatre called? Can you attend during the day and when is the ticket office open?

Vocabulary

a estreia	opening/première
o concurso de máscaras	masked competition
noite do terror	night of horror
noite da fantasia	fancy dress night
divirta-se!	have a good time/enjoy yourself!
a não perder!	not to be missed!
1º prémio	1st prize
o final	the final
o automóvel	car
o melhor espectáculo em cena nos palcos de Lisboa!	The best show on the stage in Lisbon's theatres!
a bilheteira	ticket office

Exercise 3

Which type of film would you choose to see? Match up the English below with the Portuguese:

um filme de suspense
um filme de amor/romance
um filme de terror
um filme de ficção científica
um musical
um desenho animado

science fiction	a cartoon	a love story	a thriller
	a horror story	a musical	

The passive

The passive translates the English:

He was killed by a bullet
Foi morto por uma bala

They were defeated by the other team
Foram vencidos pela outra equipa

Forming the passive

Use the verb **ser** + past participle; **ser** can be in any tense. The past participle agrees with the subject of the sentence as seen in the above examples:

He was killed (subject is 'he') – **Foi morto**
They were defeated (subject is 'they') – **Foram vencidos**

Por translates 'by':

Ela será atropelada *pelo* carro
She will be run over *by the* car
A janela foi aberta *pelo* homem
The window was opened *by the* man

The passive is often replaced in Portuguese by

1 using a verb in the reflexive:

Apagou-se a luz
The light was switched off (*lit*: the light switched itself off)

2 using 'they':

Pintam o edifício todos os anos
The building is painted every year
(*lit*: 'they', i.e. someone, paints the building)

The passive using estar + past participle

Whereas **ser** + past participle expresses an *action* of some kind ('was knocked down *by*'; 'were restrained *by*'), the passive using **estar** reflects a *state*. Compare:

O carro foi roubado pelo ladrão   The car was stolen by the thief
A porta estava aberta   The door was open

◯ Dialogue 5 (Audio 2: 15)
No fim de semana

An interviewer is out doing market research (pesquisa de mercado) about what people do over the weekend. He asks: O que faz . . .? What do you do . . .?

ENTREVISTADOR:	O que faz no domingo de manhã?
TRANSEUNTE 1:	Fico deitada na cama até o meio-dia. Depois, vejo televisão.
ENTREVISTADOR:	E no domingo à tarde?
TRANSEUNTE 1:	Vejo mais televisão ou oiço música. Às vezes telefono para a minha amiga para conversar.[1]
ENTREVISTADOR:	O que faz no sábado de manhã?
TRANSEUNTE 2:	Vou visitar os meus pais. Depois, vou ao super-mercado.
ENTREVISTADOR:	E no sábado à tarde?
TRANSEUNTE 2:	Saio com uns amigos.

1 More colloquial is **cavaquear** to chat/gossip. **Bater papo** (Br) to chat/gossip

Vocabulary

domingo de manhã	Sunday morning
domingo à tarde	Sunday afternoon/early evening
domingo à noite	Sunday night
sábado de manhã	Saturday morning
sábado à tarde	Saturday afternoon/early evening
sábado à noite	Saturday night

Exercise 4

Using the English words as clues can you find the Portuguese sentences in the above dialogues which are the equivalent of:

1 I stay in bed till midday (**a cama** – bed)
2 I go out with some friends (**saio** – I go out)
3 I watch more television (**vejo** – I watch)
4 I go to visit my parents (**os meus pais** – my parents)
5 I listen to music (**música** – music)
6 Sometimes I phone my friend for a chat (**telefono** – I phone)

Exercise 5

With the aid of the above can you now try to translate Dialogue 5 into English?

Exercise 6a

Here are some things people might do at the weekend. Can you say what they are, using the clues below?

ir pescar
(for this you will need a stretch of water and some bait)

lavar o carro
(more water involved here + soap)

ir velejar
(not a good hobby if you get seasick)

ler os jornais
(catch up on all the news)

Exercise 6b

Can you work out what these activities are?

1 **a ginástica**   (swing those arms!)
2 **o golfe**   (a hole in one!)
3 **o karaté**   (involves lots of chops)
4 **dançar** (Br: **bailar**)   (could include a foxtrot)
5 **a patinagem**   (a slippery hobby)
6 **pegar onda/fazer surfe**   (also requires the ocean,
                            the choppier the better)

Expressing activity

fazer → faço I do . . .   To do (e.g. aerobics)
Vou (nadar)   I go (swimming)
Vou passear   I go for a walk
Vou passear de carro   I go for a drive
Vou passear de barco   I go for a sail
jogo . . .   I play . . .

Exercise 7

Can you translate the following into Portuguese?

On Saturday morning I go to visit some friends. On Saturday afternoon I play golf and on Saturday evening I watch TV. On Sunday morning I stay in bed till midday and then I wash the car.

The present subjunctive

The present subjunctive expresses the English 'may' and 'might'. Whereas a sentence in the present indicative mood makes a statement or an assertion, a sentence in the present subjunctive mood expresses something which is open to doubt and uncertainty:

Talvez você conheça a Ana?
Perhaps you know Ana? (maybe not)
Oxalá² que tenha sorte!
I hope you are lucky! (but you might not be)
Não acho que ele estude muito
I don't *think* he studies much (you don't know for sure)
Conheces alguém que tenha um carro?
Do you know anyone who has a car? (uncertain who the person is)

---

2 **Tomara** is more common in Brazil and northern Portugal than **oxalá**.

The subjunctive also expresses emotion about something: 'I'm sorry that/I regret that . . .'

Sinto muito que não estejas cá
I'm sorry that you are not here

Forming the present subjunctive

You have, in fact, already seen the present subjunctive endings in the form of the imperative (see Lesson 4). Start from the 1st person singular (**eu**) of the present indicative and add these endings to the stem:

for **-ar** verbs   **-e -es -e -emos -em**
for **-er** and **-ir** verbs   **-a -as -a -amos -am**

Exercise 8

Write out the following verbs in the present subjunctive:

escrever (**escreva, escrevas,** etc.)   to write
transferir   to transfer
controlar   to control

Some irregular present subjunctives

Some subjunctives are not formed as described in the previous section and they are best learned individually:

dar	to give	(que) dê dês dê demos dêem
ser	to be	(que) seja sejas seja sejamos sejam
estar	to be	(que) esteja estejas esteja etc.
ir	to go	(que) vá vás vá vamos vão
saber	to know	(que) saiba saibas saiba etc.
querer	to want	(que) queira queiras queira etc.

The perfect subjunctive

This is formed by using the present subjunctive of the verb **ter** + past participle:

Não penso que ele tenha lido o livro
I don't think he has read the book

The weather (o tempo)

The seasons of the year As estações do ano

Dezembro, Janeiro e Fevereiro são os meses do inverno.
No inverno faz frio.

Março, Abril e Maio são os meses da primavera.
Na primavera faz bom tempo.

Junho, Julho e Agosto são os meses do verão.
No verão faz calor.

Setembro, Outubro e Novembro são os meses do outono.
No outono está fresco.

December, January and February are the months of winter.
In winter the weather is cold.

March, April and May are the months of spring.
In spring the weather is nice.

June, July and August are the summer months.
In summer it's warm.
September, October and November are the months of
autumn. In autumn the weather is cool.

Vocabulary

o Natal	Christmas	Feliz Natal!	Happy Christmas!
o Ano Novo	New Year	Feliz Ano Novo!	Happy New Year!
a Páscoa	Easter	Feliz Páscoa!	Happy Easter!

Exercise 9

Como está o tempo hoje?	What's the weather like today?
Faz bom tempo	The weather is good
mau	bad
faz vento	it's windy
está a chover	it's raining
faz sol	it's sunny
está a nevar	it's snowing

In answer to the question **Como está o tempo hoje?**, can you translate the following replies into Portuguese:

1 The weather is good; it's sunny.
2 The weather is bad; it's raining.
3 The weather is bad; it's windy.
4 The weather is bad; it's snowing.

Exercise 10

Read the following passage and then answer the questions:

Um director cinematográfico estava a filmar numa aldeia remota
no norte de Portugal. Apareceu um saloio que lhe disse: 'Amanhã
vai estar mau tempo. Vai chover'. No dia seguinte o saloio disse
que ía fazer bom tempo e sol e assim aconteceu durante muitos
dias. Um dia o saloio não apareceu e o director, confiando na
infalibilidade do saloio, foi a casa dele e perguntou-lhe: Que
tempo vamos ter amanhã? E o saloio respondeu-lhe: 'Não sei
patrão. Ainda não li o jornal hoje e a minha televisão está
avariada.'

1 Where is the film director filming?
2 What does he believe the bumpkin's gift is?
3 In fact the weather information comes from ...?

Vocabulary

uma aldeia remota	a remote village
um saloio	country bumpkin
mau/bom tempo	bad/good weather/
vai chover	it's going to rain
perguntou	(he) asked
respondeu	(he) replied
ainda não	not yet
o jornal	paper
li	read
está avariada	is broken down
confiando na infalibilidade de	believing in the infalibility of
o patrão	boss

Exercise 11

Look at this map of Portugal and answer the following questions about the weather.

1 Where would it be best to avoid if you wanted a peaceful, quiet day out?
2 Where would be the best place for a picnic?

3 Where would you not want to go if you hadn't packed a raincoat?

4 Look up the words for: thunder; fog; cloudy; temperature.

Exercise 12

Here are two advertisements for different types of holidays. Read them then answer the questions which follow:

A   B

Excursão Organizada!	*Parque de Campismo Flor*
Espanha!	**cem lugares para:**
Quinze dias!	**tendas/rulotes**
Hotel de luxo!	*** * * ***
Perto da Praia!	**chuveiros/electricidade**
Campo de Golf!	**loja – bar – piscina**
Esqui aquático!	**lavandaria automática**
	campo de ténis
!!!!!!!!!!!	

Vocabulary

excursão organizada (f)	package tour
quinze dias	fortnight
parque de campismo	camp site
o camping (Br)	camp site
o hotel de luxo	luxury hotel
nas montanhas	in the mountains
tendas (fpl)	tents
rulotes (mpl)	trailers/caravans
trailers (mpl) (Br)	trailers
o campo de ténis (m)	tennis court
o campo	field, countryside

In A:

1 Where is the holiday and how long is it for?
2 Is it in a basic hotel?
3 What leisure activities does this type of holiday offer?

In B:

1 How many places are available on the site and for what type of accommodation?
2 Name three facilities provided by the site.

Exercise 13

Here are some symbols of facilities offered by a camp site. Can you guess what they represent?

DUCHE QUENTE

LAVA-LOIÇAS

LAVA-ROUPAS

CORREIOS-POSTE

MUITAS SOMBRAS

PISCINA

 Dialogue 6 (Audio 2: 16)
Vamos ao Sul de Portugal

Two friends discuss possible holiday plans

FERNANDA: Vamos ao sul de Portugal, ao Algarve, de carro.
ISABEL: Mas, é uma viagem muito longa de carro. Porque não vamos de avião?

FERNANDA:	Porque eu não gosto de voar!
ISABEL:	Então, que achas fazendo excursões a pé nas férias?
FERNANDA:	É demasiado cansativo! Ficar numa pousada pode ser uma boa ideia!
ISABEL:	Seria menos caro ficar numa pensão, numa estalagem, ou mesmo, fazer campismo.
FERNANDA:	Campismo! Seria melhor ficar em casa!

Vocabulary

uma viagem muito longa	a very long journey
de carro	by car
Porque não vamos de avião?	Why not go by plane?
ao sul de	to the south of
Não gosto de voar	I don't like flying
Então, que achas ...?	Well/So, what do you think about ...?
férias fazendo excursões a pé	walking holiday
(uma excursão a pé)	(a hike)
fazendo	doing
é demasiado cansativa	it's too tiring
fazer campismo	to go camping

Ficar numa pousada pode ser uma boa ideia
Staying in a *pousada* might be a good idea
Seria menos caro ficar numa pensão
It would be less expensive to stay in a boarding house
Seria melhor ficar em casa!
It would be better to stay at home!

Where to stay

uma pousada	state-owned luxury inn
uma estalagem	an inn
uma pensão	a boarding house
uma albergaria	an inn
um turismo de habitação	bed and breakfast

Exercise 14

1 What does Isabel find unattractive about Fernanda's first suggestion?

2 How does Fernanda react to Isabel's suggestion about a walking holiday?

3 What alternative ideas does Isabel have for staying in a **pousada** and why doesn't she agree with her friend?

How much can you remember?

1 True or false?

a peça = bullfight
o cartaz = ticket
a próxima sessão = sold out

2 Can you say in Portuguese:

a little cake (**o bolo** cake)
a little dog (**o cão** dog)
a little plate (**o prato** plate)
I'm fed up! It's rubbish! I completely agree

3 What are the following:

um prémio, um concurso, o domingo de manhã, a bilheteira, uma estreia, O Natal, faz sol

4 Can you translate these into Portuguese:

a cartoon, a horror film, a thriller, karate, judo, skating, I watch TV, I go out with friends

5 True or false?

ir pescar = to play golf
lavar o carro = to chat
ler os jornais = to surf

6 What are three ways of saying that something is great?

7 Translate the following into Portuguese:

1 Why not go to Mozambique?
2 It would be a long journey
3 She would not like to fly
4 He would stay in a **pousada**
5 It is less expensive to go camping

8 Read this small passage, answer the questions, then translate it into English:

No sábado de manhã gosto de visitar os meus pais. Depois, vou ao supermercado. No domingo de manhã fico deitado na cama até o meio-dia. No domingo à tarde vejo televisão.

1 Is this person very energetic on a Sunday morning?
2 When does s/he do the shopping?
3 True or false? S/he goes to a football match on Saturday morning.
4 What does s/he do on Sunday afternoon?

10 Moro num apartamento

I live in a flat

In this lesson you will learn about

- talking about where you live
- dealing with problems in the home
- using the subjunctive mood in the past
- saying what you would do if you won a prize in the national lottery

 Dialogue 1 (Audio 2: 17)

Fala da sua casa

The following individuals were asked about where they live

ANA: Você mora numa casa ou num apartamento?
JORGE: Moro num apartamento. O edifício tem video porteiro
        . . .
ANA: Quantos quartos tem o seu apartamento?
JORGE: Tem quatro: a sala de visitas, um quarto de dormir,
        a cozinha e a casa de banho.
ANA: Tem garagem?
JORGE: Claro! Não gosto de estacionar o meu carro na rua!
ANA: Tem jardim?
JORGE: Não, mas tenho uma varanda com vista panorâmica.
ANA: E quantos apartamentos há no seu edifício?
JORGE: Não sei . . . talvez cinquenta, sessenta . . .

Vocabulary

moro (morar)	I live
a sala/a sala de visitas/	
a sala de estar	living room
um quarto	a room
um quarto de dormir	bedroom
a cozinha	kitchen
a garagem	garage
não sei	I don't know
estacionar na rua	to park in the street
a varanda	balcony
o jardim	garden
quantos?	how many?
no seu edifício	in your building
video porteiro	door entry system
vista panorâmica	panoramic view

 Dialogue 2 (Audio 2: 18)
Moro numa casa

ANA: Você mora numa casa ou num apartamento?

GRAÇA: Moro numa casa.

ANA: Quantos quartos tem a sua casa?

GRAÇA: No rés-do-chão há a sala de visitas, a cozinha, a sala de jantar e o vestíbulo. No primeiro andar há três quartos e uma casa de banho.

ANA: Há uma garagem?

GRAÇA: Há, ao lado da casa, e há um jardim também.

ANA: É uma casa, digamos, luxuosa, não é?

GRAÇA: É, sim. Há um alarme de roubo, uma antena parabólica, circuito interno de televisão em todos os quartos, vidros duplos . . .

Vocabulary

o rés-do-chão	the ground floor
o primeiro andar	the first floor
a sala de jantar	dining room
luxuosa/o	luxurious
o vestíbulo	the hall

o alarme de roubo	burglar alarm
a antena parabólica	satellite dish
o circuito interno de televisão	TV aerial
os vidros duplos	double glazing

Expressing 'to live'

In general: **viver**

> **Vivo em Moçambique**
> I live in Mozambique

In a specific place: **morar**

> **Moro numa casa em Londres**
> I live in a house in London

Exercise 1

Three people describe where they live. Using the details that they provide, can you decide which home belongs to which individual?

1

2

3

1 RUI:	Moro num pequeno apartamento que tem três quartos e uma varanda que dá para o mar. Não tenho garagem; estaciono o meu carro na rua.
2 ISABEL:	Acabei de mudar de casa e agora moro num estúdio bem perto da Ponte Vinte e Cinco de Abril em Lisboa.
3 PAULO:	Moro numa casa. Tem cinco quartos e um jardim com uma piscina. Comecei a construir uma garagem.

Vocabulary

dar para o mar	to overlook the sea
um estúdio	a studio flat
bem perto de	really near
a Ponte 25 de Abril	25th April Bridge
uma piscina	swimming pool
Acabei de mudar de casa	I have just moved house
acabar de	to have just
Comecei a construir	I have begun building
começar a	to begin to
construir	to build

More uses of bem

Vamos bem para Paris?
Are we on the right road for Paris?
(*lit.*: Are we going well for Paris?)

os bens (plural of **bem**) goods/belongings

Exercise 2

Read this passage about homes in Portugal then answer the questions which follow in Portuguese:

A maioria dos portugueses que vive nas cidades vive em apartamentos, em andares, aos quais chamam 'a sua casa', o seu lar. Uma 'casa' típica consiste em dois quartos de cama, sala de visitas, sala de jantar, cozinha e casa de banho.

1 True or false? The majority of Portuguese city dwellers live in houses.
2 How many rooms would a typical home have and what are these?

Vocabulary

andares	floors; flats	**aos quais chamam**	which they call
o seu lar	their home	(**o lar** = hearth/home)	
a maioria vive	the majority live	(**viver** to live)	
em andares	on floors	**quartos de cama**	bedrooms
cozinha	kitchen	**sala de visitas**	living room
em apartamentos	in flats/apartments		

Exercise 3

The following headings can be seen in any Portuguese newspaper property section. Can you match the English translations to their Portuguese counterparts?

compras	vendas	andares	lojas
armazéns	garagens	moradias	escritórios
prédios	quintas	terrenos	

shops	farms	warehouses	garages
buildings	houses	for sale	flats	wanted
offices	plots of land		

Exercise 4

Now look at the following advertisements and answer the questions.

Vocabulary

vende-se	for sale	marisqueira	seafood
aluga-se	to let	trespassa-se	to sublet
aldeia típica	typical village	árvores de fruta	fruit trees
rústico/a	rustic	a praia	the beach
vista para a serra	mountain view	assoalhadas (ass.)	rooms
remodelado	renovated	(also quartos)	
óptimo estado	excellent condition	lareira (f)	fireplace
estado impecável	impeccable condition	o estúdio	studio
boa oportunidade	good opportunity		

1 Which advert is for a commercial property and what type of business is involved?
2 What sort of dwelling is described in Colares?
3 Which advert would suit someone who likes a quiet life and what are the other advantages it offers?
4 Which advert would be best for someone who has to travel into the centre every day?
5 Which advert would be ideal for one person living alone?

The imperfect subjunctive

The imperfect subjunctive also expresses an uncertain, doubtful future but one which is even more remote than the present subjunctive. It translates the English, 'might' and often follows 'when', 'if', 'as soon as' and 'I wish':

Disse que escrevia (imperfect indic.)
quando tivesse tempo (imperfect subjunc.)

He said he would write (statement)
when he had time (doubtful – he might not have time)

Forming the imperfect subjunctive

Take the 3rd person plural of the preterite tense of any verb, remove the ending-**ram** and add:

-sse   -sses   -sse   -ssemos   -ssem

Example: perder *'to lose'*

perderam	they lost (preterite) → **perde-** + above endings
eu	perde*sse*
tu	perde*sses*
ele/a	perde*sse*
você	perde*sse*
nós	perdê*ssemos*
eles/as	perde*ssem*
vocês	perde*ssem*

In the **nós** form, an accent is added on the vowel before the ending:

in -**ar** verbs   –   **falássemos**
in -**er** verbs   –   **escrevêssemos**
in -**ir** verbs   –   **partíssemos**

Dialogue 3 (Audio 2: 19)
A lotaria nacional

Listen to these people who talk about what they would do if they won a big prize in the **lotaria nacional** (the national lottery). Can you guess what their dreams are?

ANTÓNIO:	Se eu ganhasse a lotaria comprava um carro de corrida ...
MARIA:	Se eu pudesse ganhar a lotaria fazia um cruzeiro, comprava muita roupa e um palacete.
MANUELA:	Se eu ganhasse a lotaria usava o dinheiro para comprar mobílias para a minha casa.
JOSÉ:	Se eu ficasse rico, deixava o meu emprego e viajava pelo mundo inteiro ...

Vocabulary

Se eu ganhasse	If I won (were to win)
Se eu pudesse ganhar	If I could win
Se eu ficasse rico	If I became rich
um palacete	a mansion
as mobílias	furnishings
um carro de corrida	a racing car
fazia um cruzeiro	I would go on a cruise
muita roupa	lots of clothes
usava o dinheiro	I would use the money
(**usar** to use)	
deixava o meu emprego	I would leave my job
(**deixar** to leave/to quit)	
viajava pelo mundo inteiro	I would travel around the world
(**viajar** to travel)	

Expressing 'to leave'

Partir   to leave (e.g. for Italy)

Deixar   to leave (e.g. a job), to give up or abandon something

Deixar de = to stop doing – **deixei de fumar**
                                    I stopped smoking
Deixar cair = to drop (*lit.* to let fall)

The pluperfect subjunctive

Use **ter** + past participle. **Ter** will be in the imperfect subjunctive:

se tivesse visitado	if I had visited
se tivesses arrumado	if you had tidied up

se tivesse decidido	if you/he/she had decided
se tivéssemos[1] mudado	if we had moved
se tivessem ido	if they had gone

1 The accent in the **nós** part of the verb shows that the stress is kept on the second syllable throughout.

Exercise 5

Read the description below of José's new flat. He describes a few details of the furnishings to a friend. He starts off in the centre of the living room. (To revise prepositions, see Lesson 4)

No centro da sala há uma mesa baixa para servir cafés, bebidas, etc. Atrás da mesa tenho um sofá. Ao lado esquerdo há uma mesinha pequena com um candeeiro eléctrico em cima. Na parede, em cima e atrás do sofá há um quadro com uma paisagem. Há uma televisão a cores ao lado direito do sofá e uma lareira ao lado esquerdo da mesinha. Há também duas poltronas.

Using the descriptions of the positions of José's furniture can you draw a plan of his living room and say what the following are in Portuguese?

colour TV, fireplace, armchairs, wall, sofa/couch, coffee table, table lamp, painting, occasional table

(Vocabulary for the rest of the items in the flat is at the end of this lesson.)

Conversation fillers

pois	well (then) so/as/since
sei lá ...	well .../who knows? ...
portanto	well/so/therefore
pois bem	well then
pois é	that's right
pois não	(at end of sentence) isn't it/don't they?
pois sim!	yes, of course!
pois não! (Br)	of course!
paciência!	oh well! (resignation)
penso que sim	I think so
penso que não	I don't think so

Dialogue 4 (Audio 2: 20)
Problemas na casa

DONA ANA: Ó Pedro, vem cá! A casa de banho está inundada. Que hei-de fazer?
PEDRO: Deve ser um cano roto. É melhor chamar o canalizador.

Vocabulary

Ó ...!	Hey ...!
vem cá!	come here!
está inundada	is flooded
que hei-de fazer?	What should I do?
deve ser um cano roto	it must be a burst pipe
é melhor chamar o canalizador	best to call the plumber

DONA ANA: Ora, esta! Agora falta-nos a luz!
PEDRO: Deve ser apenas um fusível. Vou verificar e, se necessário, ponho um fusível novo. Vou também verificar as ligações eléctricas do frigorífico e da máquina de lavar roupa. As fichas e as tomadas estão em ordem ...

Vocabulary

ora, esta!	for heaven's sake!
agora falta-nos a luz!	now the lights have gone!
deve ser apenas um fusível	it must just be a fuse
Vou verificar	I'll check
se necessário	if necessary
ponho um fusível novo	I'll put in a new fuse
as ligações eléctricas	the electrical connections
as fichas e as tomadas estão em ordem	the plugs and sockets are fine (**em ordem** in order)

DONA ANA: Mudei as duas lâmpadas que estavam fundidas na sala e fui ligar a televisão para ver a telenovela brasileira mas agora a televisão não trabalha!
PEDRO: Ah! A televisão não está avariada. O aparelho não estava ligado à corrente! Tudo o que tive de fazer foi meter a ficha dentro da tomada na parede!

Vocabulary

mudei as duas lâmpadas que estavam fundidas	I changed the two fused lightbulbs
fui ligar	I went to switch on
a telenovela brasileira	the Brazilian soap
a televisão não trabalha	the TV isn't working
(or não funciona	it's not working)
a televisão não está avariada	the TV isn't broken
o aparelho não estava ligado à corrente	the TV (i.e. apparatus – **aparelho**) wasn't plugged in
tudo que tive de fazer foi	all I had to do was
meter a ficha dentro da tomada na parede	to put the plug into the socket on the wall

There are three ways of saying that something is not working:

... não trabalha/não funciona ...
isn't working/is out of order

... está avariado/a ...
is out of order/is broken (down)

The term **o aparelho** can be used to mean 'machine/apparatus' of any kind.

Exercise 6

Can you find the Portuguese words for:

plug, flooded, plumber, a fuse, a burst pipe, fridge, washing machine, pump, lightbulbs, switch on the TV, is not plugged in, connections, socket

Exercise 7

And how would you say the following?

The fridge has broken down. I have (**tenho**) a burst pipe. I need (**preciso de**) a plumber. The TV is not plugged in. I need three lightbulbs. Do you have (**tem**) a fuse?

Exercise 8

Below is a list of electrical household items in Portuguese with a definition in English. Can you decide what these items are in English?

1 **o fogão**
(you need this to cook dinner)
2 **a máquina de lavar roupa**
(use for cleaning clothes)
3 **o frigorífico**
(handy for keeping things cool)
4 **a máquina de lavar louça**
(great for after large dinner parties)
5 **a chaleira**
(a bonus if you want a hot cup of tea)
6 **a máquina de secar roupa**
(no more damp clothes)
7 **a torradeira**
(you make toast in this)
8 **o ferro de passar a roupa**
(no more creases)
9 **a batedeira**
(cake-making made easy)
10 **o aspirador**
(your carpet's best friend)
11 **o microondas**
(for instant hot food)

Exercise 9

Look at the following index (**o índice**) from a typical Portuguese newspaper (**o jornal**) and try to answer the questions which follow.

1 What sort of 'useful information' is available?
2 You are a sports fan – which page do you turn to first?
3 You have a beach outing planned (but will it be warm?) and hope to take in a film in the evening. Which two sections would you consult?
4 You want to find out how your shares **(acções)** are getting on in the stock market **(a Bolsa)**. Which section do you turn to?

(Full vocabulary is given at the end of the lesson.)

128 PÁGINAS

ÍNDICE

Exercise 10

Now here are some examples of Portuguese headlines – **as manchetes.** Can you match each of them to their English equivalent?

1 **Pânico no supermercado – homem cai dentro do congelador**[2]
2 **Patinho bêbado depois de consumir mais dum copo de uísque**
3 **Campo de alfaces roubado – a polícia procura família de coelhos**

(a) Field of lettuces stolen – police seek family of rabbits
(b) Panic in supermarket – man falls into freezer
(c) Duck drunk after consuming more than a glass of whisky

2 **o freezer** (Br) freezer

How much can you remember?

1 Describe your flat: it has two bedrooms, a small kitchen, a living room and a bathroom. You don't have a garden but you do have a garage, a door-entry system, double glazing and satellite TV.

2 Do you remember how to say?

1 Are we on the right road for London?
2 The flat has a sea view
3 We have just moved
4 for sale
5 wanted

3 Write out the imperfect subjunctive of the verb **terminar** (to finish).

4 Can you translate these?

1 **Se eu partisse amanhã, chegava a casa mais cedo**
2 **Se ele comprasse o carro, custava muito dinheiro**
3 **Se nós viajássemos todo o dia, ficávamos muito cansados**

5 Can you name four types of room you would find in a house or flat?

6 Can you remember three expressions you could use to help fill in a conversation?

Vocabulary

Os móveis	Furniture
o quarto de dormir	bedroom
o sofá	sofa/couch
a mesinha	small table
a mesa	table
o candeeiro eléctrico	table lamp
a parede	the wall
o quadro (com uma paisagem)	(landscape) painting
as poltronas	armchairs
a televisão a cores	colour TV
as cadeiras	chairs
o aparador	sideboard
o cesto (cheio de fruta)	basket (full of fruit)
os armários (modernos)	(modern) cupboards
o fogão a gás	gas cooker
o fogão eléctrico	electric cooker
o frigorífico	fridge
a pia	sink
a mesinha de cabeceira	bedside table
a cómoda	dressing table
o guarda-roupa	wardrobe
o relógio-rádio	clock radio
a banheira	bath
o lavatório	handbasin
o espelho	mirror
a retrete	toilet
o tapete	carpet
o bidé	bidet

O índice do jornal		Newspaper index	
impressões	impressions	cartaz	showing/what's on
política	politics	cinemas	cinemas
opinião	opinion	rádio	radio
internacional	international	televisão	TV

sociedade	society	**farmácias**	chemists
desporto	sports	**transportes**	transport
artes	the arts	**classificados**	classified ads
vidas	lives	**tempo**	weather
suplementos	supplements	**país**	country
negócios	business	**programas**	programmes

11 Encontramo-nos mais tarde?

Shall we meet later?

In this lesson you will learn about:

- making friends
- expressing past experiences and future plans
- the future subjunctive
- similarities between English and Portuguese and hints for reading

---

 Situation 1 (Audio 2: 21)
Um congresso

Four people plan to meet up at a conference **(um congresso)** the following summer. In order to make the initial introductions easier, they decide to circulate a small dossier about themselves on tape before the event.

1

Nome:	**Eric Boucher**
Idade:	**35**
Profissão:	**correspondente estrangeiro**
Estatura:	**alto**
Bebida preferida:	**conhaque**
Passatempo predilecto:	**alpinismo**
Carro:	**Mercedes**

Vocabulary

o correspondente estrangeiro	foreign correspondent
a estatura	build
a bebida preferida	favourite drink
passatempo predilecto	favourite hobby
(*or* favorito – favourite)	

2

Nome:	Sarah Blackthorpe
Idade:	33
Profissão:	bibliotecária
Estatura:	baixa
Bebida preferida:	laranjada
Passatempo predilecto:	crochê
Carro:	Volkswagen

Vocabulary

a laranjada	orangeade	o crochê	crochet
a bibliotecária	librarian		

3

Nome:	Maria Napoli
Idade:	28
Profissão:	estilista
Estatura:	magra
Bebida preferida:	Martini
Passatempo predilecto:	vôo livre
Carro:	Motocicleta (Harley Davidson)

Vocabulary

a estilista	fashion designer	o vôo livre	hang gliding
a motocicleta	motorbike		

4

Nome:	Hugo Van Vliet
Idade:	40
Profissão:	advogado
Estatura:	média
Bebida preferida:	vinho tinto
Passatempo predilecto:	filatelia
Carro:	não conduzo: bicicleta

Vocabulary

o advogado	lawyer	**o vinho tinto**	red wine
a filatelia	stamp collecting	**não conduzo**	I don't drive
a bicicleta	bicycle		

Exercise 1

Using the information given above can you answer the following questions:

1 Will Maria find much in common with Hugo? Give two reasons.
2 Will Hugo find Eric's hobby appealing?
3 Which two individuals are more likely to end up at the bar?
4 What is Eric likely to make of Hugo's mode of transport?

Exercise 2

Create your own dossier using the same headings.

The future subjunctive

The future subjunctive is used to translate the future but – unlike the future indicative tense, which makes statements about the future which have an air of probability or certainty – the future subjunctive is used to translate a future which is clouded in uncertainty and doubt and is often heralded by 'when', 'if' or 'as soon as'.

Estará cansada	*quando chegar*
(future indic.)	(future subjunc.)

She will be tired   *when she arrives*
(statement)   (it's doubtful when she will arrive)

Forming the future subjunctive

Take the 3rd person plural of any verb in the preterite tense, remove the ending **-ram** and add: **-r -res -r -rmos -rem**

Example

partir	to leave
partiram	they left (preterite) → **parti** + above endings

eu	parti*r*
tu	parti*res*
ele/a	parti*r*
você	parti*r*
nós	parti*rmos*
eles/as	parti*rem*
vocês	parti*rem*

The future perfect subjunctive

This tense, formed by the future subjunctive of the verb **ter** (**tiver, tiveres, tiver, tivermos, tiverem**) + past participle, is used in a similar way to the future subjunctive tense but is not as widely used.

Se não tiveres mandado o pacote amanhã, ficarei muito zangado.
If you haven't sent the parcel by tomorrow, I will be very angry

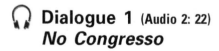 **Dialogue 1** (Audio 2: 22)
No Congresso

The four individuals finally meet

HUGO: Amanhã vou fazer turismo. Pretendo visitar todos
            os museus na cidade. Quer ir comigo?
ERIC: Infelizmente, não posso. Amanhã tenho de
            escrever um artigo para o meu jornal ...

MARIA:	Não lhe apetece assistir a um curso de saltar em pára-quedas amanhã?
SARAH:	Ah, obrigada mas não me interesso por desportos. Porque não nos encontramos mais tarde para tomar um café?
MARIA:	Combinado!

Vocabulary

fazer turismo	to go sightseeing
pretender	to plan to
quer ir comigo?	do you want to come with me?
um artigo	an article
não lhe apetece?	don't you fancy ...?
assistir a	to attend
um curso de saltar em pára-quedas*	a course in parachuting
não me interesso por	I'm not interested in
porque não nos encontramos mais tarde?	why don't we meet later?
combinado!	agreed!

*or **um curso de pára-quedismo**

Exercise 3

Can you answer the following questions in Portuguese?

1 **O que quer fazer o Hugo? (Quer fazer ...)**
2 **O que tem de fazer o Eric no dia seguinte?**
3 **A Maria convida a Sarah a assistir a um curso. Que curso?**
4 **A Sarah aceita ou recusa?**

Vocabulary

o dia seguinte	the following day	**convidar**	to invite
um convite	an invitation	**aceitar**	to accept
recusar	to refuse		

Invitations

Quer ir (ao cinema)?
Do you want to go ...?

Não lhe apetece (ir)?
Don't you fancy (going)?

Quer sair comigo?
Do you want to go out with me?

Encontramo-nos mais tarde?
Do you want to meet later?/Let's meet later

Gostava de o/a convidar ... /
Gostava de convidar você
I'd like to invite you ...

Vens ou não vens?
Are you (familiar) coming or not?

Vou **já!**
I'm coming! (Use **ir** (to go), not **vir** (to come) –
lit: 'I'm going there right away')

Accepting and refusing

Aceitar (accepting)

Gostaria muito de (ir/visitar)
I'd really like to (go/visit)

Parece-me uma boa ideia
It seems like a good idea

Porque não?
Why not?

Gostava muito
I'd like that a lot

(es)tá bom/bem
OK

O que está a passar?
What's on? (at the cinema etc.)

Recusar (refusing)

Infelizmente, não posso
Unfortunately, I can't

Acho que não é possível
I don't think it's possible

Obrigado/a, mas não me apetece ...
Thanks, but I don't fancy ...

Obrigado/a, mas não me interesso por ...
Thanks, but I'm not a fan of ...

Não posso hoje à noite, já fiz outros planos
I can't tonight, I've already made other plans

Exercise 4

Now it's your turn to speak. Using the information above, make up appropriate responses to the sentences below:

A: **Gostava de a convidar para o jantar hoje à noite**
B:
A: **Não faz mal! Em vez de hoje à noite, quer ir ao cinema no fim de semana?**
B:
A: **Um bom filme francês.**
B:

Saying how you have been feeling

The verb **andar** ('to walk/to progress') is used idiomatically to express how someone has been feeling lately:

Ando nervoso/a
I've been on edge lately

Andam despreocupados/as
They've been very happy-go-lucky recently

Small talk

If you have just met someone and don't know anything about them, you will want to find out basic things such as: 'Where are you from?', 'What's your name?', 'What do you do?', 'Are you on holiday?' and chat about the weather.

Exercise 5

We have already covered these areas but, just to refresh your memory, here are a few phrases you will need. Unfortunately the English translations have got mixed up, so first you will have to decide which is which:

Tudo bem?	Where are you from?
Como está?	What's your name?
Como se chama?	What do you do?
Donde é?	The weather is very good/bad
O que faz?	Are you on holiday?
Está em férias?	How's things?
O tempo está muito bom/mau	My name is
Chamo-me	How are you?

Exercise 6

Now look at the following captions showing different situations where people are meeting for the first time. Using the vocabulary above plus earlier vocabulary, can you create the dialogues suggested by the drawings?

1   2

1. Q: ....   A: ....

2. Q: ....   A: ....

3

4

3. Q: .... A: ....

4. Q: .... A: ....

5

6

RESTAURANTE?

5. Q: .... A: ....

6. Q: .... A: ....

What sort of person are you?

Sou ...	I am ...
vivo/a (or: alegre)	lively
dinâmico/a	dynamic
ambicioso/a	ambitious
falador/a	talkative
trabalhador/a	hardworking
eficiente	efficient
honesto/a	honest
desonesto/a	dishonest
calmo/a	quiet
preguiçoso/a	lazy

The personal infinitive

We are now familiar with infinitives such as **ser**, **ter** and **comer**. Unique to the Portuguese language is another infinitive called the personal or inflected infinitive which is a 'personalized' infinitive with personal or individual endings. It is simple to form. Take any infinitive and add the endings:

-es -mos -em

In fact, there are only three endings to learn.

Example: The personal infinitive of beber:

beber	I drink (my drinking)
beberes	you drink (your drinking)
beber	he/she drinks, you drink (his/her/your drinking)
bebermos	we drink (our drinking)
beberem	they, you (pl) drink (their/your drinking)

The personal infinitive generally follows a preposition.

Uses of the personal infinitive

1 It helps to avoid confusion about who is being referred to. Here the ordinary infinitive is used:

depois de partir = after (I, he, she, etc.?) left. *Who* exactly left? You, him, them? Use of the personal infinitive helps to specify who it was who left:

depois de partir*em* = after *they* left
(*lit.*: after *their* leaving)

Verás as montanhas ao chegares
You will see the mountains when you arrive
(*lit.*: upon *your* arriving)

2 The personal infinitive can avoid the use of the subjunctive if a preposition replaces the conjunction.

Ele vai telefonar antes que parta (subjunctive)
He is going to telephone before he leaves

Ele vai telefonar antes de partir (personal infinitive)

In impersonal expressions and verbs such as **lamentar** or **ter pena** (to be sorry) the conjunction **que** does not need to be replaced by a preposition:

É preciso que estejam lá (subjunctive)
They must be there

É preciso estarem lá (personal infinitive)
They must be there

Lamento que ela tenha tantos problemas (subjunctive)
I'm sorry that she has so many problems

Lamento ela ter tantos problemas (personal infinitive)
I'm sorry that she has so many problems

Temos pena que ele não venha (subjunctive)
We are sorry that he cannot come

Temos pena ele não vir (personal infinitive)
We are sorry that he cannot come

🎧 Dialogue 2 (Audio 2: 23)
As férias

At the conference, talk turns to how the four spent their holidays last year and what their plans are for this year

HUGO: Para as minhas férias no ano passado eu fui ao Canadá. Vi as Cataratas do Niagara. Eram lindas! Passei lá o dia inteiro ...

SARAH: Eu também vi as Cataratas há três anos!

ERIC: No ano passado eu queria ir aos Estados Unidos. Mas, infelizmente, tive de cancelar por razões de trabalho.

MARIA: Não pode ir lá este verão? Este ano eu gostaria de visitar a França ... No ano passado passei as minhas férias na África do Sul.

Vocabulary

o ano passado	last year	**vi**	I saw
fui	I went	**visitei**	I visited
passei	I spent	**eram lindas**	they were lovely
há três anos	three years ago	**não pode?**	can't you?
queria ir	I wanted to go	**tive de cancelar**	I had to cancel
gostaria de visitar	I'd like to visit	**África do Sul**	South Africa
passei lá o dia inteiro		I spent the whole day there	
por razões de trabalho		for work reasons	

Exercise 7

Translate the following passage:

No ano passado passei férias maravilhosas na praia. O tempo estava muito bom e eu fiquei¹ numa pensão muito perto da praia. Gostei imenso do mar e de todas as pessoas que encontrei. Espero regressar lá um dia.

---

1 **fiquei** and not **ficei**. To retain the 'hard c' sound (like the English 'k'), the **c** changes to **qu**. (This is an example of an orthography-changing verb, i.e. one which alters its spelling to maintain its original sound.) The rest of the verb in the preterite is as normal:

fiquei ficaste ficou ficámos ficaram

Vocabulary

na praia	on the beach
férias maravilhosas	great holiday
o tempo estava muito bom	the weather was really good
fiquei	I stayed
o mar	the sea
muito perto de	really near
gostei imenso de ...	I really liked ...
todas as pessoas que encontrei	all the people I met
espero regressar lá um dia	I hope to go back one day

Exercise 8

With the help of the additional vocabulary given below, can you create a short paragraph in Portuguese similar to that in Exercise 7 for each of the following holiday-makers:

1 Last year I had a great holiday in the mountains. The weather was very bad and I stayed in a youth hostel.
2 Last year I had a great holiday in the city of Paris. The weather was good and I stayed in a hotel.
3 Last year I had a great holiday in the lakes. The weather was great and I stayed in a **pousada** (deluxe inn).

Vocabulary

nas montanhas	in the mountains
nos lagos	at the lakes
na cidade de Paris	in the city of Paris
péssimo	awful
óptimo	great
bom	good
o hotel	hotel
a pousada	*pousada* (deluxe inn)
a pousada da juventude/	
o albergue da juventude	youth hostel

Hints for reading in a foreign language

1 First read through, trying to get the general gist.
2 Use any extra information which might be present, for example, illustrations and subheadings.
3 Try not to use the dictionary at first but do try to guess the general meaning by focusing first on words which seem similar in English. For instance, you might have already noticed similarites between words which end in '-tion' in English and -ção in Portuguese:

condição	condition
ambição	ambition

or words ending in '-able' in English and **-ável** in Portuguese:

confortável	comfortable
deplorável	deplorable

4 If a particular word in Portuguese looks familiar but you can't remember the English equivalent, try saying it out loud. For instance **condição**, when pronounced, sounds like: '*condeesow*'. This should then lead you to the English word 'condition'.

Exercise 9

Below is a list of words in English and a list in Portuguese. Using the above information can you provide in column 1 the Portuguese equivalent and in column 2, the English equivalent. The first two have been done for you.

1		**2**	
horrible	(**horrível**)	**nação**	(nation)
deplorable		**lamentável**	
variable		**incomparável**	
solution		**perfeição**	
petition		**confortável**	

A word of caution . . .

Unfortunately, this 'system' won't work for every word! For example, the English word 'marketable' translates as **comercializável**.

Prefixes

The English 'un-' (*un*happy, *un*fortunately, etc.) translates as the following:

in- as in:	**inoportuno**	untimely
im- as in:	**impensável**	unthinkable
ir- as in:	**irrepetível**	unrepeatable
des- as in:	**desfavorável**	unfavourable

English 'in-' translates as:

in- as in:	**incidente**	incident
	incapacidade	incapacity

Exercise 10

Now try to translate the following without the aid of your dictionary:

incessante, impulsivo, impossível, impulso, impreciso, imperceptível, imparcial, impetuoso

Exercise 11

Read this short passage then answer the questions which follow:

> **Para ir à fábrica vou de comboio até ao Porto e depois apanho um autocarro para a cidade. Esta manhã apanhei o carro eléctrico. Este ano faço tenções de ir ao Algarve. Mas, possivelmente, só irei lá no fim do verão.**

1 How does the writer get to the factory?
2 What did he do this morning?
3 What are his holiday plans and when is he going?

Vocabulary

até ao Porto	to Porto
apanho	I catch
apanhei	I caught
no fim do verão	at the end of summer
só irei lá	I will only go
faço tenções de ir	I intend to go

How much can you remember?

1 Can you give the Portuguese for:

my favourite drink, my favourite hobby, lawyer, librarian, profession

2 Write out the future subjunctive of **falar** 'to speak'.

3 Give three ways of refusing an invitation and three ways of accepting.

4 In Portuguese, how would you introduce yourself, ask someone their name and where they are from?

5 Name four qualities you consider yourself to have.

6 What do these translate as?

um convite, eu não conduzo, o congresso, trabalhador, calmo, eficiente, assistir a

7 Translate into Portuguese:

Last year I visited Belgium. The weather was great. I stayed in a hotel near the beach. It was very comfortable. I'd like to go to Cuba this year. Two years ago I went to the USA.

12 Exmo. Senhor...

Dear Sir ...

In this lesson you will learn about:

• setting up a business meeting by phone
• writing formal and informal letters
• office equipment
• business terms

 Dialogue 1 (Audio 2: 24)
Marcar uma reunião

Sr Dias calls Sr Silva on his mobile phone (**o seu telemóvel**)

SR DIAS:	Está?
SECRETÁRIA:	Estou. António Silva e Companhia Limitada. Faz favor. Que deseja?
SR DIAS:	Bom dia. Daqui fala Alberto Dias. Posso falar com o Sr Silva, se faz favor?
SECRETÁRIA:	Desculpe, mas o Sr Silva ainda não chegou.
SR DIAS:	Oh, que maçada! Tenho um assunto urgente a tratar com ele e preciso de marcar uma reunião juntamente com o meu sócio.
SECRETÁRIA:	Está bem. Eu posso marcar a vossa reunião. Dá jeito amanhã às três horas?
SR DIAS:	Muito bem. Então, fica combinado. Até amanhã às três.

Vocabulary

companhia limitada	limited company
(ele) ainda não chegou	has not arrived yet
que maçada!	what a nuisance!
marcar uma reunião	to arrange/fix up an appointment
preciso de	I need/have to
o sócio	partner
juntamente com	together with
Eu posso marcar a vossa reunião	I can arrange your meeting
dá jeito?	does it suit/is it convenient?
então, fica combinado	so, that's agreed

Tenho um assunto urgente a tratar com ele
I have an urgent matter to discuss with him

Talking on the phone

Revise the section 'Making a call from a phone box' in Lesson 8. Remember, when speaking on the phone, to use the following:

(you are the caller)	*(you are the recipient of the call)*
Está? (Br **Alô**)	**Estou** (Br **Alô**)
(Hello?/Are you there?)	(Hello/I'm here)

Once you get through:

Daqui fala ...	
or simply **fala ...** (name)	This is ...
Posso falar com ... (name)?	Can I speak to ...?
Pode falar mais devagar?	Can you speak more slowly?
Fala inglês?	Do you speak English?
Desculpe, eu não falo português muito bem	Sorry, I don't speak Portuguese very well
Telefono mais tarde	I'll phone later
Gostaria de cancelar a minha reunião com ...	I'd like to cancel my meeting with ...

Exercise 1

Try to translate this short telephone conversation into Portuguese:

JANE: Hello? Can I speak to the manager?
COMPANY: I'm afraid he hasn't come in yet. Is it urgent?

JANE: I'm sorry, can you speak more slowly please, I don't speak Portuguese very well.

COMPANY: Ah! Hold on. The manager has just arrived.

Vocabulary

Queria/posso falar com ...?   Could/can I speak to?
o gerente   the manager
É urgente?   Is it urgent?
não desligue   hold on

Exercise 2

Below is a transcript of a telephone conversation. Owing to the poor line, however, parts of the conversation are indistinct. Using the vocabulary below, can you complete the missing spaces to find out what is being said?

SR COELHO: ...?
SECRETÁRIA: Estou.
SR COELHO: Daqui fala o Sr Coelho. Posso falar ... o Sr Costa? É muito ...
SECRETÁRIA: ..., mas o Sr Costa ... no Porto em negócios.
SR COELHO: Porto! Que ...! Eu estou a falar do Porto!
SECRETÁRIA: Como se ... o nome da sua ...?
SR COELHO: Coelho e Irmão.
SECRETÁRIA: Não percebo. Está marcada na agenda uma ... para hoje no Porto ... o Senhor Costa e Coelho e Irmão. (*a moment later* ...)
SR COELHO: Ah! Só um ... O Sr Costa já chegou!

entre	chama	desculpe	urgente	está?
com	maçada	minuto	companhia	reunião	está

Exercise 3

Below are some pieces of equipment you can find in an office. From the list below try to match the correct Portuguese word with the item it represents.

a disquete   o computador   o fax   o teclado

a máquina de escrever   o telefone   a fotocopiadora

Vocabulary

o computador	computer
a informática	computing
o software	software
o hardware	hardware
o écran (Br a tela)	screen (computer)
a unidade de disquete	disk drive
o banco de dados	database
a fragmentadora	shredder
o calculador	calculator
o classificador	file
o líquido corrector	correction fluid
o papel	paper
os envelopes	envelopes
a caneta/o lápis	pen/pencil
o cartão de negócios	business card
homem/mulher de negócios	business man/woman
a viagem de negócios	business trip

Correspondence

Fax and memo

FAX

Para: ....

Fax Número: ....

De: .... Fax Nº: .....

Data: ...... Ref: ....

No. de páginas: ....

MEMORANDO

Para: ....

De: ....

Data: ....

Ref: ....

Vocabulary

para	to
para a atenção de	for the attention of
de	from
data	date
ref (referência)	reference
no. de páginas	number of pages
Posso enviar esta carta por fax/por email?	Can I fax/email this letter?

Letters

1 Formal business letters

English salutation	Portuguese salutation	Endings
Dear Sir Dear Sirs Dear Madam Dear Mr (Lopes) Dear Mrs (Lopes)	**Exmo. Senhor** **Exmos. Senhores** **Exma. Senhora** **Exmo. Sr Lopes** **Exma. Sra Lopes**	**Subscrevo-me** **de V. Exa(s).,** **(Muito) Atenciosamente** Yours faithfully or Yours sincerely (from one person) or **Subscrevemo-nos** **de V. Exa(s).,** **(Muito) Atenciosamente** Yours faithfully or Yours sincerely (from more than one person)
Messrs	**Ilmos. Senhores**	**Subscrevemo-nos** **de V. Sras.,** **(Muito) Atenciosamente**

2 Informal business letters

English salutation	Portuguese salutation	Endings
Dear Sir Dear Sirs Dear Madam Dear Sirs (*lit.*: Dear friends and sirs)	Caro Senhor Caros Senhores Cara Senhora Caros Amigos e Senhores	Subscrevo-me de V. Exa(s)., (Muito) Atenciosamente Yours faithfully or Yours sincerely (from one person) or
Dear José Dear Ester	Caro José Cara Ester	Subscrevemo-nos de V. Exa(s)., (Muito) Atenciosamente Yours faithfully or Yours sincerely (from more than one person)

Notes

1 **Exmo./Exma./Exmos./Exmas.** = **Excelentíssimo/a/os/as** = Most excellent Sir/Madam, etc.
2 In Brazil the equivalents of **Exmo.** etc. are:

  Ilmo./Ilma./Ilmos./Ilmas. = **Ilustríssimo/a/os/as**
  = Most Illustrious Sir/Madam, etc.

3 **V. Exa(s).** = **Vossa(s) Excelência(s)** = Your Excellency(ies)
4 **V. Sra(s).** = **Vossa(s) Senhoria(s)** = Your Lordship(s)
5 **Ilmos.** = Messrs, is used in both Portugal and Brazil
6 **(Muito) Atentamente** can replace **(Muito) Atenciosamente**

Addresses

1 Formal:

In Portugal

Exmo. Sr. J. Simões
Rua do Brasil, 61-3º esq
3900 Condeixa
Portugal

In Brazil

Ilma. D. Sra. Isabel Nunes
Av. Estação Velha, 808
6540 Portalegre
Brasil

Notes

1 'To' = **A:**
   To Mr Fernandes = **Ao Sr. Fernandes** (*lit*.: 'to the')
2 Normally after the number of the street, lane, etc, you will see:
   1° 2° 3° = 1st 2nd 3rd floor, etc.
   r/c = rés-do-chão ground floor
   dto = direito right
   esq = esquerdo left
3 The street name comes first, followed by the number

2 Informal:

In both Portugal and Brazil

Sr. Jorge Gomes
Praça dos Pombais,
I r/c dto
7654 Caia
Portugal

Sra. D. I. Castro
Beco das Flores, 6
8874 Campo Grande
Angola

Um postal

A postcard ...

10 de maio

Queridos Maria e Jorge,
um simples postal para
dizer que esperamos
poder retribuir um dia
todas as vossas atenções
na Madeira. Cá no
Porto, está a chover...
Que chatice!

Muitas saudades e
abraços,
          Graça e Paulo

Exmo. Sr. Jorge e
Sra. D. Maria Lopes
Rua do Mar,
   47-1º dto
3400
Madeira

Vocabulary

Sr. e Sra. D.	Mr and Mrs
D. = **Dona**	Mrs or Miss
Querido/a/os/as	Dear … (informal)
esperamos poder	we hope to be able
retribuir um dia	to pay you back one day
todas as vossas atenções	all your kindness
cá no Porto	here in Oporto
está a chover	it's raining
que chatice!	what a bind/pain/nuisance!
muitas saudades e abraços	missing you and sending much love
beijos	kisses/hugs
cumprimentos	best wishes

Note: for a more courteous approach, although this is an informal postcard, use the **Exmo.** form.

Exercise 4

Now fill in the blanks in this postcard:

2 de abril   *via aérea*

… Ester,
… a tua carta …
Descobri o livro que
precisas numa …
livraria de segunda
mão. … sorte!
um beijo da …,

    Teresa.

Sra. D. Ester Soares
Av. Campo, 21-3º esq
7691 Vila Nova
Moçambique

---

pequena   ontem   que   recebi   amiga   querida

Exercise 5

Below is an example of a business letter in Portuguese which has been partially translated into English. Firstly, try to fill in the missing words in English then answer the questions which follow. A full translation of the letter is at the end of the lesson.

A C Brito & Ca Lda
Avenida da Liberdade
Lisboa

n/Ref: CJK/LN   Lisboa, 14 de Julho de 20 . . .
v/Ref: L0098

Exmos. Senhores
Costa & Ca. Lda.
Rua de Portugal
8349 Luanda
ANGOLA
a.c.brito@expr.pt

Caros Amigos e Senhores,

Acusamos a recepção da v/estimada carta de 4 do corrente na qual V. Exas. nos pedem para organizarmos uma reunião para discutir as nossas necessidades de novas encomendas dos vossos produtos.

Pedimos muito desculpa por esta demora em vos responder. Contudo, achamos que podemos marcar uma reunião para o dia 25 do mês e enviaremos por fax a V. Exas. a confirmação desta data.

Entretanto, aguardando o prazer da v/visita a esta cidade, subscrevemo-nos, com os nossos mais respeitosos cumprimentos.

De V. Exas.,
Muito Atenciosamente

Director Adjunto

Dear Sirs

We thank you for your ... of the 4th inst. in which you ask us to ... a meeting in order ... our need for new orders of your ...

We ... profusely for the ... in replying. However, we think that we can ... a meeting for the 25 of the ... and we will send ... of this ... by fax.

In the meantime, we look forward to the ... of your visit to this ... Kind regards,

Yours sincerely

Assistant Director

1 The letter is in response to one sent by Costa & Co. on 8 July – true or false?
2 Costa & Co. want to arrange a meeting to buy products from Brito & Co. – true or false?
3 What does Brito & Co. apologize for?
4 What will Brito & Co. do to confirm the meeting?

More on business letters ...

Some useful phrases:

Peço-lhe mil perdões ...
Please accept my apologies ...

Queira ter a bondade de ...
Please be so kind as to ...

Agradeço-lhe que se digne ...
I should be very grateful if you would ...

Sinto muito comunicar-lhe que ...
I regret to have to inform you that ...

Envie-mo quanto antes ...
Please send me as soon as possible ...

De acordo com ...
In accordance with ...

Exercise 6

Read the following dialogue and then answer the questions which follow:

COELHO: Sei que o senhor está interessado em utensílios de metal para uso caseiro. Temos vários modelos de panelas e talheres de aço inoxidável.

PEREIRA: Sim. Estou de facto interessado. Trouxe-me um catálogo?

COELHO: Trouxe. Esses talheres são de primeira qualidade. E aqui tem as nossas listas de preços também.

Vocabulary

estar interessado em	to be interested in
utensílios de metal	metal utensils
para uso caseiro	for domestic use
vários modelos	various models
panelas e talheres de aço inoxidável	pans and stainless steel cutlery
Trouxe-me um catálogo?	Did you bring me a catalogue?
de primeira qualidade	of the finest quality
listas de preços	price lists

1 What does Sr Coelho sell?
2 Is Sr Pereira interested in his products?
3 Sr Pereira asks if Sr Coelho has brought – what?
4 Sr Coelho points out a certain product in the catalogue. What does he say about it?
5 What else has he brought?

Business terms

a gestão	administration
o serviço pós-venda	after-sales service
o custo médio	average cost
o saldo	balance
baixista	bear (market)
altista	bull (market)
anular	to cancel

os fluxos de fundos/de caixa	cash flow
a concorrência	competition
o concorrente	competitor
a procura (de consumo)	(consumer) demand
o contrato	contract
redigir um contrato	to draw up a contract
o cálculo de custos	costing
o controlo de crédito	credit control
os clientes	customers
o acordo	deal
fechar o negócio	to strike a deal
a entrega	delivery
a data de entrega/o prazo de entrega	date of delivery
desenvolver	to develop
(zona de) desenvolvimento	development (area)
o desconto	discount
expedir	to dispatch
o distribuidor	distributor
os géneros	goods
a sede social/ a matriz	head office
o importador	importer
importar	to import
investir	to invest
o investimento	investment
o empréstimo	loan
emprestar	to lend
a gestão	management
o director geral (Br o diretor geral)	managing director
o marketing	marketing
a análise de mercados/a pesquisa de mercado	market research
a reunião	meeting
as actas (Br as atas)	minutes
negociar	to negotiate
negociável	negotiable
a despesa	outlay
a percentagem	percentage
produzir	to produce
o produtor	producer
o ganho/o lucro	profit
a rentabilidade	profitability
a proposta	proposal

a quota	quota
o recibo	receipt
reembolsar	reimburse
o relatório	report
a retalho (Br o varejo)	retail
o retalhista (Br o varejista)	retailer
as vendas	sales
o contrato de compra e venda	sales contract
o gerente de vendas	sales manager
a amostra	sample
a assinatura	signature
a pequena empresa	small firm
as estatísticas	statistics
o estoque	stock
a Bolsa	stock market
o fornecedor/o abastecedor	supplier
a oferta e a procura	supply and demand
os objectivos (Br os objetivos)	targets
a feira industrial	trade fair
a transacção (Br a transação)	transaction
o transporte	transport
o movimento	turnover
o subdesenvolvimento	underdevelopment
o IVA (Br o ICM)	VAT
a mão-de-obra / a força de trabalho	workforce

Exercise 7

Can you translate the following passages into English and then answer the questions which follow. Try not to look at the vocabulary until the very last minute!

Portugal não é um país pequeno

A língua portuguesa é falada não só em Portugal, mas também num grande país, o Brasil (na América do Sul), na Guiné-Bissau, Angola, Moçambique e nas ilhas de Cabo Verde e São Tomé e Príncipe (em África), Goa, Damão e Diu (na Índia), Macau (na China), e Timor.

O português é mais falado do que o francês. A língua portuguesa é a quinta língua mais falada no mundo. Cerca de 250 milhões de pessoas falam português.

1 Portuguese is only spoken in Portugal and Brazil. True or false?
2 Are there more French speakers than Portuguese speakers?
3 Approximately how many people speak Portuguese?
4 Portuguese is the seventh most widely spoken language in the world. True or false?

Vocabulary

a língua	language
é falada	is spoken
não só em Portugal	not only in Portugal
mas também	but also
ilhas	islands
num grande país	in a big country
América do Sul	South America
é mais falado do que o francês	is more spoken than French
a quinta língua mais falada no mundo	the fifth most spoken language in the world
cerca de	around

Translation of the letter from Brito & Co.

Dear Sirs

We thank you for your letter of the 4th inst. in which you ask us to organize a meeting in order to discuss our need for new orders of your products.

We apologize profusely for the delay in replying. However, we think that we can arrange a meeting for the 25th of the month and we will send confirmation of this date by fax.

In the meantime, we look forward to the pleasure of your visit to this city.

Kind regards,

Yours sincerely

Assistant Director

13 A Internet

The Internet

In this lesson you will learn about:

- accessing the Internet
- corresponding by e-mail
- the uses of a mobile phone
- revision – some exercises!

Exercise 1

No computador *(At the computer)*

At home, Joana is working on her new computer. Can you place the correct expressions from the box below into the gaps in the text to discover what she intends to do whilst online.

Em primeiro lugar, vou _____ para _____. Depois _____ onde tenho uma conta. (...) Depois disso, _____. Ah! Não há mensagens. Finalmente, vou _____ que tem informações de viagens.

procurar o site   vou ver o meu email

escrever a minha password   entrar na Net

vou ao site do banco

Vocabulary

em primeiro lugar	firstly
a minha password[1]	my password
(also: **a palavra-chave**	password)
entrar na Net	to access the Net
depois	next/after
depois disso	after that
ir ao site/visitar o site	to go to/ to visit the site
o site do banco	the bank site
uma conta	an account
o meu email	my e-mail
(in full: **o correio electrónico**	electronic mail)
não há mensagens	there are no messages
(also: **não tenho mails**	I don't have any mail)
as informações de viagens	travel information

[1] **a minha senha** (Br) password

Exercise 2

Imagine you are Joana. In an effort to remember your movements on the computer, you have written down each step. These steps are written in English below. Try to translate them into Portuguese using the Preterite tense. (See **Lesson 3** for a re-cap on how to form the Preterite.)

1 Firstly I keyed in my password
2 Next I went to the bank site where I have an account
3 After that I checked my mail
4 Finally, I searched for the travel information site

🎧 Exercise 3 (Audio 2: 25)

Read the following passage about Internet usage in Portugal and see if you can answer the questions which follow.

Um estudo revela que em Portugal, há 670 mil assinantes da Internet, 450 mil dos quais beneficiam de acessos gratuitos, e, por força dos utilizadores brasileiros, o português é a quarta língua mais usada na Net, com um total de 4,1 milhões de utilizadores.

1 How many subscribers to the Internet are there in Portugal?
2 Can you pick out the word for *"users"* in Portuguese?
3 What factor contributes to so many people in Portugal using the Internet?
4 True or False: Because of the amount of Brazilian users, Portuguese is the sixth most used language on the Internet.

🎧 Exercise 4 (Audio 2: 26)

Many expressions connected with computers and the Internet in Portuguese are similar to, or exactly the same, as those in English. Listen first to the recordings if you have them, then try to match up the following Portuguese expressions with their correct English translations from the box below.

**a sala de chat   o scanner   a Tecnologia de Informação
o programa   o browser   o hacker [2]   o Servidor da Internet
passear na Net [3]   o Shopping online   a Internet   o modem
o Banco online**

> the Internet   Internet Provider   online banking
> to surf the Net   online shopping   chat room
> browser   modem   scanner   Information Technology
> hacker   programme

---

[2] also: **o pirata informático** computer pirate
[3] **navegar na Net** (Br) to surf the Net

Enviar um email *Sending an e-mail*

Exercise 5

In Lisbon, Alexandra sends an e-mail to her company's overseas office in Brazil. Below you will find a partial translation into English of her e-mail message. With the aid of this, plus the vocabulary which follows, can you fill in the blanks to decipher why Alexandra is writing to her Brazilian colleague, Ester? You will find a full translation of the e-mail in the exercise key.

Alexandra Machado, 25/6/01   18.20   página 1 de 1

De:	Alexandra Machado@livros.inc.pt
Para:	Ester Soares@livros.inc.br
Enviado:	Terça-feira, 25 de Junho de 2001 18.20
Assunto:	Conferência em Vídeo

Querida Ester

Poderias organizar uma conferência em vídeo para quinta-feira, 18 de Julho, entre os escritórios de Lisboa e Rio, por favor, afim de discutirmos a estratégia de vendas para o ano que vem?

A propósito, muito obrigada pela página da Net que construiste para o escritório do Rio – parece muito melhor! Agora, é tão fácil para entrar e download a informação, e os gráficos são excelentes.

Conforme pedido, envio como attach a lista de fornecedores de DVD na Europa.

Muitas saudades
Alexandra Machado
Directora Executiva

Translation:

Dear Ester

_____ a video conference for _____, between the Lisbon and Rio _____ , _____ next year's _____ ?

By the way, thank you for _____ that you built _____ – it looks much better! Now it is so

_____ to _____ and _____ information, and the graphics are excellent.

As requested, _____ the list of _____ in Europe.

All the best,
Alexandra Machado
Sales Executive

Vocabulary

organizar	to set up
os escritórios	offices
afim de discutirmos	so that we can discuss
a estratégia de vendas	sales strategy
construir uma página da Net	to build a Web page
entrar	to access
download (a informação)	to download (information)
envio como attach	I attach
enviar como attach	to send an attachment
(also: **enviar um attachment**	to send an attachment)
os fornecedores	suppliers

 Reading aloud a Portuguese e-mail address (Audio 2: 27)

maria@uol.com.pt   "maria arroba uol ponto com ponto pt"

 Dialogue 1 (Audio 2: 28)
O shopping online
Joana chats about the merits of online shopping with a work colleague, Manuel

MANUEL: No fim de semana fui a 4 livrarias diferentes e nenhuma delas tinha o livro que eu queria. No fim, tive que o encomendar. Mas que perda de tempo!

JOANA: Eu também fui às compras. Comprei um CD para dar à minha irmã pelo dia dos seus anos e um ramo de flores para a minha tia que está no hospital – tudo isto sem necessidade de sair de casa.

MANUEL: Ah, já sei ... usaste o shopping online! Mas é seguro fornecer os detalhes do teu cartão de crédito pela Internet?

JOANA: Ah sim, é cem por cento garantido. Tenho o e-card, que é um cartão exclusivo para compras na Internet. Nesta semana eu até reservei um vôo para Londres online. É super pràctico!

Vocabulary

as livrarias	bookshops
tive que o encomendar	I had to order it
sem necessidade de sair de casa	without setting foot outside
fornecer os detalhes	to provide details
reservei um vôo	I booked a flight

Exercise 6

With the help of the vocabulary in Dialogue 1, can you translate the following sentences into Portuguese:

1 He ordered 5 books online
2 She buys all her CDs using her computer
3 They provide their credit card details
4 You booked a flight to London online

A World Wide Web *The World Wide Web*

If you have access to the Internet, why not try looking at the following Portuguese sites:

www.portugal-info.net	for news on all things Portuguese
www.beachcam.pt	for news on beaches (**a praia** – beach)
www.portugalinsite.pt	for news on where to stay etc.
www.vialivre.com	for news on traffic (**o tráfego /o trânsito** – traffic)
www.radiocomercial.pt	for news / music etc. (**as notícias** – news; **a música** – music)
www.tvi.pt	**Televisão Independente** (Independent Television)

Some Portuguese newspapers to try:

<u>Daily</u>:

Diário de Notícias	*www.dn.pt*
Jornal de Notícias	*www.jn.pt*
O Público	*www.público.pt*
Correio da Manhã	*www.correiomanha.pt*
Desporto Digital	*www.desportodigital.com*

<u>Weekly</u>:

O Expresso	*www.expresso.pt*

Exercise 7

Look at the following expressions in Portuguese relating to e-mail. Insert against each the correct English translation from the box below, then try to find out what Alberto used his e-mail for on one special occasion.

escrever a sua password _____

enviar uma mensagem _____

enviar um attachment _____

ir ver o seu email _____

não tenho mails _____

o meu endereço email _____

to send a message	to key in your password
I don't have any mail	to send an attachment
my e-mail address	to check your e-mail

Q   What did Albert use his e-mail for last year?

A   **O ano passado, o Alberto enviou por email um cartão de Natal virtual a todos os seus colegas de trabalho.**

Exercise 8

O telemóvel The mobile phone

Francisco is in the middle of a busy day. Read the passage below and see if you can answer the questions which follow.

Francisco pega no telemóvel⁴ e consulta na base de dados dos seus clientes o nome da pessoa com quem tem a próxima entrevista. Depois da entrevista, ele consulta a agenda electrónica e verifica que tem um almoço com um cliente importante. Liga para a *Churrascaria Central* e reserva uma mesa para as duas horas da tarde.

⁴ **o celular** (Br) mobile phone

1 Francisco wants to find out the name of the client with whom he has his next interview. How does he do this?
2 How does Francisco find out who he has a lunch appointment with?
3 Finally, who does Francisco ring and for what reason?

Vocabulary

pega no telemóvel	(he) picks up the mobile phone
a base de dados	database
os clientes	clients
a próxima entrevista	the next interview
a agenda electrónica	electronic organizer
liga para ...	he dials/rings/calls ...
a churrascaria	restaurant specializing in barbecued dishes

 Some more computer terms (Audio 2: 29)

a informática	computing
o monitor	monitor
a impressora	printer
o PC	PC

o laptop/o palmtop	laptop/palmtop
o disco rígido	hard disk
a disquete	floppy disk
a memória	memory
clicar	to click on
o ficheiro	document/file
o rato	mouse
a janela	window
o CD-ROM	CD-ROM
o DVD	DVD
o vírus	virus
passear na Net	to surf the Net
download	(to) download
upload	(to) upload
o comércio electrónico	e-commerce
o engenho de busca	search engine

How would you manage in these situations?

1 Based on Lessons 1 and 2:

1 You are in a café in Lisbon and have to call the waiter over and order a beer, a strong black coffee, a cake and a cheese sandwich.

2 You get talking to a stranger at the next table by asking him the time. You introduce yourself, tell him where you come from and what you do and ask where he is from. You tell him you like/dislike Lisbon/Portugal.

2 Based on Lessons 3 and 4:

1 You go into a hotel to ask for a room for three nights with a shower. To save time the clerk fills out the check-in form (a ficha) for you, asking: your name, age, date of birth and where you come from. What replies would you give?

2 Later you want to visit the centre of town but manage to lose your way. You stop someone and ask: 'Excuse me, how do I get to the centre?' You cannot understand their reply, however, so you ask them to please speak more slowly.

3 Later in the evening you go out for dinner. You call the waiter over and ask for a table for two. From the menu you choose:

soup, chicken and salad and a bottle of white wine. When the meal is over you ask for the bill.

3 Based on Lessons 5 and 6:

1 You decide you need to buy a sweater as you forgot to pack one. You find a shop, go in and ask to see some sweaters, size 40. You decide you want a blue one and ask how much it is and can you try it on.
2 You want to visit the Gulbenkian Museum which is a little bit outside the centre of Lisbon. As you are in a hurry you hail a taxi. What do you tell the driver?
3 Later that day you decide to hire a car to see a bit more of the country. You want a small car for the week. Your next step is to buy petrol. You stop at a small petrol station and ask for a fill-up.

4 Based on Lessons 7 and 8:

1 You wake up the following day with a slight toothache and go to the local chemist's, asking if they have something for the pain.
2 Later, feeling much better, you go to the post office and ask for 16 stamps for the USA. You also need to change some traveller's cheques at a bank. Whilst you are there you ask what the exchange rate is.

5 Based on Lessons 9, 10 and 11:

1 You decide to go to see a play later in the week. Ask for two seats in the stalls and ask what time the play starts.
2 In the afternoon you go to see a film. Ask for two tickets. Before the film starts you order two beers.
3 Back at the hotel you get talking to a member of staff about where you went on holiday last year (to Italy) and where you are planning to go next year.
4 Whilst chatting you decide to mention that the TV in your room is not working and also that there are no towels.

Reference grammar

Nouns and gender

In Portuguese nouns can be either masculine or feminine:

casa (f)	**homem** (m)	**rapariga** (f)	**urso** (m)
house	man	girl	bear

The ending of a noun gives a clue as to whether it is masculine or feminine. Nouns:

1 ending in -**o** -**im** -**om** -**um** are generally masculine.
2 ending in -**a** -**ã** -**gem** -**dade** -**ice** -**ez** -**ção** -**são** are generally feminine.

Forming the feminine

If a word in the masculine form ends in -**o**, then remove this and add an -**a**:

menino	boy	**menina**	girl

If the masculine noun ends in a consonant, add an -**a**:

cantor (m)	**cantora** (f)	singer

If the masculine word already ends in an -**a** there is no change:

jornalista   journalist (both male and female)

Plural of nouns

1 Nouns ending in an unstressed vowel, add -**s**:

bica	**bicas**

2 Nouns ending in **-r or -z, add -es:**

vendedor   **vendedores**

3 Nouns ending in an **-s** where the final syllable is stressed, add **-es:**

país   **países**

Where the last syllable is not stressed, there is no change:

lápis   **lápis**

4 Nouns ending in **-m** becomes **-ns:**

homem   **homens**

5 Nouns which end in **-ão** have three possibilities in the plural:

(a) **-ão → ões**   (the most likely possibility)

colecção   **colecções**   collection/s
organização   **organizações**   organization/s

(b) **-ão → -ães**

pão   **pães**   bread/loaves

(c) **-ão → -ãos**

irmão   **irmãos**   **brother/s**

6 Nouns which end in **-l** drop the **-l** and add **-is:**

móvel   **móveis**   furniture

Words ending in **-il** have two possible endings: **-is** or **-eis**. This changes according to whether the **-il** is stressed. If stressed, add **-is**. If not stressed, add **-eis:**

stressed: **barril**   **barris**   barrel/s
unstressed: **fóssil**   **fósseis**   fossil/s

Articles

The definite article – 'the'

	(m)	(f)
(sg)	**o**	**a**
(pl)	**os**	**as**

The definite article agrees in number and gender with the noun it represents.

o livro	the book	**os livros**	the books
a mesa	the table	**as mesas**	the tables

The indefinite article – 'a, an'

	masc	fem
sing	**um**	**uma**
plural	**uns**	**umas**

The indefinite article also agrees with the noun it represents.

um jornal   a newspaper (m)   **uma revista**   a magazine (f)

Adjectives

These agree in gender and number with the word to which they refer and usually follow this word. The feminine is formed by changing the -**o** on the masculine adjective to an -**a:**

um filme chat*o*	a boring film
uma peça chat*a*	a boring play

If the adjective ends in an -**r** then simply add an -**a:**

falador (m)   **faladora** (f)   chatty/talkative

Plurals of adjectives

If the adjective ends in a vowel, add -**s:**

masculine:		*feminine:*	
honesto	(s) →	**honesta**	(-**o** → -**a**)
honestos	(pl) →	**honestas**	(-**os** → -**as**)

If the adjective ends in an -**e**, simply add -**s:**

triste →   **tristes**   (both m and f)

For other adjective plurals follow the rules for the plural of nouns.

Demonstrative adjectives and pronouns

	This *These*	*That* *Those*	*That* *Those*
ms	este	esse	aquele
fs	esta	essa	aquela
mpl	estes	esses	aqueles
fpl	estas	essas	aquelas
	isto	isso	aquilo

Possessive adjectives and pronouns

Singular:

	ms	fs	mpl	fpl
My, mine	o meu	a minha	os meus	as minhas
your	o teu	a tua	os teus	as tuas
his, her,	o seu	a sua	os seus	as suas
your				

Plural:

	ms	fs	mpl	fpl
our	o nosso	a nossa	os nossos	as nossas
your(vós)	o vosso	a vossa	os vossos	as vossas
their,	o seu	a sua	os seus	as suas
your				

These possessive adjectives change according to the *object* referred to and not the owner of the object.

her car	o seu carro	their car	o seu carro
her pens	as suas canetas	his pens	as suas canetas
my books	os meus livros	my pens	as minhas canetas

Personal pronouns

eu	I
tu	you (m + f)
você	you (m + f)
o senhor	you (m)
a senhora	you (f)
ele	he, it
ela	she, it
nós	we
vocês	you (mpl + fpl)
os senhores	you (mpl)
as senhoras	you (fpl)
eles	they (mpl)
elas	they (fpl)

These subject pronouns are often omitted in Portuguese as the verb ending gives information about who is being referred to. They can also be used for emphasis:

O senhor Castro? Ele ainda não chegou.
Mr Castro? He hasn't arrived yet (but the others have).

Adverbs

These are formed by adding **-mente** to the end of a feminine adjective.

		adverb	
duvidoso (ms)	**duvidosa** (fs)	→ **duvidosamente**	doubtfully

Where there is no change in the feminine adjective, such as those ending in **-e** or **-z**, simply add **-mente**.

		adverb	
feliz (ms)	**feliz** (fs)	→ **felizmente**	happily

Prepositions

Some common ones are:

a	to/at
em	in/on
de	of/from
por	by/through

debaixo de	under/below
em cima de	on top of
longe de	far from
para	for, to, towards

Questions

Simply use a questioning tone in your voice:

Ela conhece o Paulo	She knows Paulo
Ela conhece o Paulo?	Does she know Paulo?

Following a question word such as **como**, **onde** or **quem**, the order of subject and verb changes as in English:

O Paulo está em casa	Paulo is at home
Onde está o Paulo?	Where is Paulo?

Verbs

The infinitive

This is the whole verb (= the English verb '*to* run/buy', etc.). Portuguese has three types of verb groups or conjugations and these end in either -**ar**, -**er** or -**ir**. *Examples:*

comprar to buy   **decidir** to decide   **beber** to drink

The personal infinitive

Portuguese has another infinitive which, as the name suggests, is a 'personalized' infinitive. It is very simple to form. Take any infinitive and add the endings:

-**es** -**mos** -**em**

There are only three endings to learn.

Using the personal infinitive

1 To indicate more clearly the person being referred to:

Depois de partires, o Jorge chegou
After you left (your leaving) Jorge arrived

2 As an alternative to the subjunctive in certain cases, by replacing the conjunction with a preposition:

Estou a preparar uma refeição no caso que venha (subjunctive)
I'm preparing the dinner in case he comes

Estou a preparar uma refeição no caso de vir
(personal infinitive)

The present indicative

This tense is used to state (a) normal occurrences or (b) facts.

(a) **A loja abre às nove horas** The shop opens at 9.00 a.m.
(b) **Não como fruta**   I don't eat fruit

The present indicative endings are added to the stem of the verb (minus the -**ar**, -**er**, -**ir** ending). *Examples:*

falar to speak	**beber** to drink	**partir** to leave
falo	**bebo**	**parto**
falas	**bebes**	**partes**
fala	**bebe**	**parte**
falamos	**bebemos**	**partimos**
falam	**bebem**	**partem**

Irregular verbs

Do not follow the above pattern of 'regular' stem + endings. Some of the most frequently used irregular verbs are given at the end of this section.

Orthography-changing verbs

These are verbs which change their spelling in order to maintain their original sound. *Some examples:*

c before **e** → **qu** (**fiquei** – from **ficar**)
c before **o** → **ç**   (**faço** – from **fazer**)

Radical-changing verbs

These are verbs which have changes to their 'root' or 'stem'. This occurs mostly to -**ir** verbs in the present indicative tense (and, as a result, in the present subjunctive tense). For example, in the **eu** part of the verb:

e → i	**mentir** to lie	**(eu) minto**
	preferir to prefer	**(eu) prefiro**
	sentir to feel	**(eu) sinto**

The present continuous tense

This uses the verb **estar** (to be) + **a** + infinitive. This tense is used for actions which are in progress and which have an air of continuity about them.

estamos a falar	we are talking
	(i.e. we are *in the middle of* talking)
estava a chorar	he was crying
	(i.e. he was *in the process of* crying)

The gerund

This is formed by removing the final -r of any infinitive and adding -ndo and is the equivalent of the English present participle '-ing' in 'running', 'eating', etc.:

dançando dancing **cantando** singing

Estar + gerund is another way to form the present continuous tense. This method is more common in Brazil: **estou comendo** I am eating.

The passive
This is formed using either the verb **ser** or **estar** + past participle and is the equivalent of 'was/were':

O livro foi escrito por José Saramago (**foi** from ver **ser** = action)
The book was written by José Saramago

O livro estava escrito em inglês (**estava** from verb **estar** = state)
The book was written in English

Preterite tense

This is used for actions in the past which are complete:

Ontem comprei um par de sapatos
Yesterday I bought a pair of shoes

To form, remove the -ar, -er or -ir from any regular verb and add:

for -**ar** verbs:	**ei aste ou ámos aram**
for -**er** verbs:	**i este eu emos eram**
for -**ir** verbs:	**i iste iu imos iram**

Imperfect indicative

This past tense is used for events in the past which have no exact time limits, or an habitual action in the past ('he used to ... every summer').

To form, remove the -**ar**, -**er** and -**ir** endings from the three verb conjugations and add:

-**ar** verbs: -**ava** -**avas** -**ava** -**ávamos** -**avam**
-**er** and -**ir** verbs: -**ia** -**ias** -**ia** -**íamos** -**iam**

There are four irregular verbs in this tense:

ser	to be	**era eras era éramos eram**
ter	to have	**tinha tinhas tinha tínhamos tinham**
vir	to come	**vinha vinhas vinha vínhamos vinham**
pôr	to put	**punha punhas punha púnhamos punham**

The future indicative

To form this tense add the following endings to the infinitive of any of the three groups of verbs. The endings are the same for the three groups.

-**ei** -**ás** -**á** -**emos** -**ão**
beber → **beberei beberás beberá beberemos beberão**
I shall/will drink, etc.

Three exceptions: **fazer**, **dizer**, **trazer**.

The future perfect

Use the future tense of **ter** (to have) + past participle.

Terão fechado a porta   They will have shut the door
Terá visto o filme   He will have seen the film

The future tense can also result from the present tense of the verb **ir** ('to go') + infinitive. This tense expresses the English 'I'm going to (eat)', 'we are going to (go out)', etc.

Vou visitar uma amiga
I'm going to visit a friend

Vai arrumar a sala
She is going to tidy up the living room

The conditional tense

This expresses the English 'you would go', etc. and is formed by adding one set of endings to all three groups of verbs in their infinitive state:

-ia   -ias   -ia   -íamos   -iam

Comprariam a casa	They would buy the house
Comeria o bolo	He would eat the cake
partiríamos	we would leave

Three exceptions: **fazer, dizer, trazer**.

The conditional perfect tense uses the conditional of the verb **ter** + past participle and is the equivalent of the English 'you would have bought'.

Terias comprado o vestido	You would have bought the dress
Teríamos visto o filme	We would have seen the film

The perfect tense

To form this tense use the present indicative of the verb **ter** + past participle. This tense expresses repeated events or states in the past which continue to have an effect in the present.

Tenho estado triste
I have been feeling sad (recently and still am)

Temos estudado muito
We have been studying a lot (lately and still are)

The pluperfect tense

This tense expresses the English 'we had (left)' and is formed by the imperfect indicative of **ter** + past participle:

Tinha ouvido a música
He/she/you had listened to the music

Tínhamos partido cedo
We had left early

Note: The simple pluperfect tense also exists, which has the same meaning as the pluperfect above. This tense is never used in speech

238

but can replace the pluperfect tense in written language. An example of the simple pluperfect:

comprara **compraras** **comprara** **compráramos** **compraram**

The imperative

This is for commands or instructions:

compra	come	parte	(tu)
compre	coma	parta	(você)
compremos	comamos	partamos	(nós)
comprem	comam	partam	(vocês)

It is formed by removing the -**ar**, -**er** or -**ir** of a verb and adding the above endings. For irregular verbs see verb tables.

The past participle

To form, remove the -**ar**, -**er** or -**ir** endings of any verb, adding:

for -**ar** verbs: -**ado** **falado** spoken
for -**er** verbs: -**ido** **comido** eaten
for -**ir** verbs: -**ido** **decidido** decided

There are a number of irregular past participles. See the irregular verbs at the end of this section.

The subjunctive mood

The present subjunctive

This is used to express something which is open to doubt:

Talvez estude? Perhaps he is studying?

It also expresses an emotional response to situations:

É pena que você não venha It's a shame you're not coming

To form this, take the **eu** part of any present indicative verb, remove the ending and add:

for -**ar** verbs: -e -es -e -emos -em
for -**er** and -**ir** verbs: -a -as -a -amos -am

ter (pres. indic. **tenho**): remove the -**o** → **tenh-
tenha, tenhas, tenha** etc.

Não penso que ele coma muito
I don't think that he eats a lot

Imperfect subjunctive

This is similar in use to the present subjunctive but indicates situations which are even more remote and uncertain. To form, take the 3rd person plural (**eles/elas**) of any verb in the preterite tense, remove the -**ram** ending and add the following endings:

-sse -sses -sse -sse -ssemos -ssem

These endings apply to all three verb groups.

Perfect subjunctive

This is formed from the present subjunctive of **ter** + past participle:

(que) tenha mandado   (that) I have sent
(que) tenhamos lido   (that) we have read

Pluperfect subjunctive

This is formed from the imperfect subjunctive of **ter** + past participle:

Não sabia se ele tivesse visitado o museu
I didn't know if he had visited the museum

Future subjunctive

To form this, start from the 3rd person plural of any verb in the preterite tense, remove the -**ram** and add:

-r -res -r -rmos -rem

The future subjunctive conveys the idea of the future, but one which is uncertain. Whereas in English we can use the present tense to indicate a future event, for example, 'When I arrive, I'll telephone', in Portuguese the future subjunctive is used after 'when' because it is uncertain *when* I will arrive.

A note on vós

Vós is a personal pronoun meaning 'you' (pl) but it is not used in everyday conversation throughout Portugal. Since the **vós** forms have been omitted from the conjugations in the following section, here is a summary of the endings for these forms in the indicative mood:

	-ar	-er	-ir
present	-ais	-eis	-is
preterite	-astes	-estes	-istes
imperfect	-áveis	-íeis	íeis
future	-eis	-eis	-eis
conditional	-íeis	-íeis	-íeis

Irregular verbs

Dar ('to give')   *Indicative mood*

Present	dou	dás	dá	damos	dão
Preterite	dei	deste	deu	demos	deram
Imperfect	dava	davas	dava	dávamos	davam
Future	darei	darás	dará	daremos	darão
Conditional	daria	darias	daria	daríamos	dariam
P. infin.	dar	dares	dar	darmos	darem
Imperative		dá	dê	demos	dêem
Past participle	dado				

Subjunctive mood

Present	dê	dês	dê	demos	dêem
Imperfect	desse	desses	desse	déssemos	dessem
Future	der	deres	der	dermos	derem

Dizer ('to say')   *Indicative mood*

Present	digo	dizes	diz	dizemos	dizem
Preterite	disse	disseste	disse	dissemos	disseram
Imperfect	dizia	dizias	dizia	dizíamos	diziam
Future	direi	dirás	dirá	diremos	dirão
Conditional	diria	dirias	diria	diríamos	diriam
P. infin.	dizer	dizeres	dizer	dizermos	dizerem
Imperative		diz	diga	digamos	digam
Past participle	dito				

Subjunctive mood

Present	diga	digas	diga	digamos	digam
Imperfect	dissesse	dissesses	dissesse	disséssemos	dissessem
Future	disser	disseres	disser	dissermos	disserem

Estar ('to be')   *Indicative mood*

Present	estou	estás	está	estamos	estão
Preterite	estive	estiveste	esteve	estivemos	estiveram
Imperfect	estava	estavas	estava	estávamos	estavam
Future	estarei	estarás	estará	estaremos	estarão
Conditional	estaria	estarias	estaria	estaríamos	estariam
P. Infin.	estar	estares	estar	estarmos	estarem
Imperative		está	esteja	estejamos	estejam
Past participle		estado			

Subjunctive mood

Present	esteja	estejas	esteja	estejamos	estejam
Imperfect	estivesse	estivesses	estivesse	estivéssemos	estivessem
Future	estiver	estiveres	estiver	estivermos	estiverem

Fazer ('to do/make')   *Indicative mood*

Present	faço	fazes	faz	fazemos	fazem
Preterite	fiz	fizeste	fez	fizemos	fizeram
Imperfect	fazia	fazias	fazia	fazíamos	faziam
Future	farei	farás	fará	faremos	farão
Conditional	faria	farias	faria	faríamos	fariam
P. infin.	fazer	fazeres	fazer	fazermos	fazerem
Imperative		faz	faça	façamos	façam
Past participle		feito			

Subjunctive mood

Present	faça	faças	faça	façamos	façam
Imperfect	fizesse	fizesses	fizesse	fizéssemos	fizessem
Future	fizer	fizeres	fizer	fizermos	fizerem

Ir ('to go')   *Indicative mood*

Present	vou	vais	vai	vamos	vão
Preterite	fui	foste	foi	fomos	foram
Imperfect	ia	ias	ia	íamos	iam
Future	irei	irás	irá	iremos	irão
Conditional	iria	irias	iria	iríamos	iriam
P. infin.	ir	ires	ir	irmos	irem
Imperative		vai	vá	vamos	vão
Past participle		ido			

Subjunctive mood

Present	vá	vás	vá	vamos	vão
Imperfect	fosse	fosses	fosse	fôssemos	fossem
Future	for	fores	for	formos	forem

Poder ('to be able to')   *Indicative mood*

Present	posso	podes	pode	podemos	podem
Preterite	pude	pudeste	pôde	pudemos	puderam
Imperfect	podia	podias	podia	podíamos	podiam
Future	poderei	poderás	poderá	poderemos	poderão
Conditional	poderia	poderias	poderia	poderíamos	poderiam
P. infin.	poder	poderes	poder	podermos	poderem
Imperative		pode	possa	possamos	possam
Past participle		podido			

Subjunctive mood

Present	possa	possas	possa	possamos	possam
Imperfect	pudesse	pudesses	pudesse	pudéssemos	pudessem
Future	puder	puderes	puder	pudermos	puderem

Pôr ('to put')   *Indicative mood*

Present	ponho	pões	põe	pomos	põem
Preterite	pus	puseste	pôs	pusemos	puseram
Imperfect	punha	punhas	punha	púnhamos	punham
Future	porei	porás	porá	poremos	porã
Conditional	poria	porias	poria	poríamos	poriam
P. infin.	pôr	pores	pôr	pormos	porem
Imperative		põe	ponha	ponhamos	ponham
Past participle		posto			

Subjunctive mood

Present	ponha	ponhas	ponha	ponhamos	ponham
Imperfect	pusesse	pusesses	pusesse	puséssemos	pusesem
Future	puser	puseres	puser	pusermos	puserem

Querer ('to want')   *Indicative mood*

Present	quero	queres	quer	queremos	querem
Preterite	quis	quiseste	quis	quisemos	quiseram
Imperfect	queria	querias	queria	queríamos	queriam
Future	quererei	quererás	quererá	quereremos	quererão
Conditional	quereria	quererias	quereria	quereríamos	quereriam
P. infin.	querer	quereres	querer	querermos	quererem
Imperative		quer	queira	queiramos	queiram
Past participle		querido			

Subjunctive mood

Present	queira	queiras	queiras	queiramos	queiram
Imperfect	quisesse	quisesses	quisesse	quiséssemos	quisessem
Future	quiser	quiseres	quiser	quisermos	quiserem

Ser ('to be')   *Indicative mood*

Present	sou	és	é	somos	são
Preterite	fui	foste	foi	fomos	foram
Imperfect	era	eras	era	éramos	eram
Future	serei	serás	será	seremos	serão
Conditional	seria	serias	seria	seríamos	seriam
P. infin.	ser	seres	ser	sermos	serem
Imperative		sê	seja	sejamos	sejam
Past participle		sido			

Subjunctive mood

Present	seja	sejas	seja	sejamos	sejam
Imperfect	fosse	fosses	fosse	fôssemos	fossem
Future	for	fores	for	formos	forem

Ter ('to have')   *Indicative mood*

Present	tenho	tens	tem	temos	têm
Preterite	tive	tiveste	teve	tivemos	tiveram
Imperfect	tinha	tinhas	tinha	tínhamos	tinham
Future	terei	terás	terá	teremos	terão
Conditional	teria	terias	teria	teríamos	teriam
P. infin.	ter	teres	ter	termos	terem
Imperative		tem	tenha	tenhamos	tenham
Past participle		tido			

Subjunctive mood

Present	tenha	tenhas	tenha	tenhamos	tenham
Imperfect	tivesse	tivesses	tivesse	tivéssemos	tivessem
Future	tiver	tiveres	tiver	tivermos	tiverem

Ver ('to see')   *Indicative mood*

Present	vejo	vês	vê	vemos	vêem
Preterite	vi	viste	viu	vimos	viram
Imperfect	via	vias	via	víamos	viam
Future	verei	verás	verá	veremos	verão
Conditional	veria	verias	veria	veríamos	veriam
P. infin.	ver	veres	ver	vermos	verem
Imperative		vê	veja	vejamos	vejam
Past participle		visto			

Subjunctive mood

Present	veja	vejas	veja	vejamos	vejam
Imperfect	visse	visses	visse	víssemos	vissem
Future	vir	vires	vir	virmos	virem

Vir (to come)   *Indicative mood*

Present	venho	vens	vem	vimos	vêm
Preterite	vim	vieste	veio	viemos	vieram
Imperfect	vinha	vinhas	vinha	vínhamos	vinham
Future	virei	virás	virá	viremos	virão
Conditional	viria	virias	viria	viríamos	viriam
P. infin.	vir	vires	vir	virmos	virem
Imperative		vem	venha	venhamos	venham
Past participle		vindo			

Subjunctive mood

Present	venha	venhas	venha	venhamos	venham
Imperfect	viesse	viesses	viesse	viéssemos	viessem
Future	vier	vieres	vier	viermos	vierem

Key to exercises

Lesson 1

2

A: Excuse me, what's your name?
B: My name is Jorge, and what's your name?
A: My name is Luisa. Pleased to meet you.
A: Good evening, how are you?
B: I'm very well, thanks, and you?
A: I'm very well, thanks.

3

ele é, nós somos, vocês são, tu és, eu sou, elas são, você é

4

Olá! Como está? Estou bem, obrigado/a. Chamo-me ... Como se chama? Você é de França? Ah, você é de Inglaterra! Sou da Holanda. Muito prazer!

5a

Sou brasileira	I am Brazilian
Sou português	I am Portuguese
Ele é angolano	He is Angolan
Você é inglesa?	Are you English?
Ela é escocesa	She is Scottish
Sou holandês	I am Dutch

5b

1 Apresento-lhe o Tom; (ele) é de Inglaterra; é inglês
2 Apresento-lhe a Gabriella; (ela) é de Itália; é italiana
3 Apresento-lhe o Alberto; (ele) é de Angola; é angolano
4 Apresento-lhe o Hans; (ele) é da Alemanha; é alemão

6

1 Você é inglesa? 2 Sou escocês 3 Ele é português
4 Ela é brasileira? 5 Você é angolana

7

1 o telemóvel 2 a mulher 3 umas bolachas 4 os relógios
5 uns gelados 6 as colinas

8

1 umas nuvens 2 os pratos 3 uns pentes 4 as praias

9

1 o tapete 2 a cadeira 3 o lápis 4 uma revista 5 um carro

10

1 Kathleen é irlandesa 4 Ela é holandesa 5 Você (Matthew) é
inglês e eu sou (Jane) escocesa 6 Andrew é escocês mas
Jules é francês

11

1 False. Jorge is from Brazil.
2 He says: I'd like you to meet Paulo. He is from Portugal; he's
   Portuguese.
3 He wants to know what nationality Isabel is.
4 That Isabel is not Italian, she is Brazilian as well.

12

The missing items are: **uma sanduíche de queijo, um bolo, uma cerveja, uma água mineral com gás**

How much can you remember?

1 LIDIA: Como se chama?
PABLO: Chamo-me Pablo.
LIDIA: Você é espanhol?
PABLO: Sou. Sou de Madrid. E você?
LIDIA: Sou portuguesa, sou de Portugal.

2 At 9 a.m. **Bom dia!**; At 6 p.m. **Boa tarde!**; At 11 p.m. **Boa noite!**

3 **Você é inglês? Donde é? Como se chama? Chamo-me ...; sou de Itália**

4 (a) **uma imperial, um chá, uma bica**
(b) You would eat **um bolo**, not the others
(c) You would not drink **uma sanduíche**

5 1 **Boa tarde, como está?**
2 **Como se chama?**
3 **Donde é?**
4 **Tudo bem?**
5 **Qual é a sua nacionalidade?**

6 **Chamo-me ... Sou ... Sou de ...**

7 1 They are Brazilian 2 Rio de Janeiro in Brazil 3 They come to Portugal every year to visit their brother
Carlos and Fernanda are Brazilian. They live in Rio de Janeiro in Brazil. They come to Portugal every year to visit their brother José who lives in Oporto.

Lesson 2

1

vivo, vives, vive, vivemos, vivem
divido, divides, divide, dividimos, dividem

2

Gosto de roupa; gostamos de fruta; gostam de viajar; gosta do cinema francês; gostas do rádio; gostam das casas modernas

3

Gostam de desportos; gostam de jogar futebol; gostam de viajar; gostam de cinema; não gostam da comida chinesa; não gostam de palavras cruzadas; não gostam de tempo frio; não gostam de transporte público.

5

Ele canta o fado; trabalha num clube em Albufeira no Algarve. Ele é casado mas separado. Mora num apartamento perto da praia. Gosta de tocar a guitarra; de arte. Não gosta de violência; de intolerância. Ele é bastante tímido mas gosta muito de se divertir.

6

1 In Algés in the outskirts of Lisbon. 2 The mother is a telephonist, the father is a garage mechanic.

7

JORGE: Sou cantor. Sou casado. Moro em Lisboa numa casa. Sou tímido. Gosto de ópera; não gosto de futebol.

CLARA: Sou cantora. Sou solteira. Moro em Luanda numa casa. Sou preguiçosa. Gosto de andar; não gosto de desporto.

8

médica; jornalista; padeira; gerente; pintora; carpinteira; jornalista

9

1 The one asking for **cabeleireiras/os**. Yes, the pay is good.
2 Good appearance, ambition, dynamism and a good communicator.
3 The one looking for sales assistants.

10

1 Paulo's free days are Monday and Friday, 2 He is not available on Thursday. 3 False: he is not busy on Friday. 4 At the weekend he rests (Saturday) and visits friends (Sunday).

11

optimista – pessimista
impaciente – calma
inteligente – estúpido
trabalhador – preguiçoso

12

1 **São duas e um quarto** 2 **É uma menos um quarto** 3 **É uma hora** 4 **São cinco e vinte**

13

1 **às quatro menos um quarto** (24hr clock: **às quinze e quarenta e cinco**)
2 **às quatro menos vinte** (24hr clock: **às quinze e quarenta**) or **às onze menos cinco** (24hr clock: **às vinte e duas e cinquenta e cinco**)
3 **à uma e meia** (24hr clock: **às treze e trinta**)
4 three: 15 minutes of Open University; the Saturday Tarzan film; Jason Donovan live.

14

A janela está aberta; O carro é azul; A menina é inglesa; Ele está triste; Elas estão na cozinha; Estremoz é uma cidade em Portugal.

15

1 He describes himself as quite tall and dark.
2 He is a doctor and works in a hospital in the centre of the city (Rio).
3 False: he likes computers.

I'm a doctor and I live in a flat in Rio de Janeiro. I work in a hospital in the city centre. I'm quite tall and dark. I like computers. I don't like being ill.

How much can you remember?

1

1 Gosto da música jazz, não gosto de política.
2 Trabalho numa companhia no Porto às quartas-feiras.
3 Ele é sueco, bastante tímido, mas optimista.

2

1 wanted/required 2 intelligent 3 ugly 4 the newspaper 5 calm 6 the flat 7 a magazine 8 short 9 the beach

3

1 as casas 2 pessimistas 3 os cinemas 4 os pintores

4

1 a médica 2 a senhora 3 a cantora 4 a jornalista 5 solteira 6 tímida

5

É meio-dia e meia, São duas e um quarto,
São quinze e quarenta e cinco, São nove horas

half past two, midnight, twenty past nine,
one o'clock, ten past seven, three o'clock

Lesson 3

1

1 Miguel is 32/**O Miguel tem 32 anos**
2 How old is Maria?/**Quantos anos faz a Maria?**
3 When is your birthday?/**Quando é o dia dos seus anos?**
4 It's my birthday/**É o dia dos meus anos**

2

1 ANA: Nasci na Madeira; o dia dos meus anos é a seis de
            Maio; tenho treze anos.
2 ROBERT: Nasci na Irlanda; o dia dos meus anos é a quatorze
            de Agosto; tenho vinte e quatro anos.
3 PEDRO: Nasci em Espanha; o dia dos meus anos é o dia um
            de Março; tenho quarenta e dois anos.
4 MARIA: Nasci no Brasil; o dia dos meus anos é a vinte e nove
            de Dezembro; tenho trinta e seis anos.

3

ANTÓNIO: My name is António, and what's your name?
MANUELA: My name is Manuela. Where are you from?
ANTÓNIO: I'm from Lisbon, and you?
MANUELA: I'm from Coimbra. I'm 19. How old are you?
ANTÓNIO: I'm 25.

4

1 Five: herself, her parents, her brother and sister.
2 Brother: Zé. Sister: Cámi.
3 Her brother is 20, her sister is 16.
4 Cristina was born in Brazil; her brother and sister in Portugal.

5

CRISTINA: o meu porta-moedas; a minha maquilhagem; os meus
            óculos; as minhas vitaminas.

ANTÓNIO: a minha carteira; a minha agenda; as minhas chaves;
os meus óculos de sol.

6

JOSÉ: Hi, Teresa. Do you have a large or small family?
TERESA: I have a large family; three sons and a daughter. Vasco
is the eldest and Clara the youngest ... the ages vary
between 30 and 15 years of age.
JOSÉ: Your husband is retired, isn't he? Do you still work?
TERESA: I'm a housewife. I always have lots to do!

7

1 **o restaurante onde fui ontem.** 2 **Onde fui eu?** 3 **Eu passei o dia
na praia.** 4 **Tomei banhos de sol.**

8a

**encontrei, encontraste, encontrou, encontrámos, encontraram;
escondi, escondeste, escondeu, escondemos, esconderam; decidi,
decidiste, decidiu, decidimos, decidiram**

8b

1 **Foi o José** 2 **Foi o Pedrinho** 3 **Foi o António** 4 **Foi a Dona Augusta**
5 **Foi a Rosa** 6 **Foi a Maria Lucinda** 7 **Foi a Teresa** 8 **Foi o Sr Silva**
9 **Foi a Susana** 10 **Foi o casal Sousa**

9

**Faz favor! Queria uma mesa para uma pessoa. Está óptima. Tem
a lista se faz favor? Sim, se faz favor. Queria uma sopa de feijão,
as sardinhas assadas com batatas fritas e uma garrafa de vinho
branco. A conta se faz favor.**

10

1 chicken soup 2 The meat comes with rice; the fish comes with
potatoes 3 lettuce and tomato 4 False: Dessert consists of fruit –
oranges, apples or grapes.

How much can you remember?

1 **Quantos anos tem? Quantos anos faz?**
2 **Quando é o dia dos seus anos?**
3 **Tenho pressa**
4 **Nasci em Londres**
5 **O meu irmão tem dezasseis anos; a sua irmã tem dez anos**
6 **as suas chaves e a sua carteira**
7 **Queria uma mesa para dois e a lista (a ementa) se faz favor**

2

1 **cheio** 2 **minha chama** 3 **tem** 4 **nasceu**

3

1 **os meus irmãos** 2 **o seu carro** 3 **os seus óculos de sol** 4 **o meu porta-moedas** 5 **os seus livros** 6 **a sua caneta**

5

sessenta e seis, setenta e três, cento e um, vinte e três, sete, oitenta e sete, dois mil, duzentos e sete, oito, noventa, quarenta e cinco, seiscentos e setenta e nove, dez, um/uma, trinta e seis

6

o jantar =	dinner
a ceia =	supper
o pequeno-almoço =	breakfast
o almoço =	lunch

7

I was born in London. I am 22. My birthday is on the 15th May. How old is Paulo? He is 40. His birthday is on the 1st of December.

8

1 His neighbour and friend, Sr Mendes 2 To sit down 3 A drink 4 Beer 5 Telephone his wife

Lesson 4

1

Faz favor! Desculpe! 2 **Como**? 3 **Não sei** 4 **aqui** (here), **ali** (there);
cá (here), **lá** (there), **aí** (there) 5 **de nada/não tem de quê**

2

1 **dentro (da caixa)** 2 **em frente de** 3 **atrás de** 4 **em cima de**
5 **debaixo de** 6 **ao lado de**

3

perto de, debaixo de, em frente de, fora de

4

1 Can you tell me where the Chiado is? 2 The Directions are: go
straight on. Stay on this side of the street. At the end of the square
turn to the right and immediately on your left you will find a road
going up to the Chiado.

5

A

1 **Você siga sempre em frente. A sapataria fica em frente do Jardim
  da Estrela**
2 **Você siga sempre em frente, atravesse a rua Correia Teles, siga
  sempre em frente, e depois vire à esquerda**
3 **Você siga sempre em frente. Depois, vire à direita e o hospital
  é em frente da estação**
4 **Siga sempre em frente, vire à direita e tome a segunda rua à
  direita. No fim desta rua vire à esquerda e o supermercado fica
  ao fim da rua**
5 **Os correios são já ali, à esquerda, na esquina**

B

1 **É ao lado do teatro**
2 **É atrás da esquadra da polícia**
3 **É em frente do banco.**

C

1 É perto do supermercado 2 É perto do cinema 3 É perto da tabacaria

D

1 É ao lado do banco 2 É ao lado da tabacaria 3 É ao lado da mercearia

6

Vamos a Londres e precisamos de um quarto com casa de banho. Vamos ficar dois dias. Queríamos um hotel de primeira classe

7

Vou viajar de avião e vou ficar uma semana

8

passaporte; cheques de viagem; cartões de crédito; carteira; pasta; pasta; pasta

9

1 Ele perdeu o seu passaporte; ele perdeu os seus cheques de viagem; ele perdeu os seus cartões de crédito; ele perdeu a sua pasta
2 a sua carteira e a sua pasta
3 a sua pasta

10

1 Queria um quarto de casal com chuveiro, televisor e telefone para uma semana
2 Queria um quarto simples com banho, telefone e chuveiro para quinze dias
3 Queria um quarto de casal com duas camas, rádio e televisor para duas noites. Tem elevador?

11

1 Desculpe, mas não há toalhas/luz
2 Desculpe, mas não há telefone/papel higiénico
3 Desculpe, mas não há televisor

12

1 Desculpe, no meu quarto a persiana não funciona; o televisor está avariado.
2 Desculpe, no meu quarto o telefone está avariado; o rádio está avariado; o chuveiro não funciona
3 Desculpe, no meu quarto a retrete não funciona; a luz não funciona

How much can you remember?

1

1 Queria reservar um quarto de casal com pensão completa para seis noites
2 Dê-me o seu número de telefone. De nada
3 Perdi a minha carteira, as minhas chaves, o meu passaporte e os meus cartões de crédito
4 Reservaram um quarto de casal com duas camas com chuveiro

2

sem banho =	without bath
um quarto de casal =	a double room
vire à direita =	turn to the right
no fim desta rua =	at the end of this road

3

reservar: reservei	to reserve
atravessar: atravessei	to cross
seguir: segui	to follow
virar: virei	to turn
subir: subi	to go up
confirmar: confirmei	to confirm

4

1 **Vão atravessar a rua** 2 **Vou reservar um quarto** 3 **Ela vai virar à esquerda**

5

1 **Pode-me dizer onde é o banco/os correios/a estação de caminho de ferro/a biblioteca/a estação dos autocarros?**

6

faz favor! desculpe! com licença!

7

debaixo de, atrás de, em cima de, junto de, longe de, ao lado de, perto de, à direita de, ao lado de

8

1 Is there a hotel near here? 2 Can you tell me where the theatre is? 3 Where is the mini-market? 4 Where is the post office?

9

felizmente	=	fortunately
encontrar	=	to find
avião	=	plane
reservar	=	to reserve
que pena!	=	what a pity!
quinze dias	=	a fortnight

10

uma cama, um rádio, um telefone, toalhas, um televisor

11

1 the Continental Hotel 2 cross this avenue, go down that road there opposite/in front, at the end of the road turn to your left and you will find the hotel very close by on your right; directions given

by a policeman 3 the Hotel Marisol 4 whether the Marisol Hotel
will be more expensive than the Continental

Lesson 5

1

saldo sale; **preços baixos** low prices; **caixa** cash desk;
aberto open; **saída** exit; **entrada livre** come in and browse;
fechado closed; **IVA incluído** VAT included

2

Um par de alpercatas pretas, se faz favor
A minha medida é trinta e sete
Sim, se faz favor. Estas estão um pouco grandes. Tem um
tamanho abaixo?
Obrigado/a. Gosto destas ... Fico com elas. Quanto custam?
Posso pagar com cheque?

3

2 **Este comboio é mais rápido do que este**
3 **Este livro é mais interessante do que este**
4 **Estes sapatos são mais modernos do que estes**

4

1 **Estes sapatos são mais caros do que estes**
2 **Ela é tão alta como o seu pai**
3 **O comboio é mais rápido do que o autocarro**
4 **Ele é tão inteligente como o seu irmão**

5

pouco – muito; mais – menos; grande – pequeno; maior – menor;
óptimo – péssimo

8

1 **Pode-me mostrar uma camisola verde?**
2 **Queria uma T-shirt de algodão**

3 **Posso ver um par de sapatos pretos**
4 **Queria uma blusa verde clara**
5 **Pode-me mostrar uma gravata cinzenta de seda**

9

a farmácia, a pastelaria, uma livraria, a papelaria, o cabeleireiro, a lavandaria automática, os correios

10

1 a shirt 2 red 3 size (40) 4 Where is the fitting room? Can I pay by cheque? The price is very good
   I'd like to buy a shirt please. Do you have other colours? I prefer the red one. My size is 40. Where is the fitting room? The price is very good. Can I pay by cheque?

11

baker's – **a padaria**
tobacconist's – **a tabacaria**
minimarket – **o minimercado**
butcher's – **o talho**
fish shop – **a peixaria**
grocer's – **a mercearia**

12

a tabacaria – os cigarros
a farmácia – os remédios
a frutaria – a fruta
a livraria – os livros
o correio – os selos
a padaria – o pão
a feira da ladra – coisas em segunda mão

13

2 um pacote de manteiga e um pacote de café
3 meio litro de vinho
4 pode-me dar duzentos gramas de queijo
5 três quilos e meio de batatas

6 queria dois quilos de cebolas
7 um tubo de pasta de dentes/queria sabão
8 Dê-me quatro quilos de açúcar

How much can you remember?

1

1 **Posso pagar com cartão de crédito?**
2 **Qual é a sua medida? 3 ficam-lhe bem; fica-me bem**
4 **Preciso dum tamanho acima 5 Fico com eles/elas**
6 **Posso experimentar? É mesmo uma pechincha**

2

1 **este** 2 **aquelas** 3 **este** 4 **estas** 5 **isto**

3

1 **tão** 2 **mais** 3 **menos** 4 **o melhor**

4

1 a dress 2 it was too big 3 buy a pair of high-heeled shoes and
a small handbag

Lesson 6

2

**o duty-free, o cartão de embarque, o horário de partidas, não-
fumadores, o controlo dos passaportes, a sala de espera, a porta
de embarque**

3

2 **Ele irá ao check-in** 3 **Ele irá ao controlo dos passaportes** 4 **Ele
visitará o duty-free**

4a

Excuse; loudspeaker; flight; time; flight; arrive

4b

apertar; cintos de segurança
refrescos; bebidas alcoólicas
comprar; cigarros; loção para depois de barbear

5

Qual é a sua nacionalidade?
Mostre-me o seu passaporte
Quanto tempo vai ficar?

6

1 The writer is going to travel to Canada to visit his/her parents
2 Half past nine; over five hours
3 Go to the check-in desk and passport control
4 False: the writer hates flying

I'm going to travel to Canada to visit my parents. The flight will leave London at half past nine and will last more than five hours. Before boarding the plane, I have to go to the check-in desk and to passport control. I must admit that I don't like flying at all but, in this case, I have to!

7

terá ido; terá reclamado; terá passado; terá dito; terá apanhado

8

proibido estacionar no waiting; **ocupado** engaged; **empurrar** push; **cancelado** cancelled

9

Quando é o próximo comboio para Coimbra? Quanto custa uma ida e volta? Queria um horário se faz favor. Queríamos três idas para Lisboa. De que linha parte o comboio?

10

1 trolley service
2 reservation
3 **Comboio Intercidades** intercity train; **Comboio Inter-Regional**
   train which runs between regions; **Comboio Regional** train which
   runs within a region; **Comboio não-diário** train which does not
   run every day

11

1 I go by car 2 I go by underground 3 I go by bus 4 I go on foot
5 I go by taxi 6 I go by tram

12

1 Yes (Renault Clio); 30,200 escudos 2 Comprehensive insurance,
unlimited mileage and VAT 3 25 years 4 40,000 escudos 5 No

13

semáforos traffic lights; **dê prioridade** give way; **obras** roadworks;
sentido único one-way street; **desvio** diversion; **auto-estrada**
motorway; **peões** pedestrians; **limite de velocidade** speed limit

14

1 Two thousand escudos of unleaded please!
2 I'd like ten litres of unleaded petrol
3 Please check the oil
4 Can you check the tyre pressures?
5 I need more water in the radiator
6 Can you fill it up please!

15

1 **Faz favor de verificar o óleo e também a pressão dos pneus.
   Preciso de mais água no radiador e três mil escudos de gasolina
   sem chumbo. Penso que tenho um furo num pneu.**

How much can you remember?

1

1 Três mil escudos de gasolina sem chumbo, se faz favor
2 Onde é o controlo dos passaportes?
3 Que vôo anunciam?
4 Quando é o próximo comboio para ...?
5 Não tenho nada a declarar

2

1 comido, dado, sido, visitado, esperado, verificado
2 feito, escrito, visto, posto, dito

3

engaged, roadworks, push, no waiting, pedestrians, diversion, give way

4

1 Uma ida se faz favor 2 Sou espanhol/a 3 Dez litros se faz favor

5

1 False: **a hora de chegada** = the arrival time
2 False: **um atraso** = a delay
3 False: **a sala de espera** = the departure lounge
4 False: **a hospedeira** = the air hostess
5 False: **o cinto de segurança** = the safety belt
6 False: **um lugar de não-fumadores** = a no smoking seat

Lesson 7

1

1 7.00 a.m. 2 The bathroom 3 In his bedroom 4 In the kitchen
5 He leaves home 6 He jogs for half an hour

2

levanto-me às ... horas, lavo-me na casa de banho às ... horas. Visto-me no meu quarto. Como o pequeno-almoço às ... horas. Saio de casa e vou ...

3

invejosamente jealously, **serenamente,** serenely, **evidentemente** obviously, **triunfantemente** triumphantly

4

A REVISTA:	A que horas se levantou?
JORGE:	Levantei-me às sete horas.
A REVISTA:	Onde se lavou?
JORGE:	Lavei-me na casa de banho.
A REVISTA:	Onde se vestiu?
JORGE:	Vesti-me no meu quarto.
A REVISTA:	Onde se sentou para comer o pequeno-almoço?
JORGE:	Sentei-me na cozinha.
A REVISTA:	A que horas saiu de casa?
JORGE:	Saí de casa às oito horas.
A REVISTA:	E depois?
JORGE:	Fiz jogging por meia hora

5

Present indicative	*Preterite tense*
queixamo-nos	**queixámo-nos**
queixam-se	**queixaram-se**
queixas-te	**queixáste-te**
queixa-se	**queixou-se**
queixo-me	**queixei-me**

6

1 **se levantou** 2 **sentámo-nos** 3 **se deitaram** 4 **se esqueceu**

7a

1 walk 2 run 3 lift 4 push 5 pull

7b

1 To put the ball in the opponents' net as many times as possible
2 Two teams; on a rectangular piece of ground

Football is a ball sport in which two teams play on a rectangular piece of ground. The object of the game is to put the ball into the opponents' net as many times as possible (to score goals).

8

1 **nós líamos**	we were reading
2 **ela ia ao teatro**	she was going to the theatre
3 **você conduzia lentamente**	you were driving slowly
4 **eu estudava**	I was studying
5 **elas tinham muitos problemas**	they had (were having) lots of problems

9

1 **(ele) pintava** ... 2 **(ele) bebia** ... 3 **(ele) fazia a barba** ...

10

daríamos, seríamos, estaríamos, veríamos, viríamos, teríamos, faríamos

11

2 **estou com dor de dentes**
3 **dói-me a garganta**
4 **dói-me o braço**
5 **estou com dores no estômago**
6 **doem-me as costas (as costas** means 'back' (pl), so the verb **doer** is in the plural)
7 **parti o joelho**

12

2 **Arranjei-o** 3 **Vendi-a** 4 **Você tinha-as**

13

1 **Dei-lhe um relógio** 2 **Não lhe disse as notícias** 3 **Comprou-lhe os bolos** 4 **Explicou-nos o problema**

How much can you remember?

1

levantar-se, vestir-se, lavar-se, sentar-se

2

1 **levantei-me às ... horas**
2 **deitei-me às ... horas**
3 **lavo-me na casa de banho**

3

Usually I get up at 8 a.m., wash and dress. I eat breakfast in the kitchen. I leave home at 8.45 a.m. I go to my job in the city centre.

4

1 **A que horas saiu de casa?**
2 **Onde se sentou para comer o pequeno-almoço?**
3 **Onde se vestiu?**

5

to get angry, to remember, to be mistaken, to complain, to cut oneself, to sit down, to wash

6

respirávamos, comia, partia, andavam

7

Imperfect tense of **ter**: **tinha, tinhas, tinha, tínhamos, tinham**
Conditional tense of **ter**: **teria, terias, teria, teríamos, teriam**
Conditional tense of **fazer**: **faria, farias, faria, faríamos, fariam**

8

estou constipado/a; dói-me a cabeça; sinto-me tonto/a; e estou com dores no ouvido

9

falo-lhe	I speak to her (or to him/to you)
falei-te	I spoke to you
falaram-me	they spoke to me
falou-nos	he (or she/you) spoke to us
fala-lhes	he (or she/you) speaks to them

10

1 7.30 a.m.
2 why he gets up so early
3 he has to go to work and his office is very far away

Lesson 8

1

1 Queria fazer uma chamada para Londres. Posso ver a lista telefónica? Qual é o indicativo do país para Inglaterra e o indicativo da zona para Londres?
2 Dez selos para os Estados Unidos, se faz favor.
3 Tem algumas cartas dirigidas a (name), se faz favor?

2

1 **viajado** 2 **mandado** 3 **comprado** 4 **visto** 5 **estado** 6 **treinado**

3

Levante o auscultador – lift receiver
Espere o sinal de marcar – wait for the dialing tone
Introduza a moeda – insert coin
Marque o número – dial number

4

1 tinha 2 tinha 3 tinha

Crossword

Horizontal	Vertical
1 **Algarve**	2 **Lisboa**
5 **Estoril**	3 **Ano**
6 **Hora**	4 **Vaidade**
8 **Ar**	7 **Amo**
9 **Comer**	

5

Bom dia, posso trocar estes cheques de viagem, se faz favor? Estou na Pensão Bonita, na Rua Gil Vicente. Qual é o câmbio?

6

1 It is vibrant and dynamic
2 It is a country full of large forests and natural resources
3 The mixture of different races. This produces a varied and exuberant culture and folklore

7a

Bom dia, queria abrir um depósito à ordem com um livro de cheques e um cartão bancário. Queria também um cartão para o terminal caixa e um extracto de conta mensal.

7b

1 Do you have a character reference?
2 Do you want a deposit account?
3 Do you want a cash-point card?
4 Do you have a specimen signature?

8

After inserting the card and keying in your pin number, select the desired amount by pressing the requisite keys. If the amount required is not shown, use the 'Other Withdrawals' key and, using the numeric keyboard, type in the required amount.

9

Your secret pin number is personal and non-transferable: memorize it, do not write it on the card or on any other place or document that may be lost or stolen along with the card or reveal it to anyone.

10

1 **as televisões** 2 **os aviões** 3 **as ligações** 4 **amáveis** 5 **portunhóis** 6 **radicais**

How much can you remember?

1

1 **Queria seis selos para Irlanda**
2 **Queria fazer uma chamada. Tem a lista telefónica?**
3 **Qual é o indicativo do país para Escócia? Qual é o indicativo da zona para Edimburgo? Que cabine telefónica?**
4 **não tenho estudado muito**
5 **o auscultador; o número; o sinal de marcar; ser desligado; estar impedido**

2

1 She had left when the postman arrived
2 We had put the cups in the kitchen
3 I had bought a sandwich to carry out
4 Can I change a travellers cheque?
5 What is the rate?
6 A bank card; cash-point machine

3

as ligações, os irmãos, os pães, azuis, os hotéis

4

a organização; a mão, o cão, difícil

5

This morning I went to the post office to make a call. The clerk there told me that I had to wait a bit because there was a queue. Whilst I was waiting, I looked for the international code for Mozambique and also the area code for Maputo. I dialled the number. It was engaged. I dialled the number again ... Ah! This time it was ringing ... I said 'Hello?' But nobody replied! I was cut off!

Lesson 9

1

Queria quatro plateias, no meio da sala 2 Queria um camarote para o próximo sábado. Está esgotada! 3 Seis bilhetes de bancada sol para hoje, se faz favor. Tem um cartaz?

2a

PAULO: Penso que o filme é chato. A história não presta para nada e a actuação é uma porcaria.

ISABEL: Não concordo contigo. A história não é horrível, é bestial! Também acho que a actuação está bem. Na verdade, o filme é óptimo!

PAULO: Ora essa! É tão chato que me vou embora!

2b

1 **Carnaval** poster. Four days. The final of the masked competition; a car 2 From Wednesday to Saturday at 10 p.m., Sundays at 4 p.m.; Open theatre. You can go every day; from 2–10 p.m.

3

um filme de suspense	a thriller
um filme de amor/romance	a love story
um filme de terror	a horror story

um filme de ficção científica	a science fiction film
um musical	a musical
um desenho animado	a cartoon

5

1 ENTREVISTADOR: What do you do on Sunday morning?
  TRANSEUNTE 1: I stay in bed till midday. Afterwards, I watch TV.
  ENTREVISTADOR: And on Sunday afternoon?
  TRANSEUNTE 1: I watch more TV or listen to music. Sometimes I phone my friend to chat.
2 ENTREVISTADOR: What do you do on Saturday morning?
  TRANSEUNTE 2: I go and visit my parents. Later, I go to the supermarket.
  ENTREVISTADOR: And on Saturday afternoon?
  TRANSEUNTE 2: I go out with a few friends.

6a

1 to go fishing 2 to wash the car 3 to go sailing 4 to read the papers

6b

1 gymnastics/aerobics 2 golf 3 karate 4 dancing 5 skating 6 surfing

7

No sábado de manhã vou visitar uns amigos. No sábado à tarde jogo golfe e no sábado à noite vejo televisão. No domingo de manhã fico deitado/a na cama até o meio-dia e depois lavo o carro.

8

escreva, escrevas, escreva, escrevamos, escrevam
transfira, transfiras, transfira, transfiramos, transfiram
controle, controles, controle, controlemos, controlem

9

1 **Faz bom tempo; faz sol** 2 **Faz mau tempo; está a chover** 3 **Faz mau tempo; faz vento** 4 **Faz mau tempo; está a nevar**

10

1 In a remote village in the north of Portugal 2 To predict the weather 3 From TV and the newspaper

11

1 **Coimbra** 2 **Albufeira** 3 **Lisboa** 4 **o trovão; o nevoeiro; nublado; a temperatura**

12

A: 1 A fortnight in Spain 2 No, its a de luxe hotel 3 Beach; golf; water-skiing
B: 1 100 places for tents or trailers/caravans 2 laundrette **lavandaria automática**; shop **loja**; swimming pool **piscina**

13

hot showers, dishwashing facilities, clothes washing facilities, post office, lots of shade, pool

14

1 Isabel thinks it's a very long journey by car. 2 Fernanda thinks a walking holiday would be too tiring. 3 Isabel suggests a boarding house, an inn or to go camping; she doesn't agree with Fernanda about the *pousada* suggestion because it's too expensive.

How much can you remember?

1

a peça = play; **o cartaz** = poster; **a próxima sessão** = the next show

2

um bolinho; um cãozinho; um pratinho; estou farto/a!; é uma porcaria!; concordo completamente contigo

3

a prize, a competition, Sunday morning, ticket office, a première, Christmas, it's sunny

4

um desenho animado, um filme de terror, um filme de suspense, o karaté, o judo, a patinagem, vejo televisão, saio com amigos

5

False: **ir pescar** = to fish
False: **lavar o carro** = to wash the car
False: **ler os jornais** = to read the papers

6

é óptimo!; é bestial!; é bacana!

7

1 **Porque não vai a Moçambique?** 2 **Seria uma viagem muito longa** 3 **(Ela) não gostaria de voar** 4 **(Ele) ficaria numa pousada** 5 **É menos caro fazer campismo**

8

1 No, s/he stays in bed until mid-day 2 On Saturday morning after visiting his/her parents 3 False 4 Watches TV

On Saturday morning I like to visit my parents. Afterwards, I go to the supermarket. On Sunday morning I stay in bed until mid-day. On Sunday afternoon I watch TV.

Lesson 10

1

Rui: figure 3 2 Isabel: figure 1 3 Paulo: figure 2

2

1 Falsa: a maioria vive em apartamentos
2 Seis: dois quartos de cama; sala de visitas; sala de jantar; cozinha
e casa de banho

3

shops **lojas**; farms **quintas**; warehouses **armazéns**;
garages **garagens**; buildings **prédios**; houses **moradias**;
for sale (or sales) **vendas (vende-se** for sale); flats **andares**;
wanted **compras**; offices **escritórios**; plots of land **terrenos**

4

1 A seafood restaurant; the one advertising **restaurante marisqueira**
2 A splendid house with six bedrooms, living room with fireplace,
dining room, four bathrooms, garage, 5,000 square metres of
land, in impeccable condition
3 The one advertising **moradia rústica** (rustic dwelling); it has a
mountain view and is 15 km from the beach
4 The one for **Queluz de Baixo** which has a **local central** (central
location)
5 the one in **Santos**

5

uma televisão a cores, uma lareira, poltronas, parede, sofá, mesa
baixa, candeeiro eléctrico, quadro, mesinha

6

a ficha, inundado/a, o canalizador, um fusível, um cano roto, o frigorífico, a máquina de lavar roupa, a bomba, lâmpadas, ligar a
televisão, não estar ligado à corrente, as ligações, a tomada

7

O frigorífico está avariado. Tenho um cano roto. Preciso de um
canalizador. A televisão não está ligada à corrente. Preciso de três
lâmpadas. Tem um fusível?

8

1 cooker 2 washing machine 3 fridge 4 dish washer 5 teapot
6 tumble drier 7 toaster 8 iron 9 mixer 10 vacuum cleaner
11 microwave

9

1 Chemists (p 42), transport (p 43), classified advertisements (p 46)
2 **desporto** sport (p 24) 3 **tempo** weather (p 35), **cinemas** cinemas
(p 73) 4 **Negócios**

10

1 (b); 2 (c); 3 (a)

How much can you remember?

1

**O meu apartamento tem dois quartos de cama, uma pequena
cozinha, uma sala de estar e uma casa de banho. Não tenho jardim
mas tenho garagem, video porteiro, vidros duplos e antena
parabólica.**

2

1 **Vamos bem para Londres?**
2 **O apartamento tem vista para o mar**
3 **Acabámos de mudar de casa**
4 **Vende-se (vendas) 5 Procura-se/Compras**

3

Imperfect subjunctive of **terminar: terminasse, terminasses, terminasse, terminássemos, terminassem**

4

1 If I were to leave tomorrow, I would get home earlier
2 If he were to buy the car, it would cost a lot of money
3 If we were to travel all day, we would be (become) very tired

5

uma sala de jantar, um quarto de cama, uma cozinha, uma casa de banho

6

sei lá . . .; pois . . .; portanto

Lesson 11

1

1 Not really. She has a motorbike whereas he has a bicycle; her hobby is hang gliding whereas his is stamp collecting
2 Probably not
3 Eric and Maria
4 Not very much!

3

1 **Quer fazer turismo**
2 **Tem de escrever um artigo para o seu jornal**
3 **Maria convida a Sarah a assistir a um curso de saltar de pára-quedas**
4 **Sarah recusa – ela não se interessa por desportos**

4

B Infelizmente, não posso.
B O que está a passar?
B Gostaria muito de ir/parece-me um boa ideia/porque não?

5

Tudo bem? How's things?; **Como está?** How are you?; **Como se chama?** What's your name?; **Donde é?** Where are you from?; **O que faz?** What do you do?; **Está em férias?** Are you on holiday?; **O tempo está muito bom/mau** The weather is very good/bad; **Chamo-me** My name is

6

1	Q: Bom dia, como se chama?	A:	Chamo-me ...
2	Q: Donde é?	A:	Sou de ...
3	Q: Quer café?	A:	Porque não
4	Q: Bom dia, como está?	A:	Bom dia, estou bem obrigado
5	Q: O que faz?	A:	Sou professor
6	Q: Quer comer?	A:	Quero, sim, obrigada

7

Last year I spent a great holiday on the beach. The weather was very good and I stayed in a boarding house which was very near the beach. I really liked the sea and all the people I met. I hope to go back there one day.

8

1 **No ano passado passei férias maravilhosas nas montanhas. O tempo estava muito mau e eu fiquei numa pousada da juventude**
2 **No ano passado passei férias maravilhosas na cidade de Paris. O tempo estava bom e eu fiquei num hotel**
3 **No ano passado passei férias maravilhosas nos lagos. O tempo estava óptimo e eu fiquei numa pousada**

9

deplorable	**deplorável**
variable	**variável**
solution	**solução**
petition	**petição**
lamentável	lamentable
incomparável	incomparable
perfeição	perfection
confortável	comfortable

10

incessante incessant; **impulsivo** impulsive; **impossível** impossible; **impulso** impulse; **impreciso** imprecise; **imperceptível** imperceptible; **imparcial** impartial; **impetuoso** impetuous

11

1 **By train and then bus**
2 **He caught the tram**
3 **He plans to go the Algarve at the end of the summer**

How much can you remember?

1

a minha bebida preferida, o meu passatempo predilecto/favorito, o advogado, a bibliotecária, a profissão

2

falar, falares, falar, falarmos, falarem

3

Refusing: **não posso, já fiz outros planos; acho que não é possível; infelizmente, não posso**
Accepting: **gostava muito; está bom; parece-me uma boa ideia**

4

Chamo-me ... Como se chama? Donde é?

6

an invitation, I don't drive, the conference, hardworking, calm, efficient, to attend/go to

7

No ano passado visitei a Bélgica. O tempo estava óptimo. Fiquei num hotel perto da praia. Foi muito confortável. Gostaria de ir a Cuba este ano. Há dois anos fui aos Estados Unidos.

Lesson 12

1

JANE:	Está? Posso falar com o gerente?
A COMPANHIA:	Desculpe, mas ele ainda não chegou. É urgente?
JANE:	Desculpe, pode falar mais devagar? Não falo português muito bem.
A COMPANHIA:	Ah! Não desligue. O gerente já chegou.

2

SR COELHO:	Está?
SECRETÁRIA:	Estou.
SR COELHO:	Daqui fala o Sr Coelho. Posso falar com o Sr Costa? É muito urgente.
SECRETÁRIA:	Desculpe, mas o Sr Costa está no Porto em negócios.
SR COELHO:	Porto! Que maçada! Eu estou a falar do Porto!
SECRETÁRIA:	Como se chama o nome da sua companhia?
SR COELHO:	Coelho & Irmão.
SECRETÁRIA:	Não percebo. Está marcada na agenda uma reunião para hoje no Porto entre o Senhor Costa e Coelho & Irmão.

(a moment later . . .)

SR COELHO:	Ah! Só um minuto. O Sr Costa já chegou!

3

a fotocopiadora; a máquina de escrever; o computador/o teclado; o telefone; a disquete; o fax

4

querida; recebi; ontem; pequena; que; amiga

5

Missing words: letter; arrange; to discuss; products; apologise; delay; arrange/set; month; confirmation; date; pleasure; city

Questions:
1 False: sent on 4th July
2 False: Brito & Co. want to arrange the meeting with Costa & Co. to purchase Costa's products
3 The delay in answering
4 Send a fax

6

1 Metal utensils 2 Yes 3 A catalogue 4 Cutlery sets. They are of the finest quality 5 Price lists

7   ***Portugal is not a small country***

The Portuguese language is spoken not only in Portugal, but also in a huge country, Brazil (in South America), in Guinea-Bissau, Angola, Mozambique and in the Cape Verde islands and São Tomé and Principe (in Africa), Goa, Damão and Diu (in India), Macau (in China), and Timor.

Portuguese is spoken more than French. The Portuguese language is the fifth most spoken language in the world. About 250 million people speak Portuguese.

Questions: 1 False 2 No 3 250 million 4 False

Lesson 13

1

1 **escrever a minha password**   2 **entrar na Net**   3 **vou ao site do banco**
4 **vou ver o meu email**   5 **procurar o site**

Firstly, I am going to key in my password to access the Net. Next I will visit the bank site where I have an account. (....) After that, I will check my e-mail. Ah! There are no messages. Finally, I'm going to search for the travel information site.

2

1 **Em primeiro lugar escrevi a minha password**
2 **Depois fui ao site do banco onde tenho uma conta**

3 **Depois disso, fui ver o meu email**
4 **Finalmente, procurei o site que tem informações de viagens**

3

1 670 thousand
2 utilizadores
3 they can get free access
4 False: Portuguese is the fourth most widely used language (**a quarta língua mais usada**)

4

a sala de chat	chat room
o scanner	scanner
a Tecnologia de Informação	Information Technology
o programa	programme
o browser	browser
o hacker	hacker
o Servidor da Internet	Internet Provider
passear na Net	to surf the Net
o Shopping online	online shopping
a Internet	the Internet
o modem	modem
o Banco online	online banking

5

Dear Ester

Please could you set up a video conference for Thursday, 18 July, between the Lisbon and Rio offices, in order to discuss next year's sales strategy?

By the way, thank you for the Web page that you built for the Rio office – it looks much better! Now it is so easy to access and download information, and the graphics are excellent.

As requested, I attach the list of DVD suppliers in Europe.

All the best,

Alexandra Machado

Sales Executive

6

1 Ele encomendou 5 livros online
2 Ela compra todos os seus CDs usando o computador
3 Eles fornecem os detalhes dos seus cartões de crédito
4 Você (o/a senhor/a) fez a reserva de um vôo para Londres online

7

to key in your password
to send a message
to send an attachment
to check your e-mail
I don't have any mail
my e-mail address

A

Last year Alberto sent a virtual Christmas card by e-mail to all his work colleagues

8

1 He picks up the mobile and consults his client database for the name of the person with whom he has the next interview
2 He consults his electronic organizer and confirms that he has a lunch with an important client
3 He rings the *Churrascaria Central* to reserve a table for 2pm

1

1 **Faz favor! Queria uma cerveja, uma bica, um bolo e uma sanduíche de queijo.**
2 **Faz favor, que horas são? Chamo-me ..., sou de (país), sou (profissão). Donde é? Gosto de Lisboa; não gosto de Portugal.**

2

1 **Bom dia, queria um quarto para três noites com chuveiro; chamo-me ...; tenho (vinte e cinco) anos; o dia 1 de Abril; sou de ...**

2 Faz favor, para o centro da cidade? Pode falar mais devagar?

3 Faz favor! Queria uma mesa para duas pessoas. Queria sopa, frango com salada e uma garrafa de vinho branco. A conta, se faz favor

3

1 Posso ver algumas camisolas? A minha medida é quarenta. Prefiro a azul, quanto é/custa? Posso experimentar?

2 Para o Museu Gulbenkian, se faz favor

3 Queria um pequeno carro para uma semana; pode encher, se faz favor

4

1 Faz favor, estou com dor de dentes, tem alguma coisa para a dor?

2 Queria dezasseis selos para os Estados Unidos, se faz favor. Posso trocar uns cheques de viagem? Qual é o câmbio?

5

1 Duas plateias, se faz favor; a que horas vai começar a peça?

2 Dois bilhetes, se faz favor; duas cervejas, se faz favor

3 No ano passado fui a Itália. Este ano tenho intenções de ir a . . .

4 A televisão no meu quarto não funciona e não há toalhas

Portuguese–English glossary

Brazilian (Br) words are distinguished from Portuguese (Pt) words where necessary.

a	at, to, it, the (f), you (f), her
à (contraction of a + a)	at the, to the
abaixo(de)	down, below, under
aberto	open
abraçar	to hug, embrace
abrir	to open
acabar(de)	to finish (to have just)
acampar	to camp
aceitar	to accept
acenar	to wave (hand), to nod (head)
acender	to light, to switch on
achar	to find, to discover, to think
acima	above
acontecer	to happen
acordo (m)	agreement
açougue (m)	(Br) butcher's (shop)
acreditar	to believe
adeus	goodbye
adiamento (m)	postponement, advance
adiantado	fast, early (time)
adoecer	to become ill
adorar	to adore, to love
advogado (m)	lawyer, solicitor
aeromoça (f)	(Br) air hostess
aeroporto (m)	airport
afastar	to remove, to keep away
aficionado (m)	fan, enthusiast
afinal	at last, finally
agarrar	to seize, grasp
agência (f)	agency
agência de correio	(Br) post office
agenda (f)	diary
agir	to act, to behave
agora	now
agradável	pleasant
agradecer	to thank, to be grateful for
água (f)	water
aguardar	to await
aguardente (f)	brandy
aí	there
AIDS (f)	(Br) AIDS
ainda	still, yet, even
ajuda (f)	help
ajudar	to help

albergaria (f)	inn	**aprender**	to learn
alcançar	to reach	**apresentar**	to introduce
alegre	cheerful	**aquele/a**	that, that one
além	over there, beyond	**aqui**	here
além disso	moreover	**ar** (m)	air
alface (f)	lettuce	**árbitro** (m)	referee
alfândega (f)	customs	**arena** (f)	ring, arena
algo	something	**artista** (m/f)	artist
algodão (m)	cotton	**árvore** (m)	tree
alguém	someone, some-body	**ascensor** (m)	lift, elevator
		assim	thus, like this
algum/a	some, any	**assinar**	to sign
alguma coisa	something	**assunto** (m)	subject, matter
alho (m)	garlic	**até**	up to, as far as, until
ali	there		
aliás	besides, otherwise	**aterragem** (f)	landing (aeroplane)
almoçar	to lunch		
almoço (m)	lunch	**aterrissagem** (f)	(Br) landing (aeroplane)
alto	tall		
altura (f)	height	**atirar**	to throw, shoot
alugar	to rent, to hire	**atrás**	behind
amanhã	tomorrow	**atrasado**	late
amar	to love	**atravessar**	to cross
amável	kind	**attach;**	attachment
ambiente (m)	atmosphere	**attachment** (m)	(in e-mail)
ambos	both	**auscultador** (m)	receiver (telephone)
amigo/a (m/f)	friend		
amor (m)	to love	**autocarro** (m)	(Pt) bus
andar	to go, to walk	**auto-estrada** (f)	(Pt) motorway
andar (m)	floor	**automóvel** (m)	car
angolano	Angolan	**avariado**	out of order, broken
aniversário (m)	anniversary		
ano (m)	year	**avião** (m)	aeroplane
antena (f)	aerial		
antes	before, rather	**bacalhau** (m)	dried, salted cod
anúncio (m)	advertisement	**bacana**	(Br) great, cool
ao (a + o)	to the, at the	**bagagem** (f)	luggage, baggage
apagar	to put out, to extinguish	**bagunça** (f)	(Br) mess
		bairro (m)	district, suburb
apanhar	to catch	**baixo**	low, short
apartamento (m)	flat, apartment	**balcão** (m)	balcony, circle (theatre)
após	after		

baliza (f)	net, goal	**brincar**	to have fun,
bancada (f)	row of seats		to play a joke
	(outdoors)	**brinquedo** (m)	toy
banco (m)	bank	**buraco** (m)	hole
banho (m)	bath	**burro** (m)	donkey
barato	cheap	**buscar**	to go for, to fetch
barba (f)	beard	**buzina** (f)	horn
barco (m)	boat		
barulho (m)	noise	**cá**	here
bastante	enough, quite	**cabeça** (f)	head
bate-papo (m)	(Br) chat	**cabeleireiro/a**	hairdresser
bater papo	(Br) to chat	**cabelo** (m)	hair
bêbado	drunk	**cachaça** (f)	(Br) rum
beber	to drink	**cachorro** (m)	(Pt) puppy;
bebida (f)	drink		(Br) dog
beira-mar (f)	seaside	**cada**	each
bem	well, quite,	**cada um/a**	each one
	good,	**cadeira** (f)	chair
bem vindo	welcome	**café** (m)	coffee, café
bens (mpl)	goods, belongings	**café da manhã**	(Br) breakfast
biblioteca (f)	library	**cair**	to fall down
bica (f)	strong black	**caixa** (f)	box
	coffee	**caixa de correio**	letterbox
bicha (f)	(Pt) queue	**calar**	to keep quiet
bilhete (m)	ticket	**calçar**	to put on
biscoito (m)	biscuit		(shoes, gloves)
blusa (f)	blouse	**calças** (fpl)	trousers
boa (adj f)	good	**caldeirada** (f)	fish stew
bocadinho (m)	a little bit, a little	**caldo verde** (m)	cabbage soup
	while	**calor** (m)	warmth, heat
bola (f)	ball	**cama** (f)	bed
bolacha (f)	biscuit	**camarote** (m)	cabin (ship), box
bolo (m)	cake		(theatre)
bolsa (f)	(Br) handbag;	**câmbio** (m)	foreign exchange
	(Pt) purse, pouch	**caminho** (m)	path, way
bolso (m)	pocket	**caminho de**	railway (Pt)
bom/boa	good, nice, kind	**ferro** (m)	
bonde (m)	(Br) tram	**camioneta** (f)	coach
borracha (f)	rubber	**camisa** (f)	shirt
braço (m)	arm	**camisola** (f)	sweater (Pt)
brasileiro	Brazilian	**campismo** (m)	camping
breve	short, brief, light	**campo** (m)	field

canal (m)	channel (TV)	**chatice** (f)	nuisance
canalizador (m)	plumber	**chave** (f)	key
caneta (f)	pen	**chávena** (f)	(Pt) cup
cansado	tired	**chegar**	to arrive, to be
cansar-se de	to tire of		enough
cantar	to sing	**cheio**	full
cão (m)	dog	**cheirar**	to smell
cara (f)	face	**choroso**	tearful
carne (f)	meat	**chouriço** (m)	spicy smoked
caro	dear, expensive		sausage
carro (m)	car	**chover**	to rain
carta (f)	letter	**chumbo** (m)	lead
cartão (m)	card, cardboard	**(sem)**	(unleaded)
cartaz (m)	poster	**chutar**	to kick
carteira (f)	wallet	**chuva** (f)	rain
carteiro (m)	postman	**chuveiro** (m)	shower
casa (f)	home, house	**cidade** (f)	city
casado	married	**cinema** (m)	cinema
casal (m)	couple	**claro**	bright, clear
casamento (m)	marriage, wedding	**claro!**	right!, of course!
cavaquear	(Pt) to chat	**cobrir**	to cover,
cedo	soon, early		to conceal
celular (m)	(Br) mobile phone	**código** (m)	code, postal
cem	hundred		code
cento (m)	hundred	**coisa** (f)	thing
(e um)	(and one)	**com**	with
cerca (de)	around	**comboio** (m)	(Pt) train
certeza (f)	certainty	**começar**	to begin
com certeza	certainly	**comer**	to eat
certo	certain	**comida** (f)	food
cerveja (f)	beer	**comigo**	with me
chá (m)	tea	**como**	as, like
chaleira (f)	kettle	**como?**	what?
chamada (f)	call	**comprar**	to buy
chamar	to call,	**compras** (fpl)	shopping
	(*of telephone*)	**compreender**	to understand
	to ring	**comprido**	long
chamar-se	to be called	**computador** (m)	computer
chão (m)	ground	**concluir**	to conclude,
chapa (f)	plate, disc		to end
charuteria (f)	(Br) tobacconist's	**concurso** (m)	competition
	(shop)	**conduzir**	to drive

conhecer	to know (someone/ place)	**demasiado**	too much
		demora (f)	delay
		dente (m)	tooth
consertar	to repair	**dentista** (m/f)	dentist
constipação (f)	cold	**dentro (de)**	inside
consultório (m)	surgery	**depois (de)**	afterwards, next
conta (f)	bill	**depósito** (m)	deposit, petrol
correio (m)	post office, mail		tank (in car)
correr	to run	**descansar**	to rest
corrida (f)	race, bullfight	**descer**	to go, to come
cotação (f)	rate		down
couro (m)	leather	**descolagem** (f)	take-off
cozinha (f)	kitchen		(aeroplane)
cozinhar	to cook	**desculpa** (f)	excuse, apology
criança (f)	child	**desculpe!**	excuse me!
cuidado (m)	care; worry	**desde**	since, from
cuidado!	look out!	**desejar**	to want, to wish,
cuidar de	to take care of, to look after		to desire
		desenho animado (m)	cartoon
cujo/a	whose, of which		
cumprimentar	to greet	**desligar**	to hang up
cumprir	to fulfil, to carry out		(telephone)
		despedida (f)	farewell
curto	brief, short	**despesa** (f)	expense
custar	to cost	**desporto** (m)	sport
custo (m)	price, cost	**deste (de + este)**	of this, from this
da (de + a)	of, from the	**desvio** (m)	diversion
dar	to give	**detestar**	to hate
dantes	before, formerly	**detrás**	behind
data (f)	date	**devagar**	slowly
de	of, from	**dia** (m)	day
debaixo (de)	below, underneath	**diante de**	in front of
		difícil	difficult
decerto	certainly	**dinheiro** (m)	money
decidir	to decide	**direita:**	on the right of,
declarar	to declare	**à direita de**	to the right of
dedo (m)	finger	**direito**	right-hand,
deitar	to lie down		straight
deitar-se	to go to bed	**disco rígido** (m)	hard disk
deixar	to leave, to abandon	**a disquete** (f)	floppy disk
		divertir-se	to enjoy oneself

dizer	to say, to tell	**encantado**	delighted, charmed
do (de + o)	from the, of the	**encerrar**	to lock up
doença (f)	illness	**encher**	to fill up
doer	to hurt, to ache	**encontrar**	to find, to meet
dona (f)	owner	**encostar**	to lean against
dona de casa	housewife	**enfim**	at last
dono (m)	owner	**enganar-se**	to be mistaken
dormir	to sleep	**engarrafamento** (m)	traffic jam
donde	from where	**engolir**	to swallow
(de + onde)		**enjoado**	sick
dor (f)	pain	**enorme**	huge
download (m)	(to) download	**enquanto**	while
duplo	double	**no entanto**	yet, however,
durante	during	**então**	then
durar	to last	**entender**	to understand
dúvida (f)	doubt	**entrada** (f)	entrance, entry, doorway
dúzia (f)	dozen		
		entrar	to come, to go in, to enter
e	and		
é	he, she, it is, you are	**entrar na Net**	to access the Net
		entre	between, among
écran (m)	(Pt) screen	**entrega** (f)	delivery
edifício (m)	building	**entretanto**	meanwhile
editoração electrónica (f)	desktop publishing	**entrevista** (f)	interview
		envergonhado	ashamed
ela	she, it	**equipa** (f)	team
ele	he, it	**errado**	wrong, mistaken
eléctrico (m)	(Pt) tram	**erro** (m)	mistake
elevador (m)	lift	**escada** (f)	staircase, step
em	in, on, at	**esconder**	to hide
email (m)	e-mail	**escrever**	to write
embarcar	to go on board, to embark	**escritório** (m)	office
		esgotado	sold out
embora	although, though	**esperar**	to wait, to hope
ementa (f)	menu	**esquecer**	to forget
empregado/a	employee, clerk; (Pt) waiter, waitress	**esquerda:**	on the left of,
		à esquerda de	to the left of
emprego (m)	job	**esquerdo**	left
empresa (f)	firm, enterprise	**esquina** (f)	corner
emprestar	to loan, to lend		
empurrar	to push		

está?/estou	hello? hello (on telephone)	faz favor	please
estação (f)	station, season	fazer	to make, to do
estacionar	to park	fechado	closed
Estados Unidos (mpl)	USA	fechar	to close
		feio	ugly
estar	to be	feliz	happy
este (m)	east	feriado (m)	(public) holiday
este/a	this	férias (fpl)	holidays
estes/estas	these	festa (f)	party
estrada (f)	road	ficar	to stay, to become, to be
estrada de ferro	(Br) railway		
estudar	to study	ficha (f)	token, (index) card
eu	I		
evidente	evident	fila (f)	line, row; (Br) queue
evitar	to avoid, to prevent		
		filho/a	son/daughter
explicar	to explain	filhos	children
exportação (f)	export(ing)	filmar	to film
exterior (m)	outside, exterior	filme (m)	film
extinguir	to put out (fire)	fim (m)	end
extracto (m)	extract	folha (f)	sheet, leaf
extracto de conta	bank statement	fome (f)	hunger
		fora	outside
extrovertido	extrovert	fornecer	to supply
		fósforos (mpl)	matches
fábrica (f)	factory	fraco	weak
faca (f)	knife	freguês (m), freguesa (f)	customer, client
face (f)	face		
fácil	easy	freio (m)	(Br) brake
factura (f)	invoice, bill	frente (f)	front
falador	talkative	em frente de	opposite
falar	to talk, to speak	fresco	cool
faltar	to be lacking, to miss	frio	cold
		fronteira (f)	frontier, border
farmácia (f)	chemist's (shop)	fruta (f)	fruit
farol (m)	lighthouse, headlamp (car)	frutaria (f)	fruit shop
		fumo (m)	smoke
farto	fed up	funcionário (m)	official, civil servant
fatia (f)	slice		
fato (m)	suit	fundido	fused
favor (m)	favour	fundo	deep

furo (m)	hole, puncture	**grama** (m)	gramme;
fusível (m)	fuse		(Br) grass
futebol (m)	football	**grande**	big, large
futuro (m)	future	**grátis**	free
		grato	grateful
gabinete (m)	office, study	**grau** (m)	degree, level
galão (m)	large white coffee	**greve** (f)	strike
gama (f)	scale, range	**gripe** (f)	'flu
ganhar	to win, to earn,	**grosso**	thick, rough
	to gain	**grupo** (m)	group
garagem (f)	garage	**guarda-chuva** (m)	umbrella
garçom (m)	(Br) waiter	**guardanapo** (m)	napkin
garfo (m)	fork	**guarda-roupa** (m)	wardrobe
gargalhada (f)	burst of laughter	**guardar**	to keep, to watch
garganta (f)	throat		over
garoto (m)	boy, kid; (Pt)	**guitarra** (f)	guitar
	small white		
	coffee	**há**	there is, there are,
garrafa (f)	bottle		ago
gasóleo (m)	diesel oil	**habitação** (f)	dwelling
gasolina (f)	petrol	**haver**	to have
gastar	to spend	**hipoteca** (f)	mortgage
gastos (mpl)	expenses, costs	**história** (f)	story, history
gatuno (m)	thief	**hoje**	today
gelado (m)	ice cream	**homem** (m)	man
gelar	to freeze	**hora** (f)	hour, time
gelo (m)	ice	**horário** (m)	timetable
gente (f)	people	**hospedeira** (f)	(Pt) air hostess
geral	general	**hospital** (m)	hospital
em geral	generally	**hotel** (m)	hotel
gerência (f)	management	**humor** (m)	mood, humour
gerente (m/f)	manager		
giro	turn; cute, pretty,	**ida** (f)	departure, single
(m and adj)	terrific		(ticket)
gol (m)	(Br) goal	**ida e volta**	return ticket
golo (m)	(Pt) goal	**idade** (f)	age
gordo	fat	**igual**	equal
gorjeta (f)	tip	**imediatamente**	immediately
gostar de	to like	**impedido**	engaged
gosto (m)	taste		(telephone)
gota (f)	drop	**importação** (f)	importing, import
graça (f)	charm, joke, grace	**importar**	to import

impossível	impossible	**junto (de)**	beside
impressora (f)	printer	**juros** (mpl)	interest
incluir	to include,	**sem juros**	interest-free
	to enclose	**justo**	fair, just
incomodar	to annoy,		
	to bother	**lá**	there
indicativo (m)	area code,	**lã** (f)	wool
	international	**lado** (m)	side
	code (telephone)	**ladrão** (m)	thief
indigestão (f)	indigestion	**lago** (m)	lake
informática (f)	computing	**lâmpada** (f)	light bulb
interessante	interesting	**lançar**	to throw
interior (m)	inside, interior	**lanche** (m)	snack
interromper	to interrupt	**laptop** (m)	laptop
intervalo (m)	interval	**lar** (f)	home, hearth
introduzir	to introduce	**lareira** (f)	fireplace, fireside
inútil	useless	**largo**	wide, broad
inverno (m)	winter	**lavar**	to wash
investimento (m)	investment	**lavar-se**	to wash oneself
ir	to go	**legumes** (mpl)	vegetables
ir-se embora	to go away	**lembrar**	to remind
isqueiro (m)	lighter	**lembrar-se de**	to remember
isso	that, that thing	**lento**	slow
por isso	therefore	**ler**	to read
isto	this, this thing	**levantar**	to lift, to raise
		levantar-se	to get up
já	already, now,	**levar**	to take, to
	right now		carry
jamais	never	**leve**	light, slight
janela (f)	window	**lhe**	to him, to her,
jantar (m)	dinner		to you
jantar	to dine	**lhes**	to them,
jardim (m)	garden		to you (pl)
jeito (m)	knack, skill	**libra** (f)	pound (sterling)
dar jeito	to be convenient	**licença** (f)	permission
joelho (m)	knee	**com licença**	excuse me
jogging (m)	jogging	**ligação** (f)	connection
fazer jogging	to jog	**ligar**	to tie, to connect
jogo (m)	game	**limpar**	to clean
jornal (m)	newspaper	**limpo**	clean
jovem	youth; young	**linha** (f)	line, thread,
(m and adj)			cable

lista (f)	directory (telephone), menu	**meio-ambiente** (m)	environment
livraria (f)	bookshop	**melhor**	better
livro (m)	book	**menino/a**	boy/girl
locutor (m)	radio announcer	**menor**	smaller, smallest, minor
logo	then, soon, later, right away	**mercearia** (f)	grocer's (shop)
		mesa (f)	table
longe	far, far away	**mesmo**	same
louça (f)	crockery	**metade** (f)	half, middle
lua (f)	moon	**meu/minha**	my, mine
lugar (m)	place, space	**mídia** (f)	media
luxo (m)	luxury	**mim**	me
luz (f)	light	**minha**	my, mine
ma (me +a)	it to me	(adj & pron f)	
má (adj f)	bad, evil	**minuto** (m)	minute
macio	soft, smooth	**mo (me +o)**	it to me
maço (m)	packet (cigarettes)	**moçambicano**	Mozambican
mãe (f)	mother	**moda** (f)	fashion
magro	thin	**modem** (m)	modem
maior	bigger	**modo** (m)	way, manner
maioria (f)	majority	**montra** (f)	(Pt) shop window
mais	more	**morar**	to stay (place), to reside
mala (f)	suitcase		
mamãe (f)	(Br) mum	**mos (me + os)**	them to me
mandar	to send	**mostrar**	to show
maneira (f)	way, manner	**muito**	a lot of, many; very
manhã (f)	morning		
manter	to maintain	**mulher** (f)	woman, wife
mapa (m)	map, chart	**música** (f)	music
mar (m)	sea		
marca (f)	brand, make	**na (em +a)**	in the, on the
marisco (m)	shellfish	**nada**	nothing
mas (me + as)	them to me	**nadar**	to swim
mau/má	bad, evil	**não**	no, not
medicamento (m)	medicine	**nas (em + as)**	at the (fpl)
		nascer	to be born
médico (m)	doctor	**Natal** (m)	Christmas
medida (f)	size, measurement	**necessário**	necessary
medir	to measure	**negócio** (m)	business, transaction
meio (m)	half		
meio-quilo	half a kilo	**nem**	neither, nor

nenhum/a	none, not one/any	**orçamento** (m)	budget
nesse/a	in that	**ordenado**	salary, in order
(**em** + **esse**)		**ordenar**	to order
nesses/as	in those	**organisação** (f)	organization
(**em** + **esses/as**)		**osso** (m)	bone
neste/a	in this	**OTAN**	NATO
(**em** + **este**)		**ótimo**	(Br) great
nestes/as	in these	**ou**	or
(**em** + **estes/as**)		**outono** (m)	autumn
Net (f)	Net (Internet)	**outro**	another
ninguém	nobody	**outrora**	formerly, a long
no (**em** + **o**)	in the, on the		time ago
norte (m)	north	**ouvir**	to hear
nos[1]	us, to us	**oxalá!**	let's hope; if
nos[2] (**em** + **os**)	in the/at the		only!
(mpl)		**pá** (f)	shovel; pal; mate
nós	we	**pacote** (m)	parcel
notícia (f)	piece of news	**pagar**	to pay
noticiário	radio news	**página da**	Web page
(m)		**Net** (f)	
notícias	news	**pai** (m)	father
novo	new, young	**pais**	parents
nublado	cloudy	**palco** (m)	stage
nunca	never	**pano** (m)	cloth
nuvem (f)	cloud	**papai** (m)	(Br) dad
		par (m)	pair
obra/s (f)	work(s), repairs	**para**	for, towards
obrigação (f)	obligation	**parabéns**	congratulations
obrigado/a	thank you, obliged	**parar**	to stop
ocasião (f)	occasion,	**partir**	to leave
	opportunity	**Páscoa** (f)	Easter
óculos (mpl)	glasses	**passar**	to pass, to spend
oeste (m)	west		(time); to iron
oferecer	to offer	**passatempo** (m)	pastime, hobby
olhar	to look	**passear**	to walk
onde	where	**pasta** (f)	briefcase
ônibus (m)	(Br) bus	**pasta de dentes**	toothpaste
ontem	yesterday	**pastelaria** (f)	cake shop, cafeteria
óptimo	(Pt) great	**patrão** (m)	boss, landlord
ora	now, well	**patroa** (f)	landlady
ora bem	now then	**PC** (m)	PC (personal
ora essa!	come off it!		computer)

peça (f)	piece, part, play (theatre)	**prestar**	to be of use
pedir	to ask for	**primavera** (f)	spring
pele (f)	skin	**procurar**	to look for
pelo/a	for, through,	**proibido**	forbidden
(por + o/a)	by the	**provar**	to taste, to try on (clothes)
pena (f)	suffering, pity	**próximo**	near, close, next
Que pena!	What a shame!	**puxar**	to pull
pensar	to think		
pequeno-	(Pt) breakfast	**quadro** (m)	picture, painting
almoço (m)		**qual** (pl **quais**)	which, who
perguntar	to ask	**qualquer**	any, anyone
perto	nearby	**(pl quaisquer)**	
péssimo	awful	**quando**	when
pior	worse	**quantia** (f)	sum, amount
o pior	the worst	**quantidade** (f)	quantity
pista (f)	track, trail	**quanto**	how much,
plateia (f)	stalls (theatre)		all that
pneu (m)	tyre	**quase**	almost
pó (m)	powder	**que**	who, that,
pois	well then, so, yes		which
política (f)	politics	**quê!?**	what!?
pontapé (m)	kick	**queixa** (f)	complaint
ponte (f)	bridge	**queixar**	to complain
por	for	**quem**	who (m)
por favor	please	**quente**	warm
pôr	to put	**querer**	to want
porcaria (f)	(Pt) rubbish, mess	**questão** (f)	question
porque	because	**quilo** (m)	kilo
porquê	why?	**quilómetro** (m)	kilometre
porta (f)	door	**quinze dias** (m)	fortnight
porta-moedas (m)	purse	**quotidiano**	everyday
portanto	therefore	**rádio** (m)	radio, radio station
possível	possible		
pouco	little, few	**rapariga** (f)	girl
praça (f)	square, market	**rapaz** (m)	boy
prato (m)	plate, dish	**rapidez** (f)	speed
prazer (m)	pleasure	**raramente**	seldom
precisar de	to need	**raso**	flat, low
preço (m)	price	**rato** (m)	mouse (in computing)
prédio (m)	building		

razão (f)	reason	**rossio** (m)	large square
realmente	really, actually	**roto**	torn, burst
recado (m)	message	**roupa** (f)	clothes
recear	to fear	**rua** (f)	street
receita (f)	recipe, prescription, income	**ruído** (m)	noise
		sã (adj f)	healthy, sound
recibo (m)	receipt	**saber**	to know (facts)
recolher	to collect		
reconhecer	to recognize	**sabor** (m)	taste, flavour
recreação (f)	fun, recreation	**sacar**	to take out
recusar	to refuse	**saca-rolhas** (m)	corkscrew
refeição (f)	meal	**saco** (m)	bag
regressar	to come, to go back	**saia** (f)	skirt
		saída (f)	exit
regresso (m)	return	**sair**	to go out
relógio (m)	clock, watch	**sal** (m)	salt
remédio (m)	remedy; medicine	**sala de chat** (f)	chat room (on Internet)
remoto	remote	**saltar**	to jump
renda (f)	income, rent	**sanduíche/ sande** (f)	sandwich
rentabilidade (f)	profitability		
		são/sã	healthy, sound
repousar	to rest	**sapataria** (f)	shoe shop
reprovar	to fail	**saudade** (f)	longing
rés-do-chão (m)	ground floor	**saudades**	regards (letter)
resolver	to solve, to decide	**saudável**	healthy
		scanner (m)	scanner
respeito (m)	respect	**se**	if, whether, oneself, him/her/itself
a/com respeito de	with regard to		
		secar	to dry
respirar	to breathe	**sede** (f)	thirst
responder	to reply	**secretária** (f)	secretary, writing desk
ressaca (f)	hangover		
resto (m)	rest	**seguido**	following
retrete (f)	toilet	**segunda-mão**	second hand
reunião (f)	meeting	**sem**	without
revista (f)	magazine	**semana** (f)	week
rico	rich	**semáforos** (mpl)	traffic lights
rir	to laugh		
rodovia (f)	(Br) motorway	**semelhança** (f)	similarity
romper	to break	**sempre**	always, still, yet

senão	if not, otherwise	**tamanho** (m)	size
sentar-se	to sit down	**também**	too, also
sentir-se	to feel	**tanto**	so much, many
	(happy, etc.)	**tão**	so
separar	to separate	**tarde** (f)	afternoon
ser	to be	**tarefa** (f)	job, task
serra (f)	mountain range,	**tas (te + as)**	them to you (s)
	saw	**teclado** (m)	keyboard
seu/sua	his, her(s), your(s),	**tecnologia de**	information
	its, their(s)	**informação**	technology
SIDA (f)	AIDS	(f)	
simpático	kind, nice	**tela** (f)	(Br) screen
sindicato (m)	trade union	**telemóvel**	mobile phone
site (m)	site (on Internet)	**telenovela** (f)	soap opera
só	alone	**televisão** (f)	television
sob	under	**tempo** (m)	time, weather
sobre	on, above, over	**tencionar**	to intend
sobretudo	above all	**ter**	to have
socorrer	to help	**terminal caixa**	cash-point
sofrer	to suffer	(m)	
sol (m)	sun	**terminar**	to finish
solteiro	single	**terno** (m)	(Br) suit
sono (m)	sleep	**terra** (f)	earth
sorte (f)	luck, chance	**to (te + o)**	it to you (s)
sozinho	by oneself, alone	**toalha** (f)	towel
sua	his, her(s), your(s),	**tocar**	to play (music),
(adj & pron f)	its, their(s)		to ring
subir	to go up		(telephone),
suéter (m)	(Br) sweater		to touch
sujo	dirty	**todavia**	still, however
sul (m)	south	**todo**	all, every
sumo (m)	juice	**tomada** (f)	socket
suor (m)	sweat		(electrical)
supor	to suppose	**torneira** (f)	tap
		tos (te + os)	them to you (s)
ta (te + a)	it to you (s)	**transeunte** (m)	passer-by
tabacaria (f)	(Pt) tobacconist's	**transitar**	to go, to pass
	(shop)		through
tal	such	**trânsito** (m)	traffic
talho (m)	(Pt) butcher's	**tratar**	to deal with,
	(shop)		to treat
talvez	perhaps	**travão** (m)	(Pt) brake

trazer	to bring
trem (m)	(Br) train
triste	sad
trocar	to exchange
troco (m)	change (money)
tropeçar	to trip
tudo	all, everything
turismo (m)	tourism
turismo de habitação	bed and breakfast
ufa!	phew!
uísque (m)	whisky
ultimamente	lately
um/uma	a, an, one
unir	to join
universidade (f)	university
upload (m)	(to) upload
urgente	urgent
usado	used, worn
usar	to use
útil	useful
vaga (f)	wave, vacancy
vago	vacant, vague
valer	to be worth
válido	valid
valor (m)	value, worth
vantagem (f)	advantage
variado	varied
vários	several
velho	old
vencer	to win
venda (f)	sale
vender	to sell
vende-se	for sale
ver	to see

verão (m)	summer
verdade (f)	truth
vergonha (f)	shame
verificar	to check
vestido (m)	dress
vestir	to dress
vestir-se	to get dressed
vez (f)	time, turn
vir	to come
virar	to turn
vitrina (f)	(Br) shop window
viva!	hooray!
viver	to live
você (pl **vocês**)	you
volta (f)	return, turn, curve
volver	to come back
vontade (f)	will
vôo (m)	flight
voz (f)	voice
Web (f)	Web (on Internet)
xadrez (m)	chess
xaile (m)	shawl
xícara (f)	(Br) cup
xixi (m): **fazer xixi**	to go to the toilet
zanga (f)	anger
zangar	to annoy
zangar-se	to get annoyed
zero (m)	nothing, zero
zona (f)	zone, area

English–Portuguese glossary

Brazilian (Br) words are distinguished from Portuguese (Pt) words where necessary.

a, an	**um, uma**	any	**qualquer, (pl)**
able	**capaz**		**quaisquer**
to be able (to)	**poder**	anybody/	**qualquer pessoa**
(to) access the	**entrar na Net**	anyone	
Net		anything	**algo, alguma**
address	**morada (f),**		**coisa**
	endereço (m)	arrival	**chegada (f)**
(to) advertise	**pôr um anúncio**	(to arrive)	**chegar**
advertisement	**anúncio**	as	**como, tão**
(s)	**(s) (m) (pl)**	as much/	**tanto/a/os/as**
after/afterwards	**depois de**	as many	
afternoon	**tarde (f)**	as soon as	**tão depressa**
against	**contra**	possible	**quanto**
(to) agree	**concordar, estar**		**possível**
	de acordo	(to) ask	**perguntar**
airport	**aeroporto (m)**	(to) ask for	**pedir**
all	**todo/a/os/as**	at	**em, a**
(to) allow	**permitir,**	at last	**finalmente**
	deixar	at least	**pelo menos**
alone	**só, sózinho**	at once	**imediatamente,**
almost	**quase**		**já**
already	**já**	attachment	**attach;**
also	**também**	(in e-mail)	**attachment**
always	**sempre**		**(m)**
among	**entre**	away	**fora**
and	**e**	far away	**muito longe**
angry	**zangado**	awful	**horrível, péssimo**
(to get	**zangar-se**		
become)		bad	**mau/má**
angry		badly	**mal**

bag	saco (m), bolsa (f)	breakfast	pequeno-almoço (m) (Pt); café (m) da manhã (Br)
bank	banco (m)		
bathroom	casa/sala (f) de banho (Pt), banheiro (m) (Br)	(to) bring	trazer
		(to) build	construir, estatura (f)
(to) be	ser, estar	building	edifício (m)
beach	praia (f)	bus	autocarro (m) (Pt); ônibus (m) (Br)
(to) bear	aguentar, suportar		
bed	cama (f)	business	negócio (m), negócios (mpl)
bedroom	quarto (m) de dormir, quarto de cama		
		but	mas
		(to) buy	comprar
beer	cerveja (f)	by	por, através
before	antes de		
(to) begin	começar, principiar	(to) call	chamar
		to be called	chamar-se
behind	atrás de	can (to be able)	poder
(to) believe	acreditar, crer	car	automóvel (m), carro (m)
beside	ao lado de		
besides	além de	care	cuidado (m)
better	melhor	(to) carry	levar, transportar
between	entre	cash-point	terminal caixa (m)
big	grande		
bill	conta	cassette	cassete (m)
birthday	dia de anos (m), aniversário (m)	certainly	com certeza, certamente
		chance	oportunidade (f)
to have a birthday	fazer anos	(by) chance	por acaso
		(to) change	mudar, mudança (f); trocar to (ex)change (money/things), troco (m) change (money)
black	preto, negro		
boarding/guest house	pensão (f)		
both	ambos		
bottle	garrafa (f)		
brandy	conhaque (m)		
bread	pão (m)	chat room (on Internet)	sala de chat (f)
(to) break	quebrar, partir		
breakdown (of car)	avaria (f)	cheap	barato
		chemist's (shop)	farmácia (f)

(traveller's) cheque	**cheque (de viagem)** (m)	dinner	**jantar** (m)
child	**criança** (f)	disk (floppy disk)	**disquete** (f)
choice	**escolha** (f)	(to) do	**fazer**
(to) choose	**escolher**	doctor	**médico/a; doutor/a** (academic qualification)
cigarettes	**cigarros** (mpl)		
cigars	**charutos** (mpl)		
city	**cidade** (f)	(to) download	**download** (m)
(to) climb	**subir, trepar**	(to) dress	**vestir-se, vestido** (m)
cloudy	**nublado**		
coach	**camioneta** (f)	(to) drink	**beber, bebida** (f)
coat	**casaco** (m) (Pt); **paletó** (m) (Br)	driver	**motorista** (m/f)
		driver's licence	**carta de condução** (f)
coffee	**café** (m)		
coin	**moeda** (f)		
cold	**frio** (m)	each	**cada**
(to) come	**vir**	each one	**cada qual**
to come in	**entrar**	each other	**um ao outro**
to come back	**voltar**	early	**cedo**
(to) complain	**queixar-se**	easily	**facilmente**
complaint	**queixa** (f)	east	**este** (m)
computer	**computador** (m)	easy	**fácil**
computing	**informática** (f)	(to) eat	**comer**
(to) continue	**continuar**	either	**ou**
corner	**esquina** (f)	e-mail	**email** (m)
(to) cost	**custar, custo** (m)	emergency	**emergência** (f)
(to) count	**contar**	empty	**vazio**
country	**país** (m)	English	**inglês**
(to) cover	**cobrir**	(to) enjoy	**divertir-se, gozar**
(to) cross	**atravessar**	enough	**bastante**
customer	**cliente** (m/f), **freguês/guesa**	(to) enter	**entrar**
		environment	**meio-ambiente** (m)
customs	**alfândega** (f)		
		equally	**igualmente**
dark	**escuro**	evening	**tarde** (f), **noite** (f)
darkness	**escuridão** (f)	every	**cada**
day	**dia** (m)	everybody	**toda a gente** (f) (Pt); **todo o mundo** (m) (Br)
delay	**atraso** (m)		
dentist	**dentista** (m/f)		
departures	**partidas** (fpl)	everyday	**todos os dias**
difficult	**difícil**	everything	**tudo**
(to) dine	**jantar**	except	**excepto**

excuse me	**faz favor, com licença, desculpe**	(to) forget	**esquecer, esquecer-se de**
exhibition	**exposição** (f)	fortnight	**quinze dias** (mpl),
(to) expect	**esperar, contar com**		**quinzena** (f)
		fortunately	**felizmente**
expenses	**despesas** (fpl)	friend	**amigo** (m)
(to) explain	**explicar**	from	**de**
		full	**cheio**
fabric	**tecido** (m), **pano** (m)	gate (airport)	**porta** (f) **de**
face value	**valor nominal** (m)		**embarque**
(to) facilitate	**facilitar**	gentleman	**senhor** (m),
factory	**fábrica** (f)		**cavalheiro**
(to) fall	**cair**		(m)
far	**longe, distante**	(to) get	**arranjar, obter**
fast	**adiantado, depressa**	(to) get up	**levantar-se**
		(to) give	**dar**
fat	**gordo**	glasses	**óculos** (mpl)
favour	**favor** (m)	(to) go	**ir**
fax	**fax** (m)	(to) go home	**ir para casa**
(to) fear	**recear, temer, ter medo, medo** (m)	good	**bom/boa**
		goodbye	**adeus**
		goods	**géneros** (mpl)
(to) feel	**sentir, sentir-se**	great	**grande**
(to) fetch	**buscar, ir buscar**	great!	**óptimo!**
few	**alguns/algumas/ uns/umas/ poucos/as**	(to) grow	**crescer**
		(to) guess	**adivinhar, supor**
(to) fill	**encher**		
(to) find	**achar**	hair	**cabelo** (m)
(to) finish	**acabar, terminar**	half	**meio, metade** (f)
fish	**peixe** (m)	(to) happen	**acontecer**
flat¹	**raso**	hard disc	**disco rigido** (m)
flat²	**apartamento** (m)	(to) have	**ter**
flavour	**sabor** (m)	(to) hear	**ouvir**
flight	**vôo** (m)	heat	**calor** (m)
floor	**chão** (m), **andar** (m)	heavy	**pesado**
		height	**altura** (f)
fog	**nevoeiro** (m)	(to) help	**ajudar, ajuda** (f)
(to) follow	**seguir**	here	**aqui, cá**
for	**por, para**	hi!	**olá** (Pt); **oi!** (Br)
foreign(er)	**estrangeiro** (m)	high	**alto**

hire	**aluguer** (m) (Pt); **aluguel** (m) (Br)
holiday	**feriado** (m)
holidays	**férias** (fpl)
home	**casa** (f), **lar** (m)
(to) hope	**esperar, esperança** (f)
hot	**quente**
hour	**hora** (f)
house	**casa** (f)
how	**como**
however	**contudo**
hunger	**fome** (f)
hurry	**pressa** (f)
(to) hurt	**magoar, ferir**
ice	**gelo** (m)
identical	**idêntico**
if	**se**
ill	**doente**
immediately	**imediatamente**
important	**importante**
impossible	**impossível**
in	**em**
(to) increase	**aumentar**
information	**informação** (f)
information technology	**tecnologia de informação** (f)
(to) introduce	**apresentar**
(to) invite	**convidar**
invoice	**factura** (f)
jack (tool)	**macaco** (m)
to jack up	**levantar com o macaco**
jam	**geleia** (f)
janitor	**porteiro** (m)
job	**emprego** (m)
journey	**viagem** (f)
juice	**sumo** (m) (Pt); **suco** (m) (Br)

(to be) keen on	**gostar de** (something **algo,** somebody **alguém), ter vontade de**
(to) keep	**guardar**
key	**chave** (f)
kind	**amável**
(to) know	**conhecer** (people/places), **saber** (facts, etc.)
label	**etiqueta** (f), **marca** (f)
(to) lack	**faltar, falta** (f)
(to) land	**aterrar**
laptop	**laptop** (m)
large	**grande**
last	**último**
late	**tarde, atrasado**
(to) laugh	**rir**
law	**lei** (f), **Direito** (m)
(to) learn	**aprender**
(to) leave	**partir, sair**
less	**menos**
(to) let	**deixar, permitir; alugar** (house/car)
letter	**carta** (f)
(to) lie down	**deitar-se**
life	**vida** (f)
(to) lift	**levantar, ascensor** (m), **elevador** (m)
to give a lift (in a vehicle)	**dar uma boleia dar uma carona** (Br)
(to) light	**acender, luz** (f)
(to) like	**gostar de**
(to) listen	**ouvir, escutar**
little	**pequeno, pouco**
(to) live	**viver, morar**

long	**comprido**	(to) move	**mexer-se, mover;**
(to) long for	**ter saudades de**		**mudar de**
longing	**saudades** (fpl)		(house)
(to) look	**olhar**	much	**muito**
(to) look for	**procurar, buscar**	(to) must	**dever**
(to) lose	**perder**	my	**o meu/a minha**
loud	**alto**		
low	**baixo**	name	**nome** (m)
luck	**sorte** (f)	nationality	**nacionalidade** (f)
luggage	**bagagem** (f),	near	**perto de**
	malas (fpl)	nearly	**quase**
		necessary	**necessário**
magazine	**revista** (f)	(to) need	**precisar de**
mail	**correio** (m)	neither	**nem**
(to) make	**fazer**	Net (Internet)	**Net** (f)
man	**homem** (m)	never	**nunca, jamais**
manager	**gerente** (m/f)	new	**novo**
many	**muitos/as**	news	**notícias** (fpl)
market	**mercado** (m),	newspaper	**jornal** (m)
	praça (f)	next	**próximo**
meat	**carne** (f)	nice	**simpático**
(to) meet	**encontrar**	night	**noite** (f)
meeting	**encontro** (m)	no, not	**não**
message	**recado** (m),	nobody	**ninguém**
	mensagem (f)	noise	**barulho** (m)
midday/	**meio-dia/meia-**	nor	**nem**
midnight	**noite**	north	**norte** (m)
mistake	**erro** (m), **engano**	nothing	**nada**
	(m)	now	**agora**
mobile phone	**telemóvel** (m);		
	(Br) **celular**	oath	**juramento** (m)
	(m)	(to) obey	**obedecer, cumprir**
modem	**modem** (m)	of	**de**
money	**dinheiro** (m)	office	**escritório** (m),
month	**mês** (m), **meses**		**gabinete** (m)
	(mpl)	often	**muitas vezes**
more	**mais**	on	**em, em cima de,**
morning	**manhã** (f)		**sobre**
most	**a maior**	once	**uma vez**
	parte de	only	**só, apenas**
mouse (in	**rato** (m)	(to) open	**abrir**
computing)		opinion	**opinião** (f)

opportunity	**oportunidade** (f)	quickly	**depressa**
opposite	**em frente de**	quiet	**calado**
or	**ou**	race	**corrida** (f)
(to) order	**encomendar**		(competition);
other	**outro**		**raça** (f) (people
(to) ought to	**dever**		of same group)
our, ours	**nosso/a/os/as**	railway	**caminho** (m) **de**
out	**fora**		**ferro** (Pt),
over there	**além, acolá**		**estrada** (f) **de**
			ferro (Br)
parcel	**pacote** (m),	rare	**raro, mal passado**
	embrulho (m)		(cooked)
park	**parque** (m)	(to) read	**ler**
partner	**sócio** (m)	ready	**pronto**
(to) pay	**pagar**	(to) receive	**receber**
PC (personal	**PC** (m)	(to) refuse	**recusar**
computer)		regards	**cumprimentos**
pen	**caneta** (f)		(mpl)
pencil	**lápis** (m)	(to) remain	**ficar**
people	**gente** (f), **pessoas**	(to) remember	**lembrar-se de**
	(fpl)	(to) repair	**consertar, conserto**
perhaps	**talvez**		(m)
(to) pick up	**apanhar**	(to) rest	**descansar**
pity	**pena** (f), **lástima**	rest	**resto** (m) (remain-
	(f)		der); **descanso**
(to) place	**pôr, colocar**		(m)
(to) play	**jogar** (sport);	(to) return	**voltar, regressar**
	brincar (joke);	right	**direito** (direction);
	tocar (music)		**certo** (correct)
please!	**faz favor!**	(to) ring	**tocar**
(to) please	**agradar**	room	**quarto** (m)
(to) prefer	**preferir**	(to) run	**correr**
printer	**impressora** (f)		
puncture	**furo** (m)	safe	**fora de perigo,**
purchase	**compra** (f)		**seguro; cofre** (m)
(to) put	**pôr, meter**		(for money)
		salary	**salário** (m),
quaint	**curioso, pitoresco**		**ordenado** (m)
quality	**qualidade** (f)	salesman	**vendedor** (m)
quantity	**quantidade** (f)	salt	**sal** (m)
question	**pergunta** (f),	same	**mesmo**
	questão (f)	sample	**amostra** (f)

(to) say	**dizer**	street	**rua** (f)
scanner	**scanner** (m)	strike	**greve** (f)
(on) schedule	**à tabela,**	strong	**forte**
	a tempo	suit	**fato** (m) (Pt);
sea	**mar** (m)		**terno** (m)
(to) see	**ver**		(Br)
(to) seem	**parecer**	suitcase	**mala** (f)
(to) send	**mandar, enviar**	sun	**sol** (m)
several	**vários**	sunglasses	**óculos** (mpl)
shop	**loja** (f)		**de sol**
short	**curto**	sunshine	**Sol** (m)
(to) shut	**fechar, encerrar**	(to) supply	**fornecer**
sir	**senhor**	(to be) sure	**ter a certeza**
(to) sit down	**sentar-se**	(to) surf the	**surfar na Net**
site (on	**site** (m)	Net	
Internet)		(to) switch off	**desligar**
size	**tamanho** (m)	(to) switch on	**ligar**
(to) sleep	**dormir**		
slow	**lento, devagar**	table	**mesa** (f)
small	**pequeno**	(to) take	**tomar, pegar**
(to) smoke	**fumar**		**(em)**
so	**assim, portanto**	(to) take off	**descolar** (plane),
some	**algum/a**		**despir-se**
something	**alguma coisa**		(clothes)
sometimes	**às vezes**	tall	**alto**
soon	**em breve**	tea	**chá** (m)
as soon as	**logo que, assim**	telephone call	**telefonema** (m),
	que		**chamada** (f)
(to feel) sorry	**ter pena de**	(to) tell	**dizer, contar**
for		temperature	**temperatura**
sorry!	**desculpe!**		(f)
south	**sul** (m)	than	**que, do que**
(to) speak	**falar**	(to) thank	**agradecer**
speaker	**locutor (a)**	thank you	**obrigado**
(to) spend	**gastar**	the	**o/a**
sport	**desporto** (m) (Pt),	then	**então**
	esporte (m)	there	**ali, lá, aí**
	(Br)	there is/are	**há**
stamp	**selo** (m)	thin	**magro**
station	**estação** (f)	thing	**coisa** (f)
(to) stay	**ficar**	(to) think	**pensar, achar**
still	**ainda**	thirst	**sede** (f)

this/these/ those	**este/a/es/as, esse/a/es/as, aquele/a/os/as**	vacancy	**vaga** (f), **quarto livre** (m) (room)
(to) throw	**atirar**	value	**valor** (m)
thunder	**trovão** (m)	variety	**variedade** (f)
thus	**assim**	very	**muito**
ticket	**bilhete** (m)	visit	**visita** (f)
time	**tempo** (m), **hora** (f)	wage	**salário** (m), **ordenado** (m)
this time	**esta vez**	(to) wait	**esperar**
timetable	**horário** (m)		
tired	**cansado**	waiter	**criado** (m), **empregado** (m)
to	**a, para**		
tobacconist	**tabacaria** (f)	(to) walk	**andar (a pé), caminhar**
today	**hoje**		
toilet	**retrete** (f)	(to) wake	**despertar, acordar**
too	**também**		
too much	**demasiado, demais**	(to) want	**querer, desejar**
		(to) wash	**lavar(-se)**
(to) touch	**tocar**	we	**nós**
town	**cidade** (f)	weather	**tempo** (m)
traffic	**trânsito** (m)	Web (on Internet)	**Web** (f)
traffic jam	**engarrafamento** (m)		
train	**comboio** (m) (Pt); **trem** (m) (Br)	Web page	**página da Net** (f)
(to) travel	**viajar**	well	**bem**
(to) trip	**tropeçar, viagem** (f), **giro** (m)	west	**oeste** (m)
		what?	**(o) quê?**
true	**verdadeiro**	when	**quando**
(to) try	**tentar, provar**	where	**onde**
(to) turn	**virar, voltar**	which	**qual**
ugly	**feio**	who	**quem**
unable	**incapaz**	whole	**todo, inteiro**
underneath	**debaixo de, sob**	whose	**de quem**
(to) understand	**compreender**	why?	**porquê?**
unfortunately	**infelizmente**	wife	**mulher** (f), **esposa** (f)
unless	**a não ser que**		
until	**até**	(to) win	**ganhar**
(to) upload	**upload** (m)	wine	**vinho** (m)
upstairs	**lá em cima**	with	**com**
us	**nos**	without	**sem**
useful	**útil**	woman	**mulher** (f)

(to) work	**trabalhar, trabalho** **(m)**		**vocês, os/as** **senhores/as** (pl)
worried	**preocupado**	your(s)	**teu/tua seu/sua**
worse	**pior**	yourself	**tu mesmo,**
worth	**valor** (m)		**você mesmo**
(to) write	**escrever**	young	**jovem, novo**
x-ray	**raio-x** (m),	youth	**juventude** (f)
	radiografia (f)	youth hostel	**pousada/** **albergaria**
year	**ano** (m)		(f) **de juventude**
yes	**sim**		
yesterday	**ontem**	zero	**zero** (m)
yet	**ainda, porém**	zip	**fecho-éclair** (m)
you	**tu, você,** **o/a senhor/a; vós,**		(Pt); **fecho-ecler** (m) (Br)

Topic index

The numbers refer to the lessons in the book.

Grammatical index

The numbers refer to the lessons in the book.

Printed in Great Britain
by Amazon